Ludovic Kennedy is the author of *10 Rillington Place*, *The Trial of Stephen Ward* and the bestselling *Pursuit: The Sinking of the Bismarck*. He is also extremely well-known for his numerous television appearances in *Midweek*, *Newsday* and *Tonight*.

A Presumption of Innocence
The Full Story of the Ayr Murder.

'The truth about the affair is now absolutely certain . . . and it is set out by Mr Kennedy with clarity and confidence'
New Statesman

'It is a very convincing demonstration of the ease with which a presumption of guilt, supported by a few fragments of circumstantial evidence and a coincidence or two, can entirely displace the supposed safeguard of the much acclaimed presumption of innocence, in determining the outcome of a criminal trial'
New Society

'More gripping than a well-knit murder story'
Oxford Times

'Where many so-called thrillers, which serve no other purpose, fail to thrill, it is a pleasure to find one which deals with actual events and real people, is written with serious intent and never releases its grip on the reader'
Yorkshire Post

Also by Ludovic Kennedy

10 Rillington Place
Pursuit
One Man's Meat
Sub-Lieutenant
Murder Story
The Trial of Stephen Ward
Very Lovely People
Nelson and His Captains

Ludovic Kennedy

A Presumption of Innocence

The Full Story of the Ayr Murder

Panther

Granada Publishing Limited
Published in 1977 by Panther Books Ltd
Frogmore, St Albans, Herts AL2 2NF

First published by Victor Gollancz Ltd 1976

Made and printed in Great Britain by
Richard Clay (The Chaucer Press) Ltd
Bungay, Suffolk
Set in Linotype Times

For
Tom Sargant,
Secretary of Justice

'At a trial events are often seen in a distorted perspective. A violent event has taken place, and we work backwards from it, considering primarily the evidence bearing on that event. If we work forwards in a natural sequence, from a natural starting-point, this evidence may wear a very different appearance.'

(Julian Symons: *A Reasonable Doubt*)

'It is the general habit of the police not to admit to the slightest departure from correctness.'

(Lord Devlin: *The Criminal Prosecution in England*)

CONTENTS

ILLUSTRATIONS

PREFACE TO THE ORIGINAL EDITION

When I was a boy, I used to stay often with my grandfather at his house in Belgrave Crescent, Edinburgh. He had been Professor of Public and International Law at the University, and Dean of the Faculty of Law. The top shelf of his library was filled with the distinctive red volumes of Messrs William Hodge's *Notable British Trials*. On many a winter evening, between tea and supper, I would sit on top of the library step-ladder, utterly absorbed in the transcripts of such trials as that of Dr Buck Ruxton (the Parsee dentist who cut up his wife and nurserymaid and threw the pieces into Moffat Gorge), Alfred Arthur Rouse (who strangled a tramp in his car and then set fire to it), Browne and Kennedy (who shot poor P.C. Gutteridge), Thompson and Bywaters, Crippen and Miss le Neve, Madeleine Smith and Pierre L'Angelier. An added pleasure was that Mr William Roughead, at that time general editor of the series, lived a few doors away along the Crescent, and being an old friend of my grandfather, would sometimes look in for a chat. For me it was like meeting God.

What fascinated me most about the accounts of those murders was not just the grisly gripping details, not even the breathtaking wickedness of those who had committed them, but the majesty, the ceremony, above all the exactitude of the law. It never occurred to me then that judges could be biased, that policemen could 'plant' evidence, that innocent men could be kept locked up for years. Had I been told that such things happened, even rarely, I would have disbelieved them.

Disillusionment came later and resulted in *10 Rillington Place,*[1] *Murder Story* (a play on the Craig-Bentley case) and *The Trial of Stephen Ward.* After these, I used to get letters

[1] The book that showed that John Christie had committed the murder for which Timothy Evans was hanged, and which eventually led to Evans being granted a posthumus free pardon.

from prisoners telling me they had been wrongly convicted, and seeking help. I had no doubts that many of them were speaking the truth; but not wishing to go on writing books about injustices forever, I decided to call it a day.

Then along came Meehan. There were many things that interested me about his case. Firstly, as I recount later, the chance meeting the night before the verdict with his counsel, who told me his client was an innocent man. Then the *dramatis personae*: Meehan, a criminal of unusual character and abilities; Griffiths, a weird individual in a quite different way; even the surviving victim of the attack, the bingo-hall owner Abraham Ross, somebody out of the usual run. Exceptional too were various aspects of the case, the extraordinary 'Pat and Jim' coincidence from which the whole case against Meehan stemmed, the police chase of Griffiths across Glasgow during which he killed one man and wounded a dozen others before being shot dead himself, the repeated confessions of Ian Waddell. And then, as the years went by and fresh evidence and interpretations pointed more and more towards Meehan's innocence and Waddell's guilt, the persistent refusals of successive Secretaries of State for Scotland, and of the Crown Office, to recognize that justice had miscarried. In the end it became imperative to write about it (if for no other reason – as is said of those who want to climb Everest – than because it was there).

I have reached the conclusion in the book that Meehan was wrongly convicted of the Ayr murder. Those who agree may well ask why wise men in the Crown Office – and Secretary of State's Office – who know much more about the law than I ever shall, to whom all the facts in this book were available or could have been made available – should, time and time again, have reached an opposite conclusion.

I think the answer is this: that all the investigations into Meehan's case so far have taken as their starting-point the presumption of his guilt. Fresh arguments or facts that have arisen to challenge this presumption may have knocked a few dents in it but have otherwise left it unharmed. It could not be otherwise; a verdict of guilty (however wrongly reached) brainwashes us all. If you want to find out whether a man found guilty is innocent, it is quite useless to start off with a presumption of his guilt. What you must do is go back to the beginning, start off with a presumption of his innocence, and see how far the presumption takes you; if he is truly guilty, it is unlikely to take you very far. That is what I have done in this book, as I did fourteen years ago in *Ten Rillington Place.* I hope the reader will agree that the case made out for Meehan's innocence is vastly stronger and more coherent than the case for his guilt – indeed that if you set aside the evidence about the voice 'identification' and the bits of paper, and consider afresh the evidence about the visibility and time factor, there is really no case against him at all.

Some lawyers and police officers in Scotland are already convinced that Meehan is innocent. Others, who have only a nodding acquaintance with the case, have told me that while they believe he was not guilty as charged, they think he must have been involved *in some way.*[2] This, I fear, is wishful thinking; and it comes oddly from those who normally in their professions attach such importance to facts, and so little to speculation. On the evidence available to us, either Meehan and Griffiths committed the Ayr murder or they didn't; there is nothing on which to base the theory of a half-way house.

I have a profound admiration for the Scottish legal system, which is one of the ornaments of Scotland; not only because I think it is a superior system to that of England, especially as regards the criminal law, but also because for 250 years it has helped to preserve – institutionally more than any other single factor – the identity of the Scottish nation. Will it not be diminished, people ask me, if it has to admit that it made a mistake? The answer is no. What will diminish it is if, when mistakes are made, it is thought that efforts will be made to cover them up. A law that people can have faith in is one big enough to admit mistakes, on

[2] English lawyers and police used to say just the same thing about Evans and Rillington Place.

the rare occasions they occur, and then endeavour to correct them.

In any case it is not the conduct of the law in the initial stages of the Meehan case that is at issue, but that of the police. The police in the Glasgow area have an unenviable job. On our behalf they deal with some of the most brutish villains in Britain, and on the whole they do it with courage, patience and good humour. Yet there is no burking the fact that in the Meehan case certain questions must be asked – and answered too. Does the conduct of the officers at the Identification parade, Detective Superintendent Struthers and Detective Sergeant Inglis, and of those who gave evidence about the bits of paper, Detective Superintendent Cowie and Detective Inspector Cook, leave anything to be desired? Did any of these officers, in their zeal to see justice done, to put behind bars the man whom they genuinely believed was responsible for this horrible crime, do or say anything they shouldn't have done? Certainly there are *prima facie* grounds for thinking so; and an independent official inquiry must make it its business to find out.

It would have been impossible to have written this book without the help given me by many people. Firstly Mr Abraham Ross.[3] Initially it cannot have been easy for him to discuss again a past which he must have wanted to forget, and to meet someone who had serious misgivings about his role at the Identification parade. Yet he was always unfailingly courteous and co-operative, and I greatly enjoyed our several meals and meetings. I am grateful to Mr Ross for the interesting information about his early life, also for suggesting a small number of changes in the finished script, all of which I was happy to accept.

I owe an especial word of thanks to Mr Ewan (now Lord) Stewart, who as Solicitor-General of Scotland prosecuted Meehan at his trial. Mr Stewart was under no obligation to see me at all, and many other counsel in his position would have declined to. It says much for his generosity of spirit that he invited me to his house on more than one occasion to

[3] Mr Abraham Ross unfortunately died between first publication of this book and of this edition.

discuss the case and go through his notes of evidence.

The man at the centre of it all, Patrick Meehan, has been a source of information, not only in letters and memoranda to me but to all his lawyers, going back to the time of his arrest in July 1969. Few criminals who are the subject of historical investigation can have provided their chronicler with such a mass of material, presented in such a lucid and forceful way. Over the last six years he has shown a quite amazing capacity for hanging on, refusing despite a dozen rebuffs to admit defeat, determined to go on fighting, if necessary alone, if necessary until old age, until he has been finally cleared. In Betty Meehan, whom I have come to know and admire during the past year, he has a wife of exceptional character and courage who (despite a technical divorce) has never wavered in her efforts to get his case reviewed. To her and to their son Pat, I am grateful for much useful information.

But the real 'godfathers' of this book have been Meehan's legal advisers since 1969 – Mr Nicholas Fairbairn, Q.C., M.P., counsel at his trial, Mr Joseph Beltrami, Mr Leonard Murray, Mr Ross Harper and Mr David Burnside. These gentlemen have worked on Meehan's behalf for many years, latterly without financial reward or hope of any, so profound is their belief in Meehan's innocence. In a way this is as much their book as mine, for without the benefit of their collective wisdom and experience, it would never have got off the ground. At the end of 1974 they and I, together with Frank McElhone, M.P., and Peter Watson of the *Sunday Times* formed the Patrick Meehan Committee, a body which will remain in existence until justice for Meehan, and against those who were responsible for his wrongful imprisonment, has been belatedly done.

Others to whom I wish to express grateful thanks for their help are: Mr Bruce Millar, Secretary of State for Scotland, for giving me access to the official transcript of Lord Robertson's charge to the jury at Waddell's trial; the Crown Agent and his staff; the former Crown Agent, Mr Stanley Bowen; the Clerk of Justiciary and his staff; the former Chief Constable of Ayrshire, Mr Quinton Wilson; Mr

Gordon Airs, Chief Reporter of the *Scottish Daily Record*; Mr David Scott and Mr Ken Vass of BBC Scotland; Mr Alexander Angus, former Governor of Peterhead Prison; Mrs Delia Beltrami, Mr Alan Tweedale of the *Rochdale Observer*; Mr William Carlin, Mr John McCluskey, Q.C., Mrs Grant, Mr Michael McDonald, Dr David Bremner, Sir Robert McEwen, Bart, Mrs Murray, Mr Peter Watson; and the BBC and Granada Television for the use of copyright material.

Finally I must thank my two *amanuenses*, Joyce Turnbull and Nancy Winch, for their usual tireless efforts in helping the book physically to take shape, in the high speed typing of numerous letters and drafts. Without their help, to have written and delivered to my publishers some 80,000 words in the space of only five months would have been impossible.

LUDOVIC KENNEDY

Edinburgh 1975

PREFACE TO THE PANTHER EDITION

Not long after this book was first published in January 1976 the object of writing it was accomplished. Patrick Meehan was granted a free pardon and released from nearly seven years in prison. This came about as the result of the sudden death of William (Tank) McGuinness, which enabled his solicitor Mr Jospeh Beltrami (who had also been Meehan's trial solicitor) to release the confidential admissions that McGuinness had made to him, and earlier to his own wife, of his participation with Ian Waddell in the Ayr murder. It has been suggested that I myself was in possession of this information when I came to write the book, and that was why I was able to write with such certainty. This is not so. The manuscript of my book went to the publishers in May 1975, and it wasn't until July or August that I, and other journalists who believed in Meehan's innocence, concluded from various sources that McGuinness was Waddell's accomplice. (In the original edition of the book I called Waddell's accomplice McTurk, and it was only in preparing this edition that I had the information to describe the details of McGuinness's involvement.)

No, the certainty of my belief in Meehan's innocence was based on a close examination of events before the trial, on the evidence given at the trial, and on his persistent protestations of innocence (and particularly *the nature and quality* of those protestations) after the trial. *All* my information was either available or could have been made available, had they wanted it, to the Secretary of State for Scotland and the Lord Advocate.

Mr Beltrami, however, did know from 1972, and had suspicions from as far back as 1969, that McGuinness was Waddell's accomplice. It has been debated as to whether he should have informed the Crown authorities of what he knew in order that an innocent man (and moreover one that he had defended) might be released from prison. In my view he was right not to, however frustrating for him, and however unjust to Meehan. The whole basis of the solicitor–client relationship is confidentiality, and if clients came to believe that solicitors were prepared at times to breach it, in however good a cause, they would soon lose all faith in them and cease to use their services.

Indeed in the Meehan case it is only *because* of the confidentiality of the solicitor–client relationship that Mr Beltrami came to know of McGuinness's participation in the Ayr murder, and so was able to act quickly to put things right when McGuinness died. Had McGuinness not confided in him, it is doubtful whether the unsupported testimony of Mrs McGuinness as to her husband's guilt would have carried much weight with the Lord Advocate. He had after all ignored all of Waddell's detailed, public confessions, which carried a far higher potential for proof.

From first to last the Meehan case was a denial of justice, an example of what blindness and prejudice can do to the minds of normally sensible men. In what happened many are to blame: the police for giving untrue evidence about the Identification parade and the bits of paper; the Crown Office for issuing an improper statement that was highly prejudicial to Meehan's defence; the trial judge for a prejudiced trial and an inaccurate and biased summing-up; and the Lord Advocate for not allowing Meehan's well-founded applications for Bills of Criminal Letters.

But worse was what happened later – the refusal of successive Secretaries of State and Lord Advocates for nearly seven years either to refer back the case to the Court of Appeal, or to order a public inquiry. The worst offenders were Mr William Ross, M.P., former Secretary of State, and Mr Ronald King-Murray, Q.C., M.P., Lord Advocate. Why did Mr King-Murray reject Waddell's confessions when they contained so many details about the crime and the Rosses' house – details which only could have come from someone who had been there, and nearly all of which had been confirmed by Abraham Ross to Glasgow reporters? Why did he not have Abraham Ross and the reporters interviewed by the Crown Agent to test the truth of Waddell's confessions? If he thought Waddell's confessions were untrue in substance, from where did he think that Waddell obtained the true details? If from Meehan, on what evidence? Having concluded that Waddell's confessions were untrue, why did Mr King-Murray then not have him prosecuted for attempting to pervert the course of justice?

Again, did not Mr William Ross and Mr King-Murray think that the unanimous views of Meehan's trial counsel and all four solicitors that he was innocent, of some weight – and that this, taken in conjunction with the unanimous opinions of the reviewers of this book that Meehan should be immediately pardoned or an inquiry set up, made the case for his innocence overwhelming? And if not, why not? And finally was their refusal to act due to a quite staggering blindness, or because, fearful of the official corruption and incompetence an inquiry might reveal they chose, like Nixon at Watergate, to let sleeping dogs lie? Only they can supply the answer to this? What cannot be denied is that by their inertia and negligence, and for far longer than was excusable, they hindered the course of justice.

Forewords by Patrick Meehan's Legal Advisers from 1969

I. Nicolas Fairbairn, Q.C., M.P., Counsel to Meehan at his trial.
II. Joseph Beltrami, B.L., Solicitor to Meehan from his arrest until 1971, and from 1972.
III. Ross Harper, M.A., LL.B., Solicitor to Meehan, 1971.
IV. Leonard Murray, J.P., B.L., Solicitor to Meehan from 1971.
V. David Burnside, LL.B., principal Solicitor to Meehan from 1974.

I

Nicholas Fairbairn, Q.C., M.P., Counsel to Meehan at his trial.

The duty of an advocate is to present his client's case as instructed, provided always that the instructions are not so far in conflict with the evidence that to carry them out would be to frustrate his concomitant duty to the Court.

Meehan's instructions were clear and simple. He was not guilty of the charges. On the night in question he was with a man called Griffiths in Stranraer and he had evidence which suggested that Ian Waddell was one of those who had committed the crime with which he was charged.

Apart from my duty to accept these instructions in good faith, I did not doubt after scrutinising the evidence before trial that Meehan was in fact innocent of this crime, and anything and everything that has happened since has confirmed my belief that he is serving a life sentence for a crime he had no part in committing.

The announcement by the Crown Office before the trial was both prejudicial and damaging and thoroughly improper. The trial itself was anything but fair, as the reader will see, and the exclusion of the Special Defence of Impeachment of Ian Waddell, and the admission of the manner of Griffiths' death and of his criminal record, and evidence of his possible association with the crime as evidence against Meehan, are but slight examples of the many ways in which the principle of fairness to the accused, which is paramount in the Scottish trial, was abandoned in this particular case.

The appeal was peremptorily dismissed without consideration of the important new evidence of Griffiths' voice and his stated intentions. Since then the falsification of the Identification parade which was the main plank of the Crown case and Ian Waddell's plea of guilty to charges of committing perjury at Meehan's trial, and his recent frequent admissions (in ever increasing detail) of committing this crime, confirm what was clear before, during and since the trial, that Meehan is innocent and wrongly imprisoned and that Waddell, as he has so frequently claimed, is guilty.

I myself shall not rest until Patrick Meehan is pardoned and belatedly released from his imprisonment. The people who read this book will be able to come to this conclusion on their own.

II

Joseph Beltrami, B.L., Solicitor to Meehan from his arrest until 1971, and from 1972.

In the recollections of a career encompassing the defence of literally hundreds of homicide cases the haunting shadows of one trial predominate. The case is the Trial of Patrick Connolly Meehan.

This book succinctly and accurately traces the backcloth of that sensational trial and expertly records the various strands of evidence and how they were used to convict Meehan. It recites the disturbing – and in every sense reasonable – doubts as they existed at the time and as they have been compounded since. The author has appraised the whole facts and circumstances with an open mind. His reaction is surely typical of how one thinking man, with the same knowledge of the facts, must view this developing drama.

More than five years ago I was first interviewed by press and television about the case. I was very shaken as a result of it. Even then I considered that it would rank with the notorious Trial of Oscar Slater in the annals of legal history. Subsequent events have confirmed that view and indeed indicate that the earlier case has been dwarfed by it.

It is unfortunate that in a system where fairness to the accused is our proud claim, as it is in Scotland, examples of our failure rather than our success in pursuing the truth survive to be noted by posterity. One cannot fault the jury who dealt with the case, but what would their verdict have been if they had had the opportunity to consider all the facts that have become known in the ensuing years? Yet, as time marches on, the authorities seem less inclined to admit of the possibility of error.

In my view, in the light of all the evidence which is to hand, there has been a miscarriage of justice. Careful re-investigation by the authorities is essential – despite the many instances of past inquiry – and, if I am right, justice must surely be vindicated.

III

Ross Harper, M.A., LL.B., Solicitor to Meehan, 1971.

The Trial of Patrick Meehan was not just about Meehan. The pre-trial publicity meant that the system was on trial, the Police were on trial, the dead Griffiths was on trial, and Meehan was almost an unfortunate bystander of whom it could be said that he was 'none the worse of a good hanging'.

In my brief acquaintance with Meehan he was always asking me whether I believed in his innocence. He did not accept the philosophy that a solicitor discharges his duty best by not being concerned with fundamental questions of guilt or innocence. But his attitude will be all the more understandable by the reader after he has read this book. All credit to Ludovic Kennedy who has pinpointed the weaknesses in the Crown case clearly, so that it is difficult to imagine that the authorities will refuse an independent and full scale enquiry.

For my part I have been impressed by the attitude of other prisoners to the Meehan case. Since the trial I have spoken to many convicted criminals all of whom are totally convinced that Meehan was wrongly convicted. Such unanimity and indeed forcefulness is, in my experience, unique and, in my judgment, must be of some consequence.

IV

Leonard Murray, J.P., B.L., Solicitor to Meehan from 1971.

It was on December 10th 1971 that Mrs Betty Meehan first came to see me with instructions to represent her husband.

I was not enthusiastic. He had parted company with his two previous solicitors. I viewed the whole affair with at least scepticism but I undertook to look into the matter and see what could be done for her husband.

I suppose that at that time I regarded her husband as being a bit of a crank. There had been a great deal of pre-trial publicity, which I always regard as a bad thing, and there had been if anything even more publicity since the trial concluded. That publicity had certainly not done Patrick Meehan any good. My task therefore was one which I did not look forward to with any relish.

I began a study of the papers. I suppose the first thing that struck me was just how thin the evidence against Meehan really was. In my ignorance I had assumed that the man had been convicted in the light of rather overwhelming evidence. Gradually, in the light of facts which emerged, it became almost obvious that Patrick Meehan would not have committed the murder.

I cannot say, looking back, when I became convinced that Meehan had not committed the murder. It was elsewhere reported that mine was a gradual conviction of innocence – however paradoxical that may seem. Today I have no doubt. There are far too many things which in my view are inconsistent with his guilt, for example his actions after the event, his giving the police information which inevitably led to him, the time intervals involved, his entire previous life, even his protestations of innocence.

Many convicted murderers protest their innocence after they have been convicted. In nearly twenty years' experience of practising in the Criminal Courts of Scotland I have never come across a man who protested quite as strenuously, quite as unwaveringly and quite as convincingly as has Patrick Meehan. There are aspects of the Crown case against him which trouble me not just as a lawyer but as an individual. There are aspects of the evidence which require investigation. Had the facts which are within our knowledge now, been before the Court, I am convinced that the jury would have brought in a different result. I do not hesitate to say that were Patrick Meehan to face trial today he would be acquitted. This is not a guess – it is a certainty.

V

David Burnside, LL.B., principal Solicitor to Meehan from 1974.

In November 1973 I received a letter from Mrs Betty Meehan asking me if I would be able to help her husband who was fighting against his wrongful conviction for murder. It seemed that he wanted me to proceed with a Bill of Criminal Letters against three police officers in respect of perjury and conspiracy. I replied that, provided I was satisfied that there was substance in his complaint, I would have no objection.

At our first meeting we talked for some three hours, or should I say perhaps, Meehan talked and I listened. I realised right away that this man was somewhat different from the many criminals I had met in the past. He spoke very well and very convincingly but then, of course, that could have been because he was a con-man. But, I reminded myself, this was not a con-man, this was a man who had apparently brutally and violently assaulted an elderly couple in their own home, causing one of them to die, yet that description did not appear to fit the man I was talking to. He had a wry sense of humour which he often directed against himself, but shining through everything was a passionate belief in his own innocence which I could not recollect having seen in such intensity before. Many men have gone to prison protesting their innocence, but most eventually accept the situation and work for their release. I quickly established that this was not the case with Meehan, that he had never accepted the sentence and had voluntarily spent lengthy periods in solitary confinement, deprived of the companionship of the dining room, or the work sheds.

His protestations of innocence were not merely of the emotional kind unbacked by facts, but pinpointed with almost scientific accuracy the areas of doubt which he felt had not been properly exploited at his trial. He also told me of his belief that the police officers had deliberately 'fixed' the Identification parade to ensure that Abraham Ross had the benefit of discussion with the witnesses who had already seen the parade before he was led in to identify Meehan. I left prison that day still with a degree of scepticism but already intensely interested in the case. In the months that followed I got to know the man better (although he rarely lowered a slight guard of reserve) and I became more and more convinced of his innocence. Cynics often say lawyers do nothing unless there is a handsome cheque in contemplation at the end of the exercise. I knew there was no prospect of getting paid but nevertheless I decided that I would be prepared to devote a very considerable amount of time and effort to this case, which obviously I would not have done had I thought Meehan guilty and his arguments spurious. Eighteen months and a dozen meetings with the man have made my belief in his innocence total.

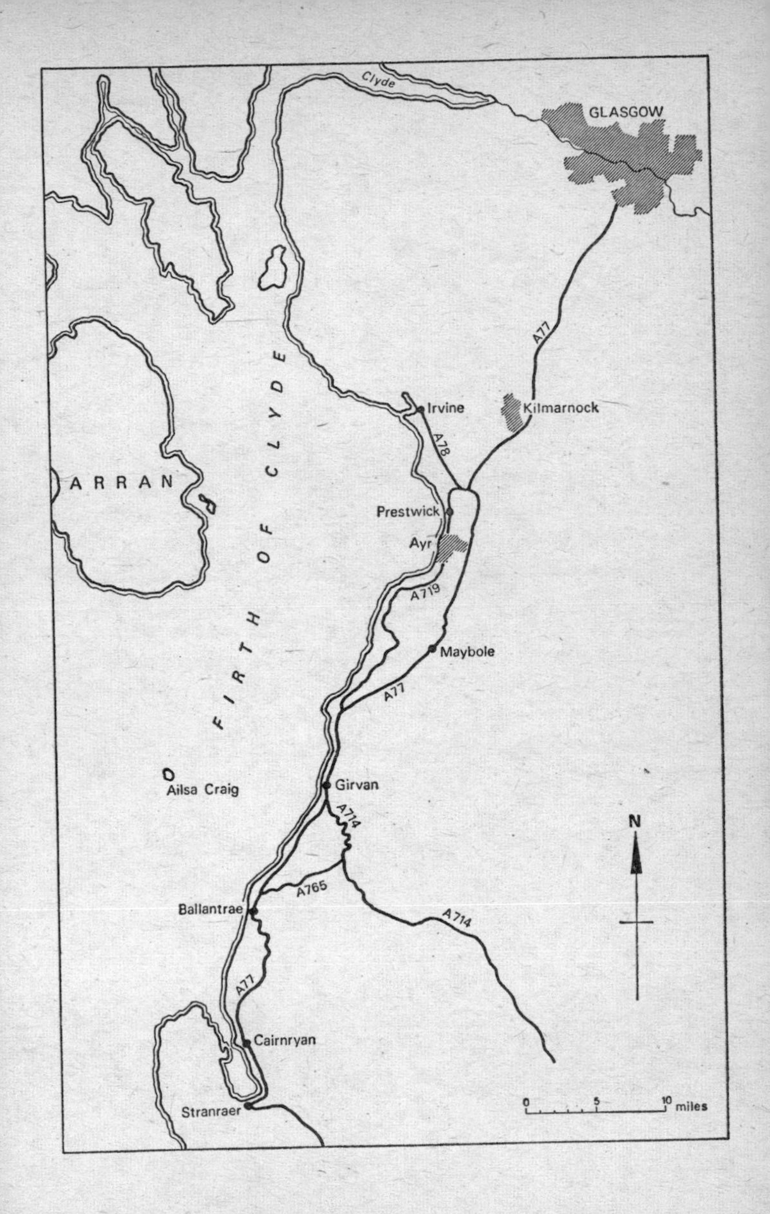

Clyde
GLASGOW
A77
Kilmarnock
Irvine
A78
FIRTH OF CLYDE
ARRAN
Prestwick
Ayr
A719
Maybole
A77
Ailsa Craig
Girvan
A714
N
A765
Ballantrae
A714
A77
Cairnryan
Stranraer
0
5
10
miles

PART I

Meehan

On the afternoon of Saturday July 5th 1969 two cars drove south separately out of Glasgow each carrying a pair of Neds or villains, each pair engaged on unlawful intent.

One of the cars was a blue Triumph 2000, with false number plates. At the wheel was an English criminal by the name of James Griffiths, a Rochdale man, aged 34, with a long, cruel record. The car was not his: he had stolen it from a motel at Gretna Green two weeks earlier. His companion was Glasgow-born Patrick Meehan, aged 42, a famous safe-blower, with an even longer record and many years of prison behind him, but nothing violent in the course of theft, nothing against the person. They were going to Stranraer, 84 miles away, to look at the motor taxation offices. If Meehan liked what he saw, he would return one night, break into the place, blow the safe and help himself to money and blank registration books that Griffiths was always needing for selling stolen cars.

The other car was a silver-grey Ford Cortina. The driver, and brains, was a criminal by the name of William (Tank) McGuinness, with a long record of housebreaking and violence; the passenger, a small-time Glasgow crook by the name of Ian Waddell. Their mission was rather different. They had information that in Ayr, only 33 miles away, there was a safe to be robbed, containing much money: it lay, they had heard, in the house of Mr Abraham Ross, a bingo-hall owner who lived with his wife Rachel at No 2 Blackburn Place, near the sea. In the night these two were going to force an entry into 2 Blackburn Place, and tell Mr Ross to give them the key of the safe. If he refused they had their own methods of persuading him; they were not fastidious people.

Meehan was a child of the Gorbals, born on April 12th 1927 in Alexander Row, one of a group of tied cottages. They were demolished soon after his birth and the family moved to a tenement flat in Oxford Street. Meehan's father was a casual labourer, a coalman mostly, 'a kind, easy-going man who boasted he had never been a day idle in his life'. There was an elder brother Frank, whom Meehan didn't get on with, and now never sees, and a younger brother George, with whom he has always kept in touch. Frank is a mechanic in Glasgow, and George a fitter with Qantas Airways in Australia. Neither Frank nor George have ever been in trouble with the law.

Meehan does not have much to say about his mother except that she was born Anne Ross and was always on the move, and 'it was her theory that I got into trouble because of Irish blood on my father's side'. (George thinks it was because their father was not strict enough.) When Meehan was five, he went to stay with his father's parents, Grandfather Billy and Granny Bina, who lived round the corner in South Portland Street – the first of many visits. Granny Bina adored him, and he was the right age for a young cousin, Patrick Connelly, who had also come to live there after his parents had died. To distinguish the two Patricks, the cousin became known as Packy and Meehan as Paddy which his family and friends have called him ever since.

Paddy loved his Irish grandparents and says that his happiest childhood memories are of his times with them. 'Granny Bina had strong political views. She supported the Irish Republican movement, was anti-English and hostile to the Police. Grandad Billy was a reader who spent his days in the local library.'

Also living in the house was Aunt Nan, the grandparents' youngest daughter, who, says Meehan, 'spent her day covering up for my cousin Packy and me'. In the Gorbals in those days there were few playgrounds, and like many of their friends the two boys played truant in the streets. 'Stealing from shop doorways was a regular sport, and fruit shops, where the fruit was put on display in the street, were our favourite targets.'

But what had started as a boyish prank suddenly turned sour. After warning by the police and the Sheriff, young

Meehan found himself, at ten, being hauled off to approved school. He soon ran away, not to his grandparents but to his parents' house in Oxford Street. He wanted his mother, and felt that if he found her, the authorities would allow him to stay with her. But there was a court order against him, and Mrs Meehan had no choice but to return him to the approved school. Perhaps if she had been able to keep him, his life would have been different.

For the next six years, that is during the latter part of his childhood and most of his adolescence, Meehan was in approved schools for persistent theft, running away from them half a dozen times, and almost as quickly being returned.

'Of the approved schools I was in, three were Catholic and one (Oakbank in Aberdeen) was for Protestant children. Of the Catholic schools – even as I look back from this distance in time – I can say nothing good. These schools were staffed by Christian Brothers who were invariably Irish, and a more ignorant, sadistic and hypocritical lot it would be difficult to find. In these schools I was beaten more times than I can count, and if my arse wasn't in tatters from constant thrashing, my knees were swollen due to hours of kneeling at prayer in the chapel. Standing for hours in the snow dressed in a nightshirt; sweeping the play-yard with a toothbrush; these were the punishments thought up by the Christian Brothers.

'Of Oakbank Approved School I can say nothing but good. There the staff were family men and cruelty did not exist. The School Director or Governor lived in the school with his wife and children. His name was McLeod, a former professional football player, and I think it significant that I was two years at Oakbank before I ran away. During my time at Oakbank I turned fourteen, was made school monitor and head gardener.'

In the end he ran away from Oakbank too. He had a girlfriend in the district, and, to earn money to take her to a café, he stole onions from the garden and sold them to an old lady. One day the old lady, thinking the onion sales were legal, came to the school to buy more. 'When I heard about it,' said Meehan, 'I took the next train to Glasgow.' He was on the run for seven months before being returned to the school and then, because it was feared he might run off with the girl, he was transferred to a senior approved school, St Johns, in Glasgow.

At sixteen he ran away from this school, committed an offence, and was arrested. To the police he admitted not only the offence, but others of which he was innocent, in order to get sent to Borstal. 'If you were committed to Borstal, you could count on being released within one year; if you were returned to approved school, you would remain there until you were eighteen – two years. The police knew what it was all about, and were quite happy to clear their books.'

Meehan's early life then, from the age of ten to eighteen, was spent in corrective institutions, and it could well be that his many adult years in prison are partly the result of that early conditioning. Years later when a judge told him that he had been a criminal since the age of nine, he was angry. 'No child of nine can be called a criminal; and no child who has a home where he is wanted should be put into an institution. Put a child into an institution and all he wants is to go home.' And he added, wryly: 'Children from a slum area are called juvenile delinquents and are sent to approved schools. Children from a middle-class area are called naughty and sent home.'

* * *

When Meehan came out of Borstal in 1945 at the age of eighteen, Grandfather Billy and Granny Bina were dead. His parents, who seldom stayed anywhere more than a few months – a restlessness that he seems to have inherited – had now moved to Moffat Street in the Gorbals. In nearby Orchard Street lived a family called Carson, the father a worker at the Rolls-Royce factory at Hillington, with two sons and a daughter. The daughter, Elizabeth, was a pretty, sensible girl of sixteen, and Meehan found himself increasingly drawn to her. She also liked him. 'He was sort of different to other boys – he wasn't interested in cars or films or football or jazz. He wasn't *a bore*.' She admired his vitality (his brothers were much quieter) and sense of fun, and the neatness of his appearance. She admired too his desire to help others, as when he became a voluntary blood donor, a practice he has continued all his life. 'He was really soft,' says Betty. Twenty-five years later this keenness to be helpful was to land him in the deepest trouble.

They were married in the John Knox Church in Glasgow's Surrey Street in September 1945, and for the occasion Meehan had 'BETTY' and a drawing of her head tattooed on his right arm. At the time of the wedding Meehan was on bail for theft, and while on bail he was caught shop-breaking. In October he was sentenced for both offences to fifteen months' imprisonment. It was not the most auspicious start to any marriage, and for a girl of less courage and character than Betty, it would probably have ended before it had begun. He came out of prison just a year later and was then called up for National Service. But like his grandparents he was too much of an individualist to accept gracefully alien disciplines; and after a few months of anti-social behaviour and pretending he couldn't read, the Army dishonourably discharged him.

On return to Glasgow he got a job as a welder at a shipyard on the Clyde, work he was to perform at intervals over the next few years. One of his workmates, by name Peter, was a dedicated Communist. Meehan was impressed by what Peter said at lunchtime meetings and by literature Peter gave him, and in 1950 he joined the Communist Party. He didn't attach much importance to this at the time (he says that after a while the propaganda bored him), but eventually it was to have far-reaching effects.

In December 1947 Meehan was arrested for blowing the safe of Cochrane's, the grocers, in Bedford Street, and in February 1948 sentenced to three years' imprisonment. Betty thinks he picked up the expertise on safe-blowing from a Canadian the first time he was in Barlinnie. 'That's always been Paddy's trouble – he can turn his hand to anything.'

So the pattern of his life was established, and he was to continue in this fashion for the next ten years; Meehan blowing safes all over Scotland, being caught and imprisoned, coming out again, sometimes for only a few months, taking casual work while planning the next 'job'. He never told Betty when he had blown a safe, but she always knew: he would come in during the early hours, tired and tense, then disappear for several days in case the police came looking for him. One of his colleagues at this time was a Glaswegian-born Lithuanian called Ramensky, a brilliant cracksman who had got the D.C.M. in the war for being parachuted behind the lines and blowing enemy safes. Betty meanwhile struggled to bring up a family. The first son Patrick was born in 1947, a daughter Sally in 1948, and another daughter Liz in 1951.

That same year Meehan got three years for blowing the safe of a bank in Alexandra Parade. He was out in 1953, and, soon after, a strange thing happened while preparing to blow a safe at J. D. Cuthbertson's, a music shop in Sauchiehall Street. He had gone to a disused basement in Renfrew Street to store explosives for use later, 'when I heard the heavy breathing of a large dog coming down the stairs. I then heard a man's voice and a few seconds later I heard the whimper of a child. There was no door to the basement cellar, and on looking out I observed a man in the act of attempting to interfere with a little girl of about four or five. I went for the man but he heard me (the cellar was full of rubble) and he made off. I chased him and he ran through the back court and escaped through a close further along. As he ran away he called out to the large dog. The dog ran after him. I returned to the child who was crying, picked her up and carried her upstairs to the front street. As far as I could see the child had not been harmed, so I left her.

'A few weeks later I found myself in Barlinnie as an untried prisoner. I was the barber and had to cut the hair of other prisoners. One day I was cutting the hair of a prisoner whose face seemed familiar to me. I couldn't recall where I had seen him before, but I got the impression that he was a bit feeble-minded.

'I was released on bail pending trial, and one day I was sitting in a tram-car when a man jumped on the platform. Running behind the tram-car was a large dog, and I immediately recognized the man as the prisoner whose hair I had cut, and as the man I saw interfering with the little girl.

'A few months later I was in Peterhead Prison when a little girl or two or three was raped and murdered not far from Renfrew Street. This became known as the "Betty Blue" case. I immediately consulted the Governor and sent off a statement with the above facts to the Northern Police Station, on the off-chance that the same man might have been responsible. In fact no arrest was ever made.'

This is Meehan's 'Good Samaritan' side – a compulsion to be helpful in matters that do not concern him, and which, because of his vulnerability as a man with a record, he would be wiser to let be. As he himself wrote of the incident years later: 'What would my position have been had the little girl been seriously assaulted and I, after the man ran off, was left to explain the situation to someone who came on the scene?' Could he but have foreseen it, something not dissimilar was to happen seventeen years later at Ayr.

In 1954 Meehan was involved in another bizarre incident, the 'springing' of Edward Martin from Peterhead Prison. He had known Martin since approved school days.

'In 1954 we were in Peterhead together. At that time Peterhead Prison had the reputation that no escapee had ever succeeded in getting clear of the area. It was believed that the road blocks set up by the police and prison staff ensured that no escapee would get through. The police and prison staff were proud of this.

'While in prison Martin confided in me that he intended to escape, and I suggested that he wait until I was released; I would assist him by bringing up a car and clothing.

'I was released December 9th 1954 and, back in Glasgow, I enlisted the assistance of two other men; John Harvey and a man I will call Darky. The plan I thought out was as follows: Darky arranged to have a prison uniform, vest and shirt, smuggled out of Barlinnie Prison, Glasgow. On this clothing we ink-marked Martin's Peterhead Prison number. The clothing was then concealed in the loft of a building in the Blackhill area of Glasgow.

'On the eve of the escape Darky remained in Glasgow.

John Harvey and myself picked up Martin when he came over and drove to a hotel a few miles west of the prison. We sat in the hotel lounge drinking, and about five hours later I phoned Darky in Glasgow. Darky then made an anonymous phone call to Glasgow Police, telling them that the escaped convict Martin was hiding in the loft of a building at Blackhill. The Police went to the loft, and did not find Martin, but they found what looked like Martin's prison clothing, and presumed Martin must be in Glasgow. Darky watched the police leave the building with the prison clothing, then he phoned me back to let me know. About an hour later Martin, Harvey and I left the hotel and drove to the west coast and down via Fort William to Glasgow. We reached Glasgow in the early hours of the following morning. We saw no road blocks.

'A few months later Martin, Harvey and I went before Lord Cameron at Aberdeen High Court; Martin charged with escaping, Harvey and I assisting escaping. I agreed to enter a plea of guilty if the Crown would drop the charge against Harvey. The Crown accepted this, Martin got 15 months, I got 12 months and Harvey was acquitted.

'To me the whole thing was just a lark. Whether the prison suit we used as a red herring caused the road blocks to be taken off is disputable. The Police say they did not fall for the trick; *but I saw no road blocks.*'

This is another side of Meehan; the man who has never grown up, the boy still playing truant in the Gorbals streets, seeking excitement and adventure for its own sake, enormously pleased at having cocked a snook at authority.

Early in 1955 Meehan took part with Ramensky in a bank raid at Oban, capital of the western Highlands, and later in the year he and a villain named Thompson broke into the temporary premises of the Commercial Bank at Beauly in Invernesshire. They blew three safes, but a safety device operated in the one that contained the most cash, and the total haul was under £400. They were caught because a Perthshire garage proprietor, who sold them petrol on the way back, thought the Humber Snipe they were driving was 'not the sort of car one usually associates with such men', and he took its number. Later, by an extraordinary chance the key of Thompson's Glasgow house was found lying in the road where he had dropped it after leaving the Bank. successfully, to get the case reviewed. By this time Archie Elliott. Elliott had first acted for Meehan five years earlier when, under Scottish Bar procedure, he found he had been allocated Meehan on the Poor Persons Roll. On this occasion (another safe-breaking) he had got Meehan off, and Meehan was so impressed that he asked for his services at the trial for springing Martin (where Elliott argued, unsuccessfully, before Lord Cameron that as Martin had not escaped from Peterhead *prison* but from an outside working-party in the dockyard, Meehan was being charged with a crime unknown to Scottish law).

The evidence against Meehan at the Beauly trial was flimsy, and he was convicted on a majority verdict. Although admitting privately that he had been involved in the raid, he was annoyed, he says, that some of the evidence against him was perjured, and he tried, in the end unsuccessfully, to get the case reviewed. By this time Archie Elliott had come to know and rather like Meehan. 'In my view,' he said, 'he wasn't capable of hurting a fly.'

Meehan got six years for the Beauly job, but with remission was due out in the summer of 1960. But Betty, whose married life to date had been spent more on her own than with her husband, decided that she had had enough, and told Paddy she wanted a separation. When he came out in June 1960 she had taken the family to live with friends, but Paddy followed her, and begged for a last chance. His obvious need for her – he has always needed her – persuaded her to change her mind; and in the summer of 1960 they left the children with Paddy's mother in Beith, Ayrshire, and flew to Canada.

They went to the west coast, to Vancouver, where Paddy got a job with a welding firm, doing much the same job as in Glasgow. Later he got work as a dining-car attendant (a job he had also done in Scotland between sentences) on the Canadian Pacific Railroad. He was on the Winnipeg run, and would be away five days at a time. Betty meanwhile had got two jobs, one in the boarding house where they were staying, another as waitress in a hotel in the evening.

But the dining-car job was seasonal, and in the autumn of 1960 Paddy got a new job as a deckhand on the *King George V*, a big cargo-boat plying between Vancouver, Nanaimo and New Westminster. It was rough work, and the weather was often foul; but he seems to have enjoyed it. Betty would fly across to Nanaimo to join him at weekends. She looks back on this period as one of the least troubled of their married life.

They hoped to save enough money to bring the children out, and start a new life. But when the *King George V* was ordered to Liverpool, Paddy decided to stay in her. In England he wired Betty money to fly home. She was met at the airport by her son Patrick, now aged thirteen, with the news that the police were looking for Paddy and he had gone into hiding. He showed up two days later, having completed another successful safe-blowing, told the family he was flying back at once to Canada (to avoid the police), and they should follow. He left almost immediately for Vancouver and two days before Christmas 1960 the family joined him there in a rented house.

For the Meehans this should have been the beginning of a new life. There were plans for opening a restaurant, and it is noticeable that in all their time in Canada Paddy went straight, tempting though it must have been to blow a safe or two in an area where his expertise was unknown. But the plans for the restaurant never materialized, and Betty, who was now pregnant again, found herself increasingly irritated and tired. So, in March 1961, after only three months in Canada, the whole family returned to Glasgow and moved into a small house in Alexandra Parade.

Betty, approaching the end of her pregnancy, was now far from well, and had to go into hospital for blood transfusions. The children were staying with Betty's stepmother in Glasgow; and Paddy lost no time in seeking out old friends:

'Within a few days I renewed my association with Edward Martin and the man I refer to as Darky. Soon after Martin and I went down to London to consult with certain London villains who required the services of a safe-blower. After about a week in London Martin and I returned to Glasgow. I told the people in London that I was not prepared to get involved in anything until my wife had had the baby.'

Back in Glasgow events took a curious turn. Martin and Darky quarrelled over money: Darky shot and wounded Martin, who was taken to the Royal Infirmary. Meehan visited him there, and one day he left the hospital to buy some things for Martin. He first went to the main Post Office in George Square to change a £100 note, and as he came out, he was hailed by a man. 'The man knew my name was Paddy and he kept snapping his fingers trying to remember my surname – so I told him. His face was not familiar, but he did convince me at that moment that he had met me years previous at Communist Party meetings. He said he was going in the direction of the hospital so I offered him a lift.'

In the car the man mentioned Peter, the Communist Paddy had met working in the shipyards ten years earlier, and with whom he had since kept up a desultory correspondence. 'He said he had read about me in the papers several times and had often discussed me with Peter. Then he asked me if the fellow who had been shot was the same fellow I had sprung from Peterhead. At the hospital we sat in the car talking and it soon became clear to me that our meeting outside the GPO was no accident. It also became clear that the conversation was being steered. The Portland spy case was mentioned, and the question of springing a spy from an English prison.'

There the conversation ended but Meehan agreed to meet the man again in a couple of days' time. 'What shall I call you?' said Meehan, as they parted. 'You think of a name,' said the man, and for want of a better Meehan said 'Hector'.

At the second meeting, says Meehan, Hector got over to Meehan three things. That Peter had put up Meehan's name as someone who might spring a spy from an English prison, but that if Meehan questioned Peter about it, Peter would deny everything. That Meehan was to keep out of trouble until Hector was in touch with him again; and that Meehan would probably have to go to East Berlin to get instructions. But, says Meehan, all this was said obliquely. 'He was very crafty. He would broach a subject, leaving me to ask the questions; and he would answer as if he was merely expressing an opinion – 'I should *think* you would have to go to East Berlin so that the people there could discuss it with you – I should *think* they would know Peter.' Hector told Meehan to say nothing to anyone of their meeting; and Meehan never saw him again.

Although this strange conversation was to stick in Meehan's mind, it would be a long time before he acted on it. Meanwhile he had no reason to be deflected from his usual mode of life. After his second son Garry was born on April 1st, he again went to London. There was the matter of the job that he and Martin had discussed before Martin was shot. He and Betty had been talking about the possibility of emigrating to Australia. If the London job came off, there would be plenty of money to pay the fares and set up house in Australia.

But the London job was an abject failure. The premises to be broken into were the Co-operative Stores at Edmonton. Meehan's services were not required for entering the place, which had already been achieved, but for vetting the explosives. On arrival with the rest of the gang he was appalled at the amount of gelignite they had placed. 'There's enough here,' he told them, 'to blow up ourselves and the whole building.' He was in the act of picking some of the gelignite out with a knitting needle when the police, acting on a tip-off, arrived, and the whole gang was arrested.

The three accomplices got sentences ranging from two and a half to five years, but for Meehan, with several convictions for safe-blowing and explosives, a punitive sentence was inevitable. On June 23rd at the Old Bailey Mr Justice Maud gave him eight years' preventive detention in the name of Patrick Carson. Betty heard the news from a friend, then rang a number in London that Paddy had given her for emergencies, to get it confirmed. For her it was the end.

Yet for Meehan it was to be only the beginning of another series of bizarre adventures. Four months after arriving in Wandsworth, he says, he received a postcard from Hector, and there was a reminder of their past conversation about going to East Germany.

In prison people have all the time in the world to plan and meditate, and the more Meehan thought about the idea of going behind the Iron Curtain, the more it appealed to him. It was another adventure, like the busting of the bank in Beauly or the springing of Martin from Peterhead, but altogether more novel and with the possibility of rich rewards. In December 1962 he attempted to escape from Nottingham Prison where he had been transferred. He failed, was awarded 28 days' solitary confinement, 9 days' bread and water and 180 days' loss of remission.

On August 20th 1963 he tried again, this time successfully. A diversion was arranged during a cricket match and in the confusion Meehan, a prisoner called Hogan and two others escaped through a fence to a road where a car was waiting. They drove to London, where the party split up. Meehan and Hogan went to Glasgow, where he saw Betty briefly at the house of friends. Next day Meehan caught a plane to Dublin, then to Frankfurt. Here, he says, he took a train to Badhersfeld where he bought a bike, and then cycled to the frontier. He started to cross it near a place called Marienborn, and was arrested by the East German police.

Having explained who he was Meehan was taken to the East German Security Police headquarters at Hohenschönhausen in Berlin. To his interrogators he offered his services: he could, he told them, arrange for any spy they wanted to be sprung from any British prison – though if a transfer of the spy to a Scottish prison could be arranged, that would be easier, as he knew the prison officers who could be bribed. According to what Meehan later told the *Daily Express* journalist, Chapman Pincher, the Communists said they were interested only in springing the famous double agent, George Blake, serving 42 years, and Helen and Peter Kroger, the Navy spies; they were not interested in Gordon

Lonsdale, as they were making other arrangements for him. They asked Meehan repeatedly about the lay-out of British prisons and escape routes, and he told them the best way of leaving Britain was by hiding in a van loaded on to the Stranraer–Larne boat. They even took him by air to a secret destination (which Meehan thinks was Moscow), where he was interrogated by more security people. Meehan also wrote essays about escaping from British prisons, but said that if they intended to spring anyone, he should be there to supervise it.

With plenty of time on his hands Meehan began to learn German, and having a facility for languages, was soon fluent in it. He got to know several other inmates of the prison, among them a girl called Inge Schmidt, with whom he was to correspond for many years, and another girl, Beatte Barwich. Her father, Professor Heinz Barwich, an East German atomic scientist, had defected to the Americans at Geneva, and as a reprisal his children had been arrested. 'Beatte Barwich was in the cell above mine,' wrote Meehan. 'The cell lavatories had a common waste pipe, and by removing the water from the S bend, one could speak through the waste pipe to the person in the cell above or below.' For three months Meehan had long talks with Beatte Barwich in German, with his head down the lavatory pan. 'It was not very dignified but it was practical.'

By December 1964 the East Germans had decided that Meehan had exhausted whatever usefulness he might have had for them. They took him to Berlin's Checkpoint Charlie and handed him over to the West Berlin authorities. From here Meehan flew to England, was arrested on arrival and sent to Wandsworth to complete his sentence.

The Special Branch were not long in calling at Wandsworth, but Meehan refused to see them. So (according to him) they adopted 'planting' tactics. 'On being detailed to do work with the Security Party (where everyone knows everyone else), I sat down next to a man I knew; but the officer came over and told me to sit in a seat which he pointed out. This was most unusual. I found myself sitting next to a man whom no one knew. After some conversation I knew instinctively he was no prisoner. After a couple of days the man started talking fluent German. He was in sympathy with the Communists: he hated the British (I don't blame him when they gave him a job like that!) and was going to run away behind the Iron Curtain when he got bail. Every day he was called away for about an hour, would come back and say, 'That was my lawyer. He expects to have me out on bail any day now. Anything I can do for you?' Meehan asked Steve Taggart, a fellow prisoner, to keep an eye on him. 'One day I was called away and shipped to Parkhurst. A few days later Steve arrived, and I asked him what happened to our friend. "As soon as you went, he disappeared," said Steve.'

At Parkhurst, in the Isle of Wight, Meehan was again 'pestered' by the Governor to speak to MI 5, but repeatedly refused. The same thing happened when he was transferred to Blundeston near Lowestoft. Then, it seems, MI 5 changed their tactics. Would Meehan help them to trace certain persons missing in East Germany? He felt he could not refuse this and agreed to an interview.

On April 2nd 1965 he was interviewed at Blundeston by a Mr Saunders of MI 5 (Saunders seems to be one of the standard names for characters from MI 5 – certainly it has a fine, Buchanesque ring about it). Saunders, says Meehan, started the conversation by asking Meehan to sign the Official Secrets Act. Meehan refused on two grounds; first because he was described on the form as an employee which he found insulting; and second because the form threatened him with imprisonment if he contravened the Act, which was absurd.

Saunders then got down to the business in hand which was not, says Meehan, to inquire about missing persons, but to find out from Meehan what had happened in Berlin. As to what Meehan said there are two versions. Meehan's is that the only spies the Communists said they wanted to spring, and intended to spring, were Blake and the Krogers; but according to the Mountbatten report on prison security,

Meehan told Saunders that the Communists 'were not much interested in Blake'.

Eighteen months later Blake was sprung in a brilliant coup from Wormwood Scrubs. Afraid the authorities might think he had some hand in it, he got a message to Chapman Pincher to visit him. This Pincher did, posing as a friend, and after a long interview he published an article in the *Daily Express* called 'My Startling Talk with Prisoner 519'. In this Pincher upheld Meehan's claim to have warned Mr Saunders that the Communists were interested in Blake. 'I have since confirmed,' wrote Pincher 'that Meehan was interrogated ... by a Senior Security official who reported the warning in writing to the Director-General of the Security Service. I have also been assured that the warning was then passed to the Home Office.'

But when the Mountbatten Report on prison security came out, it told a different story. It said that the account given by Meehan to Chapman Pincher of what he had said to Saunders differed 'in some important respects' from Special Branch records. The main difference, said Lord Mountbatten, was that Meehan had made his account to Chapman Pincher re Lonsdale and Blake match with Blake's subsequent escape and Lonsdale's subsequent exchange. 'If the references which he originally made to these two spies had been repeated in the interview, their inaccuracy would have been immediately apparent and would throw doubt on the reliability of anything else he might say.' But Lord Mountbatten did not challenge Pincher's claim to have checked that Meehan's warning to the authorities had been passed on to the Head of Security, and that they had passed it on to the Home Office. And Meehan himself says that during a later conversation with another Special Branch officer (not Saunders), the man admitted they had passed on his warning, but that the Home Office had denied it in order to cover up its own neglect.

The Mountbatten Report came out at the end of 1966. Christmas came and went, and then in the New Year of 1967, Meehan was transferred from Blundeston to Parkhurst, Isle of Wight. Here he met another prisoner whose

future was to be fatally linked with his. Hi
Griffiths.

* * *

James Griffiths was born in Rochdale, 1
1935, one of a family of seven children. He w
from the age of six, pinching things from ho the
pockets of classmates at school. 'He always liked to be seen,' said his mother, 'and attract attention to himself.' He was taken to a child guidance clinic, and later put under the supervision of a woman probation officer. But the stealing went on, and when he was nine his mother took him before the Rochdale Juvenile Court as being beyond her control. When she told the court that both her husband and herself were going out to work, the Chairman, Dr W. H. Bateman, said to her: 'It is felt you are losing more than you are gaining by not being at home looking after the children. It is absolutely essential that you should be there to give them a proper home where they would know they were being cared for.' But a year later, unable to cope with her difficult son any more, Mrs Griffiths sent the boy to an orphanage for a year. The experience had a lasting effect on him; he felt rejected.

At thirteen Griffiths was back in the Juvenile Court for breaking and entering and theft. This included a watch from his home and eleven keys from school – he said in evidence he wanted the watch and he'd starting collecting keys. Like Meehan he was sent to approved school – at a place called Newton-le-Willows. Sometimes his mother visited him. 'Even when you went,' she said, '... the only conversation you had was when you spoke, he'd answer you. He never told you anything ... bloody hell if he spoke half a dozen words. One day one of the masters came out, and I said, who's that, and he says, oh, he's a pig, he doesn't half belt you.' After approved school he stole a car in Rochdale to go joy-riding – cars were to become a lifelong passion – and, like Meehan, was sent to Borstal.

After this (again like Meehan) Griffiths went into the Army, joining the Ordnance Corps. He liked it at first, got d had two sons. But he couldn't keep out of for long. In 1956 he broke into his brother's house Rochdale and stole goods and cash, and he also admitted to stealing from an army camp. Sentence was suspended for twelve months. He then stole a motor-car from a Rochdale garage and drove it to Northamptonshire where he fitted new number plates and altered the licence. His unit left for Cyprus soon after, but on return, the following year, he was sentenced to six months' imprisonment both for the car theft and for stealing from the house of his brother. A fellow prisoner, Vincent Burke, said of him at this time: 'He was a very good-looking lad with a fine physique, powerful and attractive, especially to women. But he told a lot of lies. He said he had nine or ten G.C.E's and four or five of them were A levels, and of course he hadn't got any at all. He told me he was in the Red Devils, and when he was released from prison he had a Red Devils' uniform on with a Sergeant's stripes, but he was actually in the Ordnance Corps.' Burke's brother, who was a mental nurse, met Griffiths later and thought him a psychopath.

On finishing this sentence Griffiths found that his wife was having affairs with other men. 'So after that,' he said, 'I wasn't really interested in what she did. She just carried on in her sweet way, and I went mine.' His way consisted of a life of increasing crime and punishment. He got 18 months at Derbyshire Quarter Sessions for conspiracy to defraud and obtaining money by means of a forged instrument, and 15 months at Burton-on-Trent Quarter Sessions for stealing £10 from a dwelling-house.

He came out in 1959 and for a few years managed to avoid arrest. After each job, 'I got my money together and went abroad ... I lived in the best hotels and did what I wanted ... and when the money was getting a bit low, I came back to this country, did some more and went back abroad.' He went on: 'I've been caught two or three times, but there's more times I haven't been caught ... so I consider it was worth it.' We have his own word that he was always ready to use violence or the threat of violence. 'If there's one or two people come on the scene of the crime, and I've got no weapons at all, I'm captured unless I can do something about it. So I either carry a gun or a knife ... for self-preservation, and to cope with dogs or anything like that.'

And yet, despite his shallowness and brutality, there was another side to Griffiths. He hardly ever drank, he kept himself fit with exercises, and he loved climbing and potholing. 'Climbing is a thing you can do no matter what the weather is – whether it's snowing or raining or blowing a gale, you can still go climbing. And it's an achievement, you get a feeling you've done something. You can sit back after a really stiff climb and think "I did that" – it was good – it was hard but it was good.' And he added, comically, 'I think I'm one of the safest people to go climbing or potholing with because I ... don't want publicity. I don't want to fall off a cliff and break my arm or break my leg or get trapped down underground and have all the police digging around. Because they're going to say, "Who's this chappie? He says he's John Green. He isn't John Green, he's so and so. We know – we got his fingerprints." I mean, this sort of thing just isn't on.'

Griffiths also loved classical music, and often went to concerts. He always regretted he couldn't play an instrument. Ballet music was what first captivated him, then he progressed 'through the whole range of classical music, going right back to the fourteenth and fifteenth centuries' composers, mainly Italian'. Tchaikovsky was his favourite composer and Beethoven a close second. His favourite piece was Rimsky-Korsakov's *Scheherazade* ('I can't listen to it too often – new horizons all the time'). He thought Toscanini an overrated conductor, and most admired Klemperer and von Karajan. Though untutored, his musical appreciation was none the less genuine; and one wonders, as with Meehan, if his latent talents had been fostered earlier, whether his life might have taken a different course.

In 1963 Griffiths came back from the continent again short of funds, and took part in one of the most brutal crimes he had committed so far. He was told by a friend of a boarding house in Blackpool where there was ready cash to be found, and he picked three Rochdale men for the job. 'We went to Blackpool on the night in question and I left two of them sitting in the car opposite the house and told them that if anybody came into the house after I'd gone in, they was to follow them in and take care of them.' Griffiths with a bayonet and the other man with a gun, and both wearing nylon stocking masks, then entered the rear of the house. But the other man proved something of a liability. 'He was a right dead-beat one ... he fell flat on his face as soon as he got inside the door ... when he fell down the gun went off.'

This Chaplinesque incident roused the household, but didn't deter Griffiths from carrying on. With his bayonet he attacked two men who appeared on the scene, stabbing one on the head and in the thigh, and cutting the finger of the other. According to Roger Watson, one of the men left outside, he was then stricken with remorse. 'He later tried to make up by putting a cold compress on this chap's hand – a wet cloth and that, while the other chap was crying for his heart pills. He just tried to make amends with the fellows, he didn't want to leave them in a bad state.' Despite this thoughtfulness the two men were robbed of more than £700. Soon after, the whole gang was arrested, and two guns were found in the flat where Griffiths was living. 'Even at that time,' said Inspector Jack Hilton, 'I came to the conclusion that if he was pushed into a tight corner, he would resort to using violence.' On March 5th 1963 Griffiths was sentenced to four years' imprisonment for robbery with violence and sent first to Walton jail, Liverpool, then to Parkhurst.

In December 1965 Griffiths showed himself as clever an escaper as Meehan. One day at Parkhurst he walked away from an outside working-party, arrived at the local bus-stop just as the bus was arriving, and paid his fare to Ryde. Although he was wearing prison overalls, no one paid any attention. At Ryde he went to the ferry booking office. 'I walked over to the counter, pushed a pound across and said, "A day return". The ticket man never looked up – he just pushed a ticket across and twelve and sixpence change.' At Portsmouth Harbour station Griffiths saw a lot of police, so took a taxi to the Town station, and boarded a train there. In his compartment Griffiths noticed 'a prison officer with his wife, talking about a man putting in too many petitions or something. And he kept looking at my overalls, but he never said nothing and we both got off at London.' Griffiths was one of the very few men in Parkhurst's history to make a successful escape to the mainland.

Griffiths went up north to Scunthorpe, where he'd done jobs before. He lived in a caravan on the outskirts of the town, sheltered by a man called Wally Gow. To Gow he told fantastic stories of how he'd had a row with the Kray brothers, 'he'd had to sort them out, you know, he'd swapped shots with them and he'd a mark on his leg, he had a Sten gun and he was spraying the street with bullets, you know ... that's the sort of bloke he was.' Gow told a horrifying story of how while at Scunthorpe Griffiths and another man 'went to do a scrapyard, he was going to surprise the owner. They were waiting on either side of the gates for this bloke coming with his bit of money, or else they were going to tie him up and make him open the safe. He had a big lump of wood in his hand, and after about half an hour the door opened and someone came in and Griffiths battered him over the head two or three times. There was such a squeal, and he jumped on this figure on the ground, and it was a young kid, only about nine or eleven, and he was screaming. He said, "I've only come for my bike, mister", and Griffiths said, "How much have you got?" and the kid said, "I don't know, I think it's one and seven", and he looked in his pocket and found one and nine, and Griffiths said, "Give it to us".'

But there was always the other side of Griffiths. 'You'd never have known he was a villain because he spoke ever so proper, looked a perfect gentleman, always dressed nice and neat, and always willing to pay first.' At the time Griffiths was courting Wally Gow's sister and he made a great impression on her. 'He would always open the doors for you, so you could pass through, and pull the chair out for you to sit down first. If he was going one way, and you another, he'd always go out of his way to take you where you were going.'

At Scunthorpe, said Gow, Griffiths stole gold and jewellery (which he sold to a local fence called John Matthews) and cars – 'he had about six or seven garages in Scunthorpe and as many cars' – but in March 1966 the law once again caught up with him, and at Lindsey Quarter Sessions he was sentenced to four years on each of four charges of housebreaking, stealing, and stealing a motor-car, on top of the four years he'd already got.

Back at Parkhurst Griffiths met Meehan for the first time. Meehan noticed he didn't mix much with other prisoners, and usually exercised alone. 'I think the other prisoners looked on him as an odd character and a bit of a bore. He saw himself in the role of a gentleman crook, but the others did not accept him in that role.'

At this time Meehan used to exercise with an old friend, a Glaswegian villain called Roy Fontaine. When Griffiths heard that Fontaine had been a professional butler and in service to people like Charles Clore, he was much impressed. 'Fontaine,' said Meehan, 'had a steady stream of society magazines sent in, and Griffiths would borrow these, and having read them, would return to discuss them with Fontaine.' Griffiths greatly admired Fontaine, said Meehan, and sometimes would come and join them at exercise. Like his fellow prisoners, Meehan found Griffiths tedious. 'I would listen to him for perhaps a couple of minutes and then switch off.'

A few months later Griffiths was transferred to the prison at Gartree, near Liverpool. 'I did not even notice he had gone,' said Meehan. 'I think Fontaine told me he had gone. I had no reason to think I would ever see him again.'

Gartree was a prison for recidivist prisoners whom the authorities believe can be reformed. Griffiths thought he had been sent there by mistake. He described the place as 'a cross between Butlin's Holiday Camp and a nut-house'. During his stay a BBC Television unit came to make a film about the prison called *Out of Harm's Way* for the Sunday evening religious slot; and by chance Griffiths was one of the half-dozen prisoners interviewed.

In his careful North Country voice he spoke about his early life in Rochdale, and how he took to crime, about his love of climbing and potholing, and how much music meant to him. He admitted to being a bit of a loner – 'I don't make a habit of meeting up with a lot of people' – but set great store on personal appearance – 'If you dress fairly well and speak fairly well and got money, there's no bother' (he described himself as 'fairly well-spoken' despite his Lancashire accent). His only regrets seemed to be about his two sons. 'I don't think they'll turn out like me because they won't have the same environment. I know their grandfather and grandmother think the world of them.' He hoped they would work in steady jobs from nine to five, 'and come and go as they please, and be happy and respectable people'.

As for himself, he made it quite clear that Gartree had had no reformative influence. 'I'm not going straight when I've finished because I don't feel there's any future in going straight ... I'm going to get some money when I get out of here ... I shall either get the money and live very well in South America for the rest of my life, or get buried.'

He was asked to elaborate, and his reply was unequivocal. Under the new penal laws, he said, a man like him with more than two indictable convictions could be sent down for a long stretch, even for a quite minor offence like stealing a bottle of milk. 'So when I get out of here, I know I'm going to face a big sentence if I'm caught – fifteen or twenty-five years.' And in those circumstances his course was clear. 'I don't go out with the intention of committing violence. But if in the course of my going on a job, it means either I get caught and put in prison, or I whack somebody over the head and they die, that's their hard luck.' And there was no point on a job in turning back, 'because you get just as much for starting as you will for finishing. So if a policeman charges at me shouting "Stop, stop, stop", and he caught me a blow with that truncheon, *if I had a gun in my possession, I would use it*. In fact I *would* use it.'

Before another year was out, Griffiths was to fulfil his promise to the letter.

* * *

In Glasgow meanwhile much of the old Gorbals slum area had been demolished, and Betty and her four children had moved to the 18th floor of one of the new high-rise council flats in Old Rutherglen Road. Apart from the privacy, she didn't much like it; the lifts were usually filthy and it took an age waiting for them to come up or down. But she made the place bright and comfortable; there was quite a lot of sun and a fine view over the city.

Since Paddy's return from East Germany, it had seemed to Betty increasingly pointless to continue the marriage. She took legal advice and was told that as Paddy was not living at home at the time of his arrest for the Edmonton affair, she could get a divorce on the grounds of desertion; and she so instructed her solicitors. The children meanwhile were growing up fast. Pat, the eldest boy, was now 21, working as a statistician in a well-known Glasgow stockbroking firm, and engaged to be married. Sally had joined the Army, and was serving in Germany. She had fallen in love with a Lance Corporal and was also engaged to be married. Liz was working at a Savings Bank, but aiming to go to Teacher Training College. The 'wee boy' Garry was seven and so knew nothing of his father.

In the spring of 1968 old Mr Meehan, now living at East Kilbride, was dying of cancer. Paddy, who was due out from Parkhurst that summer, was given special leave to visit him. Pat took Garry to their grandfather's to meet him and later they came back with their father to Old Rutherglen Road. 'I hadn't seen him for four years,' Betty said, 'but he was just his usual, cheerful self. He was amazed to see the family so grown up.' Meehan was very proud of the way his children had developed ('The credit for this belongs entirely to my wife'), and the children were thrilled to see him. 'We ought to hate him,' said Pat later, 'we haven't seen him for nine-tenths of our lives, yet every time he comes back, we still like him. He's a great talker, he makes us all laugh.' Garry, noticing that the top half of his father's left-hand little finger was missing (he had lost it in an accident when a child) asked how it had happened. Meehan looked at the little boy solemnly and said, 'When your brother Pat was a wee bairn, *he sucked it right off*!'

That summer Paddy was allowed two more home visits, one in May, the other in June, just after Pat was married. On June 13th Betty's divorce was granted, and that evening she and Sally visited Paddy in Saughton Prison, Edinburgh, where he was staying the night before going back to Parkhurst. On one of these visits Paddy brought Betty a box of papers which he asked her to keep and then destroy at a later stage. This Betty did. These papers were files on Paul Kroger, which had been taken from the Governor's Office. One day a Special Branch man, an Englishman, says Betty, arrived at the flat, asking if she still had the papers, but she said she had torn them up. The Special Branch man asked if she had read them, and she said no, though she had noticed that some of the papers were written in German. Later that summer she had to go to Winchester to give evidence at the trial of the prison officer involved in the theft.

In August Paddy left Parkhurst after completing seven years of his sentence, and came back to Glasgow. He stayed with his son Pat to begin with, then gradually moved in to Rutherglen Road. Despite the divorce, it never occurred to him to do anything else, and Betty, when all was said and done, was glad of it. She found Paddy quieter and more settled. He told her he would never blow a safe again, and as events turned out he never did. He rarely had a drink, went to bed early, seldom went out except to visit his father, and when he did, said Betty, 'couldn't get home soon enough'.

At this point it might be worth taking a closer look at Paddy Meehan. He was five feet seven inches in height, had blue-grey eyes, short reddish brown hair, fair skin, and 'a florid and somewhat patchy facial expression'. He was stocky in build and always neat in appearance. He had great vitality and a rich sense of humour. Most people who met him took to him: one Glasgow CID man said he had 'a romantic touch to him' and another admitted: 'He's a devious bastard but a very likeable one.'

He was also, everyone is agreed, extremely intelligent, one who expressed himself fluently, both in speech and on paper. His children say he is a natural story-teller. During his many years inside he had done much to educate himself, and now had German O and A levels, and a shorthand speed of 140 words per minute. At Parkhurst he had the German magazines *Der Stern* and *Spiegel* sent to him, and he kept up a correspondence in German with Inge Schmidt. He had also taken courses in book-keeping and short story writing.

Despite these attainments he found it difficult to find congenial work. In October 1968 he got a job in the hardware department of Lewis's department store, but when his brother George told him that he paid as much in tax as Paddy's wage, he chucked it in disgust. In the New Year he got a job driving a van but had to leave it when unable to provide satisfactory references. He then bought himself a second-hand typewriter and taught himself typing, but that led to nothing. There were jobs available in Glasgow, but none at a wage that Paddy found acceptable and none that allowed him the independence he was used to. So gradually he made contacts with old friends in the underworld, and acted as middleman in the selling of stolen goods. It didn't bring in much, but it required little effort.

And then in the spring of 1969 Meehan found a job that suited him down to the ground, one where he could be his own master and yet earn the sort of money he wanted. It was a very simple job – fitting peep-holes in people's front doors for them to see who was calling. He even had a little card printed. 'Protect Your Family. House Security. Glass and Installation Complete £1. Mr P. Meehan.' It was a perfect example of poacher turned gamekeeper. Soon he was fitting eight or ten a day, earning fifty to sixty pounds a week, and hoping to buy a car.

But before these plans could ripen, something else happened. Returning home one day Betty found an empty cigarette packet lying on the door-mat. On it was scrawled in pencil: 'Pat. Sorry to miss you. Will phone later. Jim.'

Jim, thought Paddy, who is Jim? And when a little later Betty said that an Englishman called Jim had called, Paddy still couldn't place him. It was only when Griffiths telephoned and Paddy heard his North Country burr that he remembered who he was. Paddy asked how he knew his address, and Griffiths said he'd got it from Roy Fontaine whom he'd just visited in prison in Hull.

Griffiths came round to Old Rutherglen Road. He said he was living in a flat at Selly Oak, Birmingham, where he had a job with a jewellery firm ('he called it a "position"' commented Paddy), but he'd come to Glasgow to sell some stolen antiques: Roy Fontaine had mentioned the name of a fence whom Paddy knew. Paddy introduced him to the fence, who wasn't interested as he dealt only in jewellery and changing 'hot' money at 10 per cent. So Paddy took him to another fence, to whom Griffiths sold a stolen clock. As Griffiths had nowhere to sleep that night, they let him stay in the flat. He then went back to Birmingham.

But soon Griffiths was back in Glasgow again, this time on a semi-permanent basis. He was wanted in England for a number of crimes (passing dud cheques, stealing cars, housebreaking) and so was looking for a base north of the border. He began dropping in to Old Rutherglen Road frequently. When he said he had nowhere to stay, Paddy let him have the use of an empty flat belonging to his mother; Betty lent him some blankets, and sometimes cooked breakfast for him when he returned from some all-night journey. 'I didn't much like him,' said Betty, 'but I felt sorry for him.'

Griffiths' record describes him as being 5 foot 8 inches in height, with grey eyes, fair hair and fair complexion. Tattooed on his arm was a snake, a dagger and a skull and crossbones (Meehan's arm it will be recalled was tattooed with the word BETTY and a drawing of her head). Betty remembers Griffiths as being very young looking, well dressed and with a nice hairstyle. 'He had good manners and was always opening doors and all that. He was very quiet, though, he hardly ever spoke and then mainly about himself. He said he'd been in the army and knew karate. He liked to try and impress.' Liz, aged 18, was bowled over by him. 'You couldn't meet a nicer man. He was really suave. He told me he was the black sheep of the family. I said to my Dad how nice he was, and he said, "You don't want to believe everything he says." I think my Dad felt sorry for him – he always hates seeing people left out of things.'

Sorry for him they might be, but the Meehans were beginning to find Griffiths' frequent visits and telephone calls rather a strain. 'He didn't know anyone in Glasgow,' said Betty, 'and kept asking Paddy to take him around.' Paddy still found his conversation fairly tedious. Once Griffiths told Paddy he woke up with a foul taste in his mouth every morning and was sure he had cancer of the stomach. On another occasion, on a rare visit to a pub, Griffiths droned on 'about a man who made false passports and driving licences. He explained how to transfer a passport frank, but I can't remember a word of what he said. He also went on about silver antiques (he had a little book which gave the hallmarks). I just listened politely.'

Yet however little the safe-blower and the petty thief had in common, there was one thing each wanted from the other. Paddy knew what Griffiths wanted. 'It's my opinion Griffiths kept coming back to me because he believed that sooner or later I would hit a bank, and he wanted to be on hand when I did.' And what did Paddy know? Something quite simple: the open road. Griffiths always had a car, often a different one, all stolen. A car of his own was what Paddy had longed for during his years inside, because a car made you a free man, you could come and go as you pleased, car journeys led to danger and excitement. So when Griffiths said he knew of banks in England waiting to be hit, Paddy would go along with him, drive through the night to inspect them. Not surprisingly none took his fancy. 'I don't go to banks on someone else's say-so,' was his excuse, 'I like to judge for myself.' In fact what he'd gone along for was the ride.

* * *

And about this time, in another part of Glasgow called Barrowfield, at No 40 Mountainblue Street, a villain called William Macintyre (convictions for safe-blowing, house-breaking, assault and robbery) was visited by another villain by the name of Andrew Dick. They had first met some three years earlier when Dick used to bring cars to be repaired at a garage Macintyre used to run in Bridgeton. The garage had recently been pulled down as part of the Glasgow Corporation's Development Schemes, and Dick still owed Macintyre some £30 for work done.

Dick brought a proposition; there was a scheme afoot to break into a house in Ayrshire where lived a picture-hall owner and his wife; there was thought to be several thousand pounds cash on the premises. Ian Waddell, a mutual friend and fellow villain, who was then staying with Dick at his house in Law Street, had agreed to take part. But he couldn't drive a car. Would Macintyre be interested in providing a car, driving it to the scene of the crime and then taking part in the robbery?

Macintyre agreed to the idea, and rather than risk using a Glasgow car, travelled a few days later to Ballachulish, up on the west coast of Argyllshire at the entrance to the pass of Glencoe, and there bought a cheap powder-blue second-hand Vauxhall Victor from Chisholm's garage. Back in Glasgow he made preparations to paint the car dark blue for the robbery, then respray it with its former colour as soon as the job was completed.

First though he went round to Dick's house to hear from Waddell further details of the job. And what he heard he didn't like. The picture-hall owner and his wife, said Waddell, were an elderly couple, and it was to be a tie-up job, that is, the couple would have to be tied up while the house was ransacked and the money found. Now ten years earlier Macintyre had been questioned by the Glasgow police about a man called Levine who had died as the result of a tie-up job, and ever since then the idea of a tie-up job had made him, as he put it, 'a wee bit windy in the vernacular'. So he told Dick and Waddell he was no longer interested: they would have to find someone else for the job.

* * *

Griffiths (using the name of Douglas from a driving licence he had stolen) was now more or less semi-resident in Glasgow, and engaged heavily in crime, near and far. After leaving Paddy's mother's flat he was always on the move, seldom staying at any address for more than two or three weeks, once living in a caravan on the edge of the city as he had done at Scunthorpe when on the run from Parkhurst. He stole wherever he could, but mostly from parked cars. From a car parked outside the Scotch Corner Hotel in Yorkshire, he stole a shotgun and rifle, presumably the property of some luckless sportsman on his way to the Highlands; from a car parked outside the Connell Hotel in Argyllshire he stole another rifle and a camera. He burgled houses as near as Bearsden and as far away as Aviemore. He tried to steal a caravan from a caravan site at Loch Lomond but was foiled by the nightwatchman whom he assaulted.

And he stole cars everywhere: several in Glasgow and several more in England, mostly Triumphs and Rovers. He collected cars like boys collect the numbers of trains. 'He could tell you where a car came from,' said Paddy, 'just by looking at the number plates.' He kept each car in a lock-up he'd hired in Shawhill Road, and when he'd finished with one, he'd dump it on an empty site. After disposing of several in this way, all sticky with his fingerprints, he looked around for somewhere to dump cars where they wouldn't be found. He tried to put one into Loch Lomond but misjudged the depth, and it ended up on its side in shallow water. Then he heard of an ideal place up at Loch Awe, between Dalmally and Taynuilt, a place where the road ran between high ground on one side and deep water on the other. Here he successfully dumped three cars. On one occasion Meehan was with him. ('I could show you the exact place,' Meehan said, 'between three to five miles from the Loch Awe Hotel, near an old pump where there is a gap in the fence.')

But by now the Glasgow police were rumbling to Griffiths and his association with Meehan. Twice they called at Old Rutherglen Road looking for him, once in connection with a stolen watch, the other time to do with a stolen car. After the second occasion Betty told Paddy she didn't want to see Griffiths in the flat any more.

On the afternoon of June 20th 1969 Paddy Meehan was driving Jim Griffiths in a green Ford Cortina towards Scotch Corner from Carlisle. They were on their way to Scunthorpe where Griffiths hoped to sell some jewellery he'd stolen in the Glasgow area to the fence, John Mathews. Paddy had hired the car from a Glasgow firm because Griffiths had just dumped his last one into Loch Awe; he was hoping to steal another one during this trip.

Paddy occasionally hired a car himself when he had enough funds. Only the week before he had taken Betty and Garry in the car for a long one-day trip to the Highlands. They had got up at 4.30 and driven right up to Inverness and into Sutherland. At Golspie Paddy took a look at a bank and the local tax office, just to keep his eye in. Then they came back by Loch Ness and Fort William. Near Ben Nevis Garry had spotted a sheep stuck on a ledge, and urged his father to get out and rescue it. Paddy did so, the sheep ran away, and then Paddy got stuck. They arrived back in Glasgow at midnight. Betty said it was one of the nicest family outings they had ever had.

Approaching Scotch Corner, Paddy's car was overtaken by a car driven by a woman, a Mrs Boyle, and a few moments later this car and four others were involved in an accident. Paddy drove on to the grass verge and jumped out to see if he could be of help. He found Mrs Boyle and her husband very shaken and Mrs Boyle's knee bleeding. She said she thought she had broken it, and Paddy made her get out and walk about a little. It seemed all right, so she got back into the car and Paddy felt the knee and then tried to mop up the blood with his handkerchief. Presently a police car arrived, and Paddy went to get a bandage from the first-aid kit, but the box was empty. He then gave some help to two children in another of the cars, one with a cut lip, the other with a cut ankle.

The Boyles' car was a write-off, so after Mrs Boyle had her knee dressed at the Scotch Corner Hotel, Meehan and Griffiths decided to abandon the trip to Scunthorpe, and take the Boyles to Carlisle where they lived.

When they reached Appleby they stopped at the house of Mr and Mrs Murray. Here Paddy got out, and Griffiths took the Boyles on to Carlisle. Paddy had first met the Murrays in April when a car he was driving had had an accident near their house, and the Murrays had put him up for the night: Mr Murray was a lorry driver and Mrs Murray an attractive mini-skirted blonde. Since then he and Jim had been in the habit of looking in on the Murrays on journeys north and south (they had already stopped there earlier that day). On one visit Jim had told Mrs Murray he was a car salesman, but hoped to retire at the end of the year and buy a yacht, on another he gave her a gold brooch.[1] Like Griffiths, the Murrays called Paddy Pat.

On the way to Carlisle Jim told Mrs Boyle that his own car had recently been stolen, which was why he was driving this hired one. He said he was a dealer in antique silver, invited Mr Boyle to inspect a few pieces he had with him, and dangled a stolen lady's wrist-watch in front of Mrs Boyle's nose. Neither of the Boyles was in the mood for buying. On arrival at Carlisle Griffiths said his name was Douglas and that if they wanted to find him, he lived at 14 Burnbank Gardens, Glasgow.

Griffiths drove back to Appleby, where he and Paddy stayed drinking with the Murrays until about 2 a.m. Then they left for Glasgow, taking the same road north that Griffiths had already travelled three times that day. They reached Gretna soon after 3 a.m., and when Griffiths saw

[1] This of course was stolen and Mrs Murray later handed it in to the police.

a lot of cars parked outside the Royal Stewart Motel, he asked Paddy to drop him off. He was going to steal one of the cars with the all-purpose bunch of keys he carried and drive it to Glasgow.

Staying that night in the Royal Stewart Motel, and now asleep, were a Mr and Mrs George Moir. They had arrived from Warwick the night before in their turquoise blue Triumph MAV 810 G on their way home to Aberdeen. The night before Mr Moir, a practical man, had filled up the Triumph with ten gallons in readiness for departure in the morning. But when he got up at 7.30 and looked out of the window, the Triumph had vanished, and with it all Mr and Mrs Moir's cases, clothes, picnic gear, cushions, torches, camera, etc, all to the value of £494. They could not know that his fine new car, with all its booty, was already tucked up in Griffiths' garage in Shawhill Road, Glasgow.

That was on Saturday June 21st. On Monday June 23rd Griffiths moved from his flat in 10 Beaumont Gardens (not, as he had told Mrs Boyle, 14 Burnbank Gardens) to one in 17 Holyrood Crescent, and then three days later to an attic flat at 14 Holyrood Crescent. At this time Griffiths had a girl-friend, Irene Cameron, aged 17, a punch-type operator at the Electricity Board, and described by Betty as 'a wee girl with spectacles and a blonde beehive wig'. They had first met at a party in April but recently Griffiths had been seeing much more of her – in fact there were few evenings that she did not spend with him after her work.

They would often go out for a meal together and come back and watch TV. Irene described Griffiths as having 'a very polite English accent, but you would get an occasional word that was from Coronation Street – Cockney, it was sort of Cockney.' To Glasgow-born Irene, North Country and Cockney were one, and when things were said in 'Cockney' plays on the television, and she didn't understand them, Griffiths would explain what they meant. Similarly when she used a Scotticism like 'the midgie men'[2] she would have to tell him what she meant.

To Irene Griffiths fantasized more than to anyone. 'He

[2] Refuse collectors.

told me he was an orphan and his father used to be an army colonel, and his father was away on business and his mother had an affair with another man and the result was Jim, and when his father came back he brought Jim up as an unwanted child, he used to beat him with a stick, and he had to have his meals with the servants, not with the family.' She also knew Griffiths as Douglas, representative of a costume-jewellery firm; but it is clear from what she said later that she knew he had another life as well.

On June 26th, the day that Griffiths moved into the attic flat at 14 Holyrood Crescent, he took Irene to a concert by the Scottish National Orchestra at the Kelvin Hall. They drove there in style in Mr Moir's turquoise blue Triumph (now with false number plates) and heard a programme of Tchaikovsky (1812 Overture, Piano Concerto No 1, Symphony No 4). Earlier Griffiths had given Irene a present of some dress-material lengths he had found in the Moirs' car, but she said she didn't sew. On July 3rd Griffiths went to the Registrar's office to extract a birth certificate in the name of Francis McNeil: he wanted this to apply for another false passport. He already had two in the names of Smith and Winthrope: they were useful for identification purposes when driving stolen cars. Then on Saturday July 5th Griffiths told Irene that he had to pick a friend up that afternoon to go to Stranraer. He dropped her at St Enoch's Square, saying that he would be back late that night or early Sunday morning. He would expect her at the flat on the Sunday afternoon, and she could let herself in with her own keys.

By now Meehan had saved up enough money from the peep-hole business to put down a deposit for a car of his own, and in the last week of June he left £179 deposit with the Chequered Flag garage in London Road on a Ford Corsair. But as he wasn't a householder he was unable to raise hire purchase on the balance of the payment, and so on July 4th after only a week's driving, he took the car back. The Chequered Flag gave him a cheque for £156 (the deposit less road tax and a week's hire), and Meehan asked them to make it out in his wife's name, E. Carson, as he himself didn't have a bank account.

That night Griffiths telephoned Paddy to suggest going ahead next day with a scheme they had already discussed – motoring to Stranraer, the county town of Wigtownshire, to look at the motor taxation office. Griffiths was fed up with journeys to Loch Awe to get rid of stolen cars; if he could lay his hands on some car registration books, he could sell the cars he stole instead of dumping them. Paddy agreed to look over the county offices, and if it seemed feasible, to break into them at a later date and rob the safe of money and registration books – though how serious he was about this is a moot point.

On Saturday morning Paddy told Betty that he and Jim Griffiths were going to run down to Stranraer that afternoon to look at a car. He asked if she would like to come, but she declined.

At about four in the early afternoon Griffiths rang up from the telephone box in the courtyard below the Meehan flat to say that he had arrived (Betty no longer allowed him into the house) and soon after Paddy left to join him. Paddy was wearing a sports coat, informal trousers, suede shoes and a cap; Griffiths was wearing dark glasses by way of disguise.

As the two men travelled southwards in Mr Moir's blue Triumph, Meehan's thoughts dwelt momentarily on a strange incident that had happened a couple of weeks before. He had telephoned to his friend Inge Schmidt in Bremen to say that he and Betty were hoping to come over for a visit in July or August (it was for this trip as much as anything that Paddy had tried to buy the Ford) to visit their daughter Sally. A day or two later another Special Branch man arrived at the flat and told Paddy that if he had any plans to visit Germany in the near future, Special Branch would be glad to know when he planned to leave.

After the Special Branch man had gone, Betty said to

Paddy, 'That's a funny coincidence. How do you think they knew?' And Paddy said, 'They must be tapping the phone.'[8]

The Triumph drove through Kilmarnock, by-passed Ayr, then headed south along the coast road, with the sea to the west and the island of Ailsa Craig lying like a pudding on the horizon. After Ballantrae the car swung inland to run through the wooded valley of Glenapp. Loch Ryan, the big bay that gives access to Stranraer, came into sight, and as they passed the Lochryanhall Hotel, Griffiths remarked that on the way back they might stop and look through the cars parked there to see if there were any cameras in them.

Soon after seven that evening, Meehan and Griffiths came into Stranraer. At about the same time two girls who they were to meet in unusual circumstances later that night, Irene Burns and her friend Isobel Smith, were getting ready in Kilmarnock to go to a dance.

[8] Although Meehan attaches some importance to this incident, I do not feel it has any significance myself.

PART II

The Murder

Waddell and McGuinness had left Glasgow earlier that day in a Ford Cortina which they had hired from Carnie's Car Hire – the same firm from which Meehan had hired the Cortina in which he and Griffiths had travelled to Scotch Corner in June.

At this time Waddell was 30, with reddish hair, of a cheerful disposition and indistinct speech. His father had been a sheep-killer in the local slaughter-house, and he had an elder sister who married and emigrated to America. After National Service Waddell had various jobs, in a bakery, as a food porter in Manchester, as a storeman for tractors. He married when he was twenty-three and had a child, but separated from his wife after five years. He drifted into crime in 1964 and since then had had several convictions in Glasgow, for theft, housebreaking and carrying an offensive weapon. Today Waddell has two scars on his face as the result of a fight with a broken bottle, and a missing front tooth caused by falling down when drunk. He walks with a stoop, has a clumsy handshake and a ready smile.

McGuinness at this time was 39, a small, lean man with auburn hair and a small, foxy face. Like Meehan he was born in the Gorbals, the son of a shipyard worker on the Clyde. There were eight children in the family, but no others were ever in trouble. His future wife Agnes met him when he was eighteen, on leave from conscription in the R.A.F. She knew him as Billy, and says his mother spoiled him dreadfully after an elder brother had died by drowning. After conscription he never worked again, living on Social Security and the proceeds of crime. His offences were theft (opening lockfast premises), housebreaking, and assault with intent to rob.

Like Betty Meehan, Agnes's married life consisted of interludes between prison; and mostly by herself she brought up four children. In contrast to her husband's vicious criminal life, she saw him as 'a good family man, never lost his temper with me or the children, always very quiet-spoken. He liked watching sport on the TV. He smoked a lot and rolled his own cigarettes. He didn't like company, he was always a bit of a loner.'

On arrival at Ayr Waddell and McGuinness went to a local betting-shop where they spent a couple of hours and Waddell won some money on a horse. They then drove to Girvan to fill in time, and had a cup of tea on the front. Although McGuinness's daughter, Elizabeth, was on holiday in Girvan, they didn't see her, and after paying for the tea, returned to Ayr. Having confirmed from the telephone directory that Abraham Ross lived at 2 Blackburn Place, they drove to the house to get the lie of the land.

Blackburn Place lies in a quiet well-to-do residential area near the front. The house, a bungalow, stands at the corner of Blackburn Place, a cul-de-sac, and Blackburn Road, which runs westward to the sea. The front of the building, which is an oblong, is in Blackburn Place: the garage and north side are adjacent to No 4 Blackburn Place, while on the south side a sunken paved garden separates the property from Blackburn Road. At the back of the house is a drying-green for clothes and a summer-house, and backing on to this is the garage of the house next door. North of the garage, and situated at the far end of 4 Blackburn Place, is a telegraph pole which, Waddell and McGuinness noted, carried a telephone wire to 2 Blackburn Place.

It was now early evening. The two men went down to the front, had a meal in a café, and killed more time sitting by the sea. Their informant, perhaps unaware that Ross did not go to the Bingo Hall on Saturdays, had told them not to expect him at the house until about midnight. At about 11.30 p.m., when according to Waddell it was 'mid dark, mid night', they got into the car again and drove eastwards down Blackburn Road to the junction with Blackburn Place. Twenty yards from it McGuinness dropped off Waddell, and then went to park the car some distance away. As Waddell was waiting in Blackburn Road for McGuinness to rejoin him, a woman appeared from the next-door house, and Waddell walked briskly on. This was almost certainly Mrs Sarah Scott of 2 Blackburn Road, who was going to her garage at the time.

Then minutes later Waddell was joined by McGuinness and, the coast now being clear, they stepped over the low wall that separated Mr Ross's property from Blackburn Road, and crept across the lawn to where a chink of light showed through the curtains of the last room at the back of the bungalow. Through the window the two men saw Mr and Mrs Ross lying in twin beds, Mr Ross, who was reading, being near the window: there were two wardrobes at the far end of the room, and between the beds and the window was a dressing-table. They observed a key in the bedroom door, and wondered if it was already locked. They then withdrew to the other side of the house and inside the garage found some garden steps. McGuinness used these to get on to the roof of the garage of No 2 Blackburn Road (one side of which formed the boundary wall) and from there he climbed the telegraph pole standing in the corner of 4 Blackburn Place, and cut the telephone wires leading to the Rosses' house. He also cut a piece from the clothes-line to tie the Rosses up.

For the next hour or so Waddell and McGuinness waited quietly in the back garden. During this time they discussed what to call each other should the need arise, and decided on the two common Glasgow names of Jimmy and Pat. McGuinness was to be Jimmy and Waddell Pat. By about one o'clock, when the light in the Rosses' bedroom had been out for some time, they took off their shoes and put on home-made masks. With an iron bar and a weeding tool they had taken from the garage they crept to the window of the front bedroom, which was on the left of the front door. McGuinness levered first the weeding tool and then the bar between the bottom of the window and the sill, and pushed upwards. The latch gave without any noise, the window opened and the two men climbed in. They shut the window behind them, then groped their way across the bedroom and into the corridor. They went down it slowly, one after the other, and came to the last door on the right, the door of the Rosses' bedroom. They turned the handle quietly, then pushed. The door was not locked.

* * *

In Glasgow, at about 7 p.m., Andrew Dick, who was a great friend of Waddell, went from his house in Shaw Street round the corner to the house, in Mountainblue Street, of William Macintyre – the man he had approached and who had declined taking part in the Ayr robbery. Dick told Macintyre that he wanted to speak to him privately, so they went outside and sat in Macintyre's car. Dick said that this was to be the night of the Ayr job, and in case word got to the police of his earlier association with it, he'd be glad if Macintyre would come to his house later and provide him with an alibi: he added that he would make it worth Macintyre's while. Macintyre, to whom Dick owed money for a garage bill, agreed. He went to Dick's house in Law Street at about 10.30, stayed till two or three in the morning, and then went home.

* * *

Abraham Ross was 67 at this time, one of five children of a Glasgow Jewish family who had lived first in Govan and then the Gorbals. He was a small man, 5 foot 3 inches, and weighed under ten stone. His wife Rachel was 72: they had been married 36 years.

Ross's father was in the rag and scrap metal trade, and after leaving school Abe joined him in the business. But in 1923, when he was 21, he read that the Canadian government were offering £5 fares to those willing to take jobs on wheat farms in Saskatchewan. He accepted the offer, but found it back-breaking work and drifted down to Toronto and then New York. Here he got work as a waiter, first on 45th Street, later at a hotel on Long Island. The owner here called him Al instead of Abe, as he had a thing about Jews.

The next year Ross's girl-friend, Fanny Segal, came out

from Glasgow to join him and in 1924 they were married in City Hall, New York. The following year she had complications while expecting a child, and had to enter the City Hospital. Abe was told that she needed a blood transfusion which would cost money. He said he didn't have that much money but would wire Glasgow for it. He says he was told that they wouldn't go ahead with the blood transfusion until they had the money. He wired immediately but by the time the money arrived Fanny was dead and the child stillborn.

For the next ten years Ross worked in the States as dishwasher, bellboy and waiter, sometimes in New York, sometimes Florida. But his happiest time was when he was taken on as a waiter by H. M. Stevens, the firm that did the catering for the American race-tracks. Abe worked at White Plains, Belmont, Aqueduct, Jamaica, Laurel and all the other principal tracks. Customers left him generous tips which if he'd saved would have made him comfortably off. But he was a born gambler himself, accepted racing tips as well as the other and was often broke until next pay day.

In 1933 he returned to Glasgow and rejoined his father in the rag trade. He also married an old friend, Rachel Freedman, of another Glasgow Jewish family, and they set up house in the Shawlands area. They were very disappointed when told by a gynaecologist that Rachel would be unable to bear children.

After war broke out Ross continued in the rag trade (he says it was classed as a reserved occupation) and in 1941 when the bombing of Glasgow started, he and Rachel moved down to rented rooms in Ayr. After the war he went briefly into the second-hand car business, but returned to the rag and scrap metal trade in 1949. Inevitably he got to know many Glasgow villains, as a big proportion of stuff offered for sale was stolen. Abe says that in the rag trade the police come and inspect the books every seven days, and if you re-sell metal without letting the police inspect it, you are in danger of losing your licence.

In 1952 he bought 2 Blackburn Place and commuted to Glasgow daily. Then in 1961 he launched a business venture that was to prove highly successful. This was the purchase of a cinema in Paisley and the conversion of it into a bingo hall. This was the time when bingo was fast becoming the rage. He and three others bought the property for £8,000.

Ross's friends at this time describe him as soft-spoken, shrewd, extremely conservative. He still gambled modestly, on the pools and the horses, and was also fond of cigars. He said generously of his wife that she was 'far above my intelligence. She was a great reader and much interested in politics. Her own views were very left-wing. She was anti-apartheid, and didn't think the Queen did enough. This didn't make her popular with all our friends in Ayr.' But their marriage was a happy one.

Abe's routine at the Bingo Hall seldom varied. He went there on Mondays, Tuesdays, Thursdays and Fridays. He would rise late, breakfast in mid-morning, then after a light lunch motor up to Glasgow to fetch the cashier, then drive with her to Paisley. He would stay at the Bingo Hall until it closed, take the cashier home, then return to Blackburn Place, arriving at about 11.30 p.m. Occasionally he would bring the takings from the Bingo Hall home, and put them in a safe in the cloakroom cupboard. He always kept a lot of money in this safe anyway, both for Bingo prizes and other cash transactions.

On this Saturday July 5th, the Rosses spent most of the day at home, then in the evening at about 7 p.m. drove to Prestwick Airport for dinner. Abe had hopes of playing cards that night with a group that met regularly, but when he found they already had a full house, he took Rachel home. They spent the evening looking at television, and at about midnight went to bed. Before getting into bed Abe drew the curtains and then, as was his custom, 'pushed them apart a little before going to sleep'. In bed he read for about a quarter of an hour, unaware that through the gap in the curtains Waddell and McGuinness were watching him. Then he turned out the light.

* * *

Meanwhile fifty miles away at Stranraer Griffiths had pulled up the Triumph at Reid and Adams's filling station on the front, just along the road from the Stranraer Police Station. The time was between 7 and 7.30 p.m. In the forecourt Meehan spotted a second-hand Morris 1100 which he liked the look of, and while Griffiths was away relieving himself, he asked the attendant how much it was. The attendant, a man of 61 called Thomas Haxton, said he didn't know himself and advised Meehan to ring the main office when it opened; and on the back of a cigarette packet Meehan made a note of the firm's name.

Griffiths then drove the car across the road to the big car-park on the sea front facing the Irish boat terminal. He wanted to repair the car's traffic indicator which had broken. While he was doing this, Meehan went off to look at the motor taxation offices which were in the County building up the hill in Sun Street. When he got there he remembered he had been there before, in 1955, and that the following year his friend John Harvey, now dead, had blown the safe in the rent office. This, he says, coupled with a belief that people were living close by the motor taxation office, turned him against the idea of breaking into it.

Back in the car-park Meehan found Griffiths still trying to fix the traffic indicator. He told him he didn't fancy the motor taxation office, and they decided to go and have something to eat. Meehan said he had seen people eating in the restaurant of Spencer's Hotel in Church Street, just down the hill from the motor taxation office, so they went there. Standing outside the hotel was a maroon-coloured Volvo, and Griffiths said it had Wigtownshire number plates. Inside, it being a Saturday in mid-summer, the restaurant was crowded, and the two waitresses, Mrs Harkness, sister of the proprietress and her niece Janet Pollock, were being kept busy. Griffiths and Meehan ordered high tea. At a table near them were an English family, and Griffiths told Meehan they came from Yorkshire, he could tell by their accent. At another table was a family with a baby of about two, and Meehan saw Janet take the baby into the kitchen so as to give its parents some peace. At

8.30 it was time for Janet to go and dress for her weekly dance, and she gave Griffiths and Meehan their bill.

The two men went back to the car-park where Griffiths had a final go at repairing the traffic indicator. Meehan went off for a walk, had a couple of drinks in a pub, went to the public lavatory, and at about 10 p.m. telephoned Betty in Glasgow to say he wouldn't be back till late. He returned to the car-park and over a mug of coffee from Griffiths' flask, suggested they start moving to the Lochryanhall Hotel; but Griffiths said it was too early, a lot of people would still be about, and anyway he wanted a catnap.

So Griffiths had his catnap and Meehan went for another walk, and then around 11.30 p.m., at the time Waddell and McGuinness were approaching Blackburn Place, they left Stranraer for Cairnryan. Griffiths parked the car two or three hundred yards from the Lochryanhall Hotel, they walked back and entered an empty Ministry of Defence camp between the main road and the sea, from which they could observe the car-park and people leaving the hotel, and yet not be seen themselves. As they took up position they heard a band in the hotel playing the National Anthem. It was 11.45 p.m.

* * *

The first thing Mr Ross remembers of the events of that dreadful night was a figure leaping at him out of the darkness. His immediate reaction was that he had woken from a nightmare, then he heard his wife shouting and screaming and realized with horror it was the real thing. His assailant, who was McGuinness, slipped sideways on to the floor and Mr Ross found himself on top of him. Despite the dark he saw that McGuinness was wearing a hood on his head with slits for eyes, and, it seemed to him, some kind of smooth, one-piece nylon suiting.

Waddell meanwhile had thrown himself on top of Mrs Ross and was hitting her about the face. 'Get this cunt off me, Pat,' shouted McGuinness from the floor, so Waddell left off hitting Mrs Ross and came over and struck Mr Ross several times with the iron bar. McGuinness hit him too with the weeding tool from the garage, and when he was quiet they put him on the floor beside the dressing-table and covered his face with a blanket. Then they turned on the light. Whenever Ross tried to remove the blanket, they hit him again, although he was already bleeding profusely from the face and head. Then, to stop him moving further, they tied his hands behind his back, and also those of Mrs Ross. Mrs Ross asked Waddell, who was kneeling on her, to be careful of her chest, as she had recently had an operation.[1] As the two men talked among themselves, Mr Ross noted their distinctive Glasgow accents.

Mrs Ross, also covered by a blanket, was now quieter, though moaning and asking for an ambulance. Waddell remembers her saying, 'Are you all right, Abe?' and also telling him and McGuinness to take what they wanted and go away. She told them they would find money in one of the dressing-table drawers, and they found £200. But they had come for bigger stuff than this, and McGuinness asked Ross where the wall safe was. Ross said, truthfully enough, that he didn't have a wall safe, and each time he said this McGuinness hit him again. Then Waddell heard Ross say, 'You can kill me if you like, but I haven't got a wall safe.' Eventually he told them he did have an ordinary safe, and where to find the keys.

McGuinness took the keys and went away to the safe and opened it while Waddell kept watch in the bedroom. Presently McGuinness came back with what Waddell describes as a small case, and in this, says Waddell, was £3,000, mostly in new notes, various coins, some jewellery and a misprinted £1 note. The two men then made a thorough search of the house, pulling out drawers, breaking into cupboards, even ripping away the side of the bath to see if money was concealed there. In the bedroom they found more money in Mr Ross's trouser pocket, in new £10 numbered notes, and some American Express Travellers

[1] 'A scar was present on the left side of the chest where the breast had been removed by operation' (from the post-mortem report on Mrs Ross).

Cheques in a black plastic folder. Then Waddell noticed a gold watch on Mrs Ross's wrist, and pulled it forcibly off her. Waddell says that under one of the beds he found a shoe-box, but that it contained only a lighter, a pair of odd cuff-links and some photographs; nor did Waddell's search of Mr Ross's suits in the wardrobe reveal anything.

By this time Waddell and McGuinness were quite tired and one of them went to the front room to fetch whisky and lemonade. They had time to lose anyway as they didn't intend leaving the house until daylight so as to make their getaway less conspicuous. They sat in the kitchen drinking and talking, Waddell says for about an hour. At one point Mr Ross thought he heard one say 'They're not here yet, Jimmy', or 'He's not here yet, Jim', but he must have been mistaken, as Waddell and McGuinness had no accomplices. Once when Waddell was back in the bedroom Mrs Ross asked if Mr Ross was all right, and though Waddell could see there was blood all around him, he said he was.

Now Waddell and McGuinness decided to tie up the Rosses even more securely so that after they had gone, they would not be able to get free quickly and give the alarm. They turned them over on their backs, bent their legs behind them and tied their ankles together; and as a final refinement they tied the rope that was binding Mr Ross's legs to the rope binding his hands. The Rosses now lay on the floor like two trussed chickens. Mrs Ross again begged them to send for an ambulance, and Waddell said, 'Shut up, shut up, we'll send an ambulance,' which at the time, he says, they intended to do.

At around 5.30 a.m., when it was quite light, McGuinness left to fetch the car, which he had parked a couple of streets away; at this time on a Sunday morning, one man in the street would look less suspicious than two; also Waddell's jacket was covered in blood. But McGuinness was out of luck. As he was walking down Racecourse Road, a police panda car spotted him and drew alongside. This was a tense moment for McGuinness, for he had Mr Ross's car keys and two of Mr Ross's rings in his pocket. The officers in the car asked McGuinness who he was and where he was going. He gave a false name, said he had walked from Girvan where he had been visiting his daughter on holiday, and had missed the last bus to Glasgow. The officers took pity on him, said they would take him to the bus-station. They rode there together, catchers of criminals with a criminal who'd come hotfoot from his latest crime.

At the bus-station the police officers dropped McGuinness, said a bus would soon be leaving for Glasgow. McGuinness hung around for a couple of minutes then, much shaken, started back on foot to where he had left the car. Fearful of being picked up by the police again and this time searched, he hid the car keys and Mrs Ross's rings inside two street drains, intending to come and collect them at a later date. Then he picked up the car and drove to Blackburn Place.

It was now nearly an hour since he had left the house, and Waddell was greatly relieved to see him. He himself had had a scare when, peeping round the curtains to see if McGuinness had returned, he had noticed a police car slowly cruising down Blackburn Road (whether or not it was the one that had picked up McGuinness is not known). 'I got a real fright,' he said, 'I thought the game was up.' On his way through the kitchen Waddell noticed an alarm clock on the dresser with black and green figures. He went out of the back door, leaving it open, put on his shoes and, carrying the small case containing the money, joined McGuinness in the car.

The route to Glasgow from Blackburn Place goes through the centre of Ayr. But McGuinness was so worried about a possible second encounter with the officer in the panda car (when he would have some real explaining to do) that he and Waddell drove south out of Ayr along Racecourse Road, and made a long, roundabout sweep through Cumnock and Douglas before returning to Glasgow by the A74. Somewhere on the way they stopped at a lay-by to divide the loot. Waddell thought of all the blood Mr Ross had lost and wondered if he would die; but neither of them telephoned the police. At about 8 a.m. McGuinness dropped Waddell in Parkhead at the house of his friend

Donald Carmichael who had promised to provide him with an alibi. Later that morning Waddell burnt his blood-stained clothing on Carmichael's midden at the back. Then he went to Andrew Dick's house, told him what had happened, and gave him some money. In the evening Dick went to see Macintyre and gave him £50 – £30 for the garage bill he owed, £10 for having waited for it, and £10 for the alibi.

McGuinness arrived at his home in Milncroft Road, Ruchazie, between 11 a.m. and 12. Agnes found him 'upset and worried about something'. This was not what he had done to the Rosses at Blackburn Place, about which he said nothing, but that his presence in Ayr had been established by the police officer who had taken him to the bus-station, and was now in a position to identify him. He told Agnes of this encounter, then said he would have to go away for a few days; and he left immediately for London by car.

In Blackburn Place Abraham Ross knew the two intruders had gone because 'everything had gone all quiet'. He managed to get the blanket off his head and saw it was daylight.

* * *

Meehan and Griffiths stood in the shadows of the Ministry of Defence camp, looking at the brilliantly-lit Lochryanhall Hotel and the cars parked in front of it, and waiting for the late drinkers and visitors to leave. At about 12.30 they saw the hotel bus drive up, and a lot of people get into it and drive away. Later Sheila Prestlie, the barmaid, and a couple of friends came out of the hotel, and they heard their footsteps disappearing down the road. Later still Meehan heard a dog panting, and in the dark saw a German shepherd dog approaching: it belonged to Ambrose Stanyer, the owner of the hotel. Meehan thought it might attack them, but it turned out quite a meek dog and allowed Meehan to fondle it. The dog went back across the road and presently the main hotel lights went out. But there was still a light shining on to the car-park from Mr Stanyer's sitting-room. He was having tea and sandwiches with the band.

It was Mr Stanyer's custom to put out the sitting-room

light between 1.30 and 2 a.m. Sometime around then (Meehan thinks it was 1.45) when the band and everyone else had gone, Meehan said to Griffiths: 'This is a waste of time, we'll be here all night', but Griffiths said that as they'd waited so long, they might as well wait a little longer. Soon after the sitting-room light went out, and the whole place was in darkness.

Griffiths crossed the road, and Meehan warned him to be careful of the dog. There were now only a few cars left in the car-park. Spotting a mini-van in front of the hotel and hoping it might contain a tourist's camera, Griffiths forced the lock, opened the door and removed the interior light bulb. He did not know it was Mr Stanyer's van which he used for hotel business, and Griffiths found nothing in it but empty cartons. 'We'd better go home,' said Meehan wearily, and reluctantly Griffiths agreed. They walked back to the Triumph and started off for Glasgow. It was beginning to rain. The time was about 2 a.m. It had not been a very fruitful day's outing.

They stopped at Ballantrae on the coast for ten minutes for Griffiths to look at a Jaguar. Meehan also got out of the car and noticed they had stopped outside a shed which said 'Funeral Directors'. After leaving Ballantrae ten minutes later, Meehan pushed the seat back and dozed. Some time later he was woken by Griffiths saying, 'That's a lovely sight,' and looked up to see the lights of Prestwick Airport.

A few miles beyond the airport the lights of the Triumph picked up an unexpected sight – a very young girl standing in a lay-by to the left of the road. To Meehan she seemed about fifteen. 'That kiddy seems to be in some sort of trouble,' he said, and told Griffiths to stop. He let down the window and the girl came up and said 'Mister, gonny help me?' Meehan said, 'What's wrong?' and the girl said, 'Two men have just thrown me out of a car and driven off with my pal.' Meehan told the girl to get in and asked her when this had happened. 'Just a couple of minutes ago,' said the girl, and Meehan said to Griffiths, 'Let's catch them.' Griffiths put down his foot, and inviting the attention of any early morning police cars that happened to be about, pushed the

Triumph up to a hundred.

'What's your name?' Meehan asked. The girl said 'Irene Burns.' Meehan said, 'No friend of Rabbie's!' and laughed.

The dance that Irene Burns and Isobel Smith had been to that night in Kilmarnock ended at 2 a.m. Afterwards they felt hungry, and though they were both only sixteen, decided to hitch-hike to Prestwick Airport, eight miles away, to get something to eat. Here they met a couple of youths by the names of William Mackie and his cousin Thomas Bell, also from Kilmarnock and who had also been to the dance. They too were looking for something to eat, but the airport café was closed, so the four of them got into Mackie's car and drove to Joe's Coffee Stall in Ayr. But that had just closed too, so they returned to the airport where the two girls had a final look round, then at about 3.30 a.m. they all started off for Kilmarnock. Mackie was driving with Irene Burns beside him, Bell and Isobel Smith were in the back.

At a lay-by outside the airport Mackie pulled up the car. Hopefully he put his arm round Irene Burns, and in the back Thomas Bell did the same to Isobel Smith. Both resisted. So at another lay-by, close to a roundabout, this ungallant pair told the girls they weren't going to Kilmarnock after all, they were going to Irvine, which was in another direction, and they would have to get out. So Irene Burns got out, and Isobel Smith was about to get out when Mackie slammed the door and drove away, not back to Irvine but on towards Kilmarnock. A few moments later Meehan and Griffiths arrived.

As Mr Moir's Triumph raced off towards Kilmarnock in pursuit of Mackie and Bell, Meehan asked Irene where she came from. She told him. Having a teenage daughter of his own, he suggested it was a bit late for a young girl like her to be thumbing lifts. He asked her about the two men, and she said she thought they had been taking dope. Irene seems to have had a thing about dope, for recalling this journey later she spoke of Meehan talking very fast and of having staring eyes, and wondering if he had been taking dope. In fact Meehan is a very voluble talker, and he was staring because of the speed they were going, and eventually asked Griffiths to go slower.

They passed several cars, and then in the built-up area on the fringes of Kilmarnock, where the street lighting was on, they saw ahead of them Mackie's white Anglia. Meehan told Griffiths 'Give him your lights,' and Griffiths flashed his headlights on and off. Then, as they passed the Anglia, Meehan signalled it to stop. After both cars had stopped, Irene got out, fetched Isobel from Mackie's car, and together they got into the back of the Triumph. Isobel noticed that Griffiths had dark glasses on and that Meehan was wearing a peaked cap. 'Where do you want us to drop you off?' said Meehan, helpful as ever, and the two girls told him. They dropped one off at Hill Street and one at Wellington Street, and then they set out for Glasgow. By now it was getting light.

It was about 4.30 a.m. that Griffiths left Paddy at Old Rutherglen Road. Letting himself into the flat, he woke Betty ('He's that clumsy,' said Betty, 'he'd wake the dead'). He said nothing of what he had been doing at Stranraer, but then he never did. But he told her about the two girls and chasing the white car. He said the girls were no more than fifteen or sixteen, and he couldn't get over them being allowed out at that time of night. 'He was quite upset about it,' said Betty.

Meehan slept late, got up in mid-morning, and then told his daughter Liz about the two girls. She thought it rather shocking too, for although she was eighteen, her mother didn't like her to stay out late without ringing in or saying where she would be. In the afternoon Paddy's thoughts turned again to buying a car, and he looked for the cigarette packet on which he'd written the name of the Stranraer garage that was selling the Morris 1100. He couldn't find it, but remembering that the Stranraer Police Station was near the garage, he telephoned them, and Police Cadet Pirrie told him the garage was Reid and Adams. Having discovered from the book that the foreman's home number was listed as well as the office one, he rang up the home number to find out the price. The telephone was answered by the foreman's son, a boy of fifteen, who said his father was out. Meehan said he would call later but didn't. A friend called Joe McLean came round to say he'd been involved the night before in some row at a deaf mute's party, and Paddy went off with him to try and get it sorted out.

Over at Holyrood Crescent Irene Cameron let herself into Griffiths' flat at about mid-day. She found him asleep in bed. Later he woke up and dressed, and they drove in the Triumph to the Glasgow Sunday market called the Barrows. On the way Griffiths told Irene about how he and Pat had waited for two hours outside the Lochryanhall Hotel, and how frustrating it had been, and then of the incident with the two girls. At the Barrows Griffiths inquired for the man who had the silver stall, but he wasn't there. He and Irene drove back to the flat.

In the bedroom of 2 Blackburn Place Abraham Ross looked about him, saw through his left eye (the other was clotted with blood and badly damaged) the chaos of the room, his blood all round him, his wife also lying helpless on the floor. He tried to move but found it impossible. However his wife's legs were not tied to her hands, and he asked her if she could get to the telephone that lay on a table between the beds. She managed to crawl over there and lift the receiver, but the line was dead.

As the day wore on Abe made several attempts to loosen his bonds, but without success. Outside in Blackburn Road he heard cars and people passing at intervals, and he shouted and screamed as loud as he could to try and attract attention. But his voice wasn't strong enough, nobody heard him. Evening came on, and then night, and now the Rosses had been lying helpless on the floor for nearly twenty-four hours without food or water. In the early hours of Monday morning Abe heard Rachel making a gurgling noise in her throat. 'I knew then that she was going.'

The Rosses' dreadful ordeal finally ended at 9 a.m. on the Monday morning when their domestic help, Mrs Grant, arrived for work. She knew something was wrong, for Sunday's milk and papers were still on the step, and the back door was wide open. She put the milk on the kitchen table, then heard Mr Ross's voice calling feebly from the bedroom, 'Who is that?' She said it was her. 'Thank God!' was the reply. 'Get the Police. We have been murdered.' Mrs Grant ran into the hall, dialled 999 on the other extension, and found the line dead. Then she went into the bedroom and saw the scene of horror. 'Get a knife and cut me loose,' said Mr Ross. But Mrs Grant was too appalled to act on her own, and ran out of the house to Mrs Adamson's opposite, and asked her to telephone the Police.

The Police arrived immediately, and before the ambulance came to take the Rosses to hospital, Sergeant Clark took a brief statement from Mr Ross. As a result of that, and a further statement made to Sergeant Aitchison in hospital, in which Mr Ross said his attackers called each other Pat and Jim or Jimmy the Ayr police say they sent out this telex that afternoon to all police forces in central and western Scotland (*mis-spellings as in the original*):

OUR REFERENCE 587/69
ABOUT 1.30 AM ON 6TH INST THE A.D. TOW MEN MASKED WITH NYLON STOCKINGS ENTERED BUNGALOW AT 2 BLACKBURN PLACE, AYR AFTER CUTTING TELEPHONE WIRES AND FORCING WINDOW WITH WOODEN JEMMY. THEY BOUND OCCUPIER AND HIS WIFE WITH NYLON STOCKINGS AND CLOTHES LINE TAKEN FROM CRYING GREEN AND BEAT THEM UP UNTIL THEY DISCLOSED WHEREABOUTS OF MONEY AND HOUSE SAFE KEY, APPROXIMATELY £1,000 STOLEN OF WHICH £300 IS BELIEVED TO BE BANK OF SCOTLAND £10 NOTES AND IN SEQUENCE AND £100 NOTE FROM UNKNOWN BANK. VICTIM IS PROPRIETKR OF A PAISLEY BINGO HALL.
DISCRIPTION OF MEN (1) 6 FEET, SLIM BUILD REFERRED TO AS 'JIM'
(2) SMALLER THAN NO. I. REFERRED TO 'PAT'

CRIME NOT DISCOVERED TILL 8 AM TODAY ANY INFORMATION TO FORCE H.Q. AYR (TEL: 64087)
MESSAGE ENDS TIMED AT 0353 HRS.

On Monday July 7th Meehan telephoned Reid and Adams in the morning and was told by Mr Downie, the Sales Manager, that the price of the 1100 was £465, which was more than he had expected. Mr Downie mentioned another 1100 which was going for £325, but Meehan said he wasn't interested. Later in the day Meehan took his son Pat to a garage in James Street to look at second-hand cars there, but saw nothing he liked.

Betty meanwhile had gone to her branch of the Clydesdale Bank to try and cash the cheque for £156 from the Chequered Flag: Griffiths had mentioned that his Scunthorpe fence, John Mathews, sometimes had good, cheap, second-hand cars, and they had made a plan to motor down there and try and buy one. But Mrs Meehan was told that as she didn't have as much as £156 in her account, she would have to wait until Wednesday before the cheque could be cleared.

That afternoon, on television and in the Glasgow *Evening Citizen*, news of the Ayr robbery broke; how the Rosses, both old people, had been savagely attacked in the middle of the night, then been left tied up all weekend in their ransacked house; and how Mrs Ross was now seriously ill in hospital. Everywhere the reaction to the news was shock and revulsion, and a desire for the perpetrators to be caught. Liz Meehan suggested to her father that the two youths in the white car might have had something to do with it, and shouldn't he tell the Police?

That evening the Meehans went to a comedy at the cinema. Afterwards Paddy found a friend called John Macfadden and his wife waiting outside. Macfadden had recognised Paddy in the cinema by his loud, distinctive laugh.

During that night meanwhile, at Ayr County Hospital, Rachel Ross's strength began to ebb. On her arrival there, she had been examined by the Surgical Registrar, Dr David Bremner, who found her 'very cold, semicomatose and having difficulty breathing'. He asked her what had happened and she replied, 'He knelt on my chest ...' This was all she said, and soon after she relapsed into unconsciousness. As the night wore on, said Dr Bremner, it was obvious that she was slowly 'drowning' in her own secretions, and in the early hours of Tuesday July 8th, despite all the doctors' efforts to revive her, she died.

The public were greatly shocked. If their mood the day before had been one of disgust, it was now one of anger; many people felt they would like to kill the murderers themselves. The Meehans felt as outraged as anyone, Betty and Liz in particular, but Paddy too. 'Because I am a criminal,' he once wrote, 'that does not mean that I do not have just the same feelings and reactions to events as anyone else.' The public, unmindful of how disparate crimes are, has a habit of lumping criminals together, of thinking that a man with a record for a certain offence is sympathetic to all other offences, even capable of committing them. This is not so. Most felons disapprove of sexual offences, particularly where they concern children: others have no sympathy for traitors; and those who commit non-violent crimes are repelled by crimes of violence. For 25 years Meehan had specialized in the crime of blowing safes in public or semi-public buildings. A crude, brutal crime like the Ayr murder, that of breaking into a private dwelling-house and beating up the occupants, was wholly foreign to his nature.

The Ayr Police responded promptly to public outrage. At Police Headquarters a special operations centre was set up, and officers started making inquiries at the first of some 15,000 houses in the town. In thousands of handbills distributed to shops and offices, in announcements in cinemas, dance-halls, restaurants and hotels, on television and radio and in the press, the Police renewed their request for any information, however trivial, that might help them in their inquiries. As a result they received hundreds of messages, most quite valueless. Abraham Ross offered a reward of £200 for information that might lead to the apprehension of the criminals, and an anonymous donor offered a further £800. That night the Police telephoned to the *Police Gazette* an announcement for the following day's issue:

SPECIAL NOTICES

MURDER

Ayrshire, Ayr. Between 01.30 hrs and 03.30 hrs 6th inst. two men with nylon stocking masks entered the bungalow occupied by Abraham Ross (66 yrs.), at 2 Blackburn Place, Ayr, after cutting the telephone wires and forcing front bedroom window with garden weeding tool (taken from garage). The occupier and his wife were bound hand and foot with nylon stockings and a clothes line (cut from drying green). Mr Ross was beaten up and stabbed in the neck and back until he disclosed the whereabouts of money and house safe key. Approx. £1,000. was stolen, of which £300. is believed to be new £10. B of E notes, in sequence, and a £100 note, bank unknown. (Details not to be divulged to Press). Crime was not discovered until 08.00 hrs. 7th inst. when both were removed to local hospital where Mrs Rachel Ross (72 yrs), died at 02.15 hrs. 8th inst. A post mortem is being held.

The after-described 2 MEN are wanted for interview—(1) MAN, referred to as Jim, b. 1929–1949 (20/40 years) 5ft 8in/6ft. slim build, wearing dark clothing, upper garment possibly cardigan or pullover. (2) MAN referred to as Pat, b. 1929–1949 (20/40 yrs), smaller than No. 1., clothing may bear traces of blood.

Any information or suggestions to be forwarded to Det. Supt., Ayr, Tel.No.Ayr 64087.

Meanwhile, in view of what Ross had later told the Police about the two men having Glasgow accents, the Glasgow police started routine inquiries among the city's villains. And one of the men they decided to interview was Ian Waddell.

Now normally the name of Waddell would have been fairly low down on any list of those wanted in connection with such a crime, if indeed on it at all. He was a petty crook. He had no record of violence, and his participation in such an enterprise, so far from Glasgow, would have been thought to have been beyond his powers. But before Mrs Ross died, Waddell had been blabbing; blabbing to Donald Carmichael, to Andrew Dick and others, and spending money too; and within a day or two of the crime it was common knowledge in the Glasgow underworld that Waddell had taken part in it. Police informants had passed this news on, and now the Police sought him out for questioning.[2]

When Waddell heard the Police were looking for him, he was naturally very worried. So he asked his friend John Skivington, manager of the Club Bar in the Gallowgate, what he should do, and Skivington said he should get hold of a solicitor right away. Waddell didn't know any solicitors, so Skivington suggested his own, Mr William Carlin; and after Waddell had peeled off £200 in new notes of the money from Mr Ross's safe, they went to Mr Carlin's office in St Vincent Street.

Waddell told Mr Carlin that the Police wanted to interview him in connection with the Ayr murder, and that although he had had nothing to do with it, he would like Mr Carlin to act for him if he was charged. He (or it may have been Skivington, there is some dispute) then gave Mr Carlin the ten new £20 notes, which Mr Carlin subsequently put into his client's account. A day or two later Mr Carlin accompanied Waddell to the Central Police Station for his interview with Detective Chief Inspector Sam Macalister. This was the officer who had once visited Meehan's flat in search of Griffiths; he is a heavily-built, sandy-haired man, described by those who knew him as 'the old-fashioned type of Glasgow cop, not likely to change his mind once it's made up'. Macalister may have thought it strange that a

[2] I have been told by a former Detective Superintendent in the Glasgow CID that one of his paid informers came to him a week after the crime with the news that Waddell had taken part in it. This officer is prepared to confirm this information to any official inquiry.

small-time crook like Ian Waddell should, if in the clear, find it necessary to bring a solicitor with him, but he was entirely within his rights. The interview, which Carlin described as 'a very lengthy interrogation', lasted an hour, and Waddell stuck closely to his alibi of having been all night in Carmichael's house. Mr Carlin was surprised at how clear Waddell's recollections seemed to be. Later Carmichael was interviewed twice and confirmed Waddell's story; and Waddell was not interviewed again.

Free of danger Waddell now went on a spending spree. He had already changed £400 in new notes from, he says, the manager of the Reekie Linn Bar, and with this and the rest of the money he gambled heavily on the horses with bookmakers at Parkhead Cross, he bought several new suits at Claude Alexander's in Parkhead, other things at a shop in Westmuir Street, and in Cowcaddens; he spent a lot of it on drink and he gave some to friends. Once in the Crest Bar in the Gallowgate William Macintyre asked if he would loan him £10 to tax a car, and Waddell replied, 'If you'd been with me on that job, you wouldn't have need of £10.' Within six or seven weeks of the robbery, all Waddell's share of the proceeds had gone.

On the Monday or Tuesday following the crime, and while McGuinness was still in London spending some of the proceeds from it, Agnes McGuinness took her son Billy aged three to the Eye Infirmary. On the way home she stopped at a newsagent to buy sweets for Billy, and saw the headlines about the Ayr break-in. In her own words, 'I put two and two together and was extremely worried.'

A week later her husband returned from London, having heard of Meehan's arrest on the car radio while driving home. Agnes told him straightaway that she thought what had happened in Ayr was dreadful. 'He told me the death should never have occurred, and had not been intended to happen. He said that someone was supposed to have phoned Ayr police after the robbery to advise them to go to the house. This person had panicked and failed to do this, and this is what caused the death.' This looks as though it was a third person who had agreed to telephone the police, but just who (Dick? Carmichael?) has never been discovered. Agnes went on: 'I asked him about the injuries to Mr Ross and he said it was "the big one" who hit him.[3] He also said he would not harm the old lady because she had just had a breast operation.' A little later McGuinness took the balance of his share of the money from Mr Ross's safe, and banked it in his account at the Shettleston Road branch of the Royal Bank of Scotland.

There is little news of Griffiths on the Monday, although Irene Cameron saw him in the evening, and found him his usual self. On the Tuesday morning he telephoned a man who was advertising a flat in Marywood Square, and in the afternoon he drove there in the Triumph, and paid £16 for two and a half weeks' rent, using the name of Francis Macneil. He said he was an antique silver merchant, and had trouble at his previous flat when silverware was stolen from his car. Francis Macneil was the name in which he had just filled in a passport application, and the same day Meehan endorsed the application in the name of John Fee. On the Wednesday Griffiths took the application form to the Passport Office and asked for the passport to be sent to Marywood Square; but he told the clerk he didn't need it till the 19th. Whether Griffiths took the flat in Marywood Square simply as a safe place to receive the passport, or because he intended to move house yet again, or as a dumping ground for stolen goods, is not known.

That day, Wednesday July 9th, the papers were again full of developments in the search for the murderers of Mrs Ross. It was now clear to the Ayr police from the evidence found at the Rosses' house that the intruders had been there several hours. Detective Superintendent Struthers, in charge of the case, told this to the press, and James McKillop of the *Glasgow Herald* printed it in his paper the next day. Accordingly the police put out a further appeal for information from those who had been driving cars in the area between midnight and 6 a.m. One driver who had been in the area at that time was of course the police officer who

[3] Later McGuinness admitted to Agnes that his partner in the Ayr crime was Waddell.

had taken McGuinness to the bus-station. But incredibly, this vital piece of information was not followed up.

But there was another driver in the general area at the material time, and that was Paddy Meehan; and when his daughter Liz read that Superintendent Struthers was even asking people 'to pass on information anonymously', she again suggested to her father that the two youths who had been driving with the two girls near Prestwick might have been involved; after all, they were only a few miles from the scene of the crime in the middle of the night when it happened. Betty, who didn't want Paddy to get any nearer the Police than he need, played down the suggestion, said wisely enough that men who had just committed that sort of crime would hardly be likely to start picking up girls who might later identify them.

But Liz persisted, and because Paddy loved her and had always had this thing about being helpful, and because the Police had said they would welcome information anonymously, he agreed to telephone the Ayr police in the afternoon, when Betty was out of the house. But he knew as he waited for the number to ring that, because of what he and Griffiths had been doing that night, he had to be careful what he said.

Detective Constable Daniel Scott answered the call, and Meehan said he had some information regarding the Ayr murder. Scott asked Meehan to give his name and address, but Paddy refused. So Scott took the message, and on a Police message form wrote it down:

> At 4.30 am morning of murder two of caller's friends driving towards Kilmarnock on Ayr–Kilmarnock road picked up girl unknown. Girl said she and pal – female – picked up by two youths from Glasgow in car – white coloured old type, no make. Youths threw her out and drove away with friend – girl said men were 'doped up'. Caller's friend gave chase – caught up with white car, girl got out – did not note registration number. Youths might have done Ayr murder.

Scott asked Meehan for the name and address of his friend, the particulars of his car, the names of the girls, etc, but all these either Meehan wouldn't give or said he didn't know. But he did suggest that if the Police put an advertisement in the newspaper asking the two girls to come forward this might lead them to the two men. He told Liz what he had done, and she seemed pleased.

About an hour later Meehan remembered his joke with Irene about 'No friend of Rabbie's!' and that she had said her name was Burns. So he called Detective Constable Scott again, and told him this. There are not many Burns in Kilmarnock, and soon after the second call police cars were on their way to visit them, including Irene's aunt at 81 Hillhead Avenue.

Earlier that day Betty had drawn from the bank the £156 cash of the Chequered Flag repayment, and given it to Paddy. Now he waited for Griffiths who had promised to drive him to Scunthorpe to look for a car as soon as the money came through. With other monies he had, Meehan had a total of £181: Betty said she doubted if he would get much of a car for that.

At about 10 p.m. Griffiths dropped Irene Cameron at her parents' home at Castlemilk, then picked up Meehan at Old Rutherglen Road, and the pair set off south, driving through the night as they had done four days earlier on the way back from Stranraer. They stopped briefly at a hotel in Appleby, where Griffiths pinched a few things from cars parked there, and they arrived at Scunthorpe in the morning. John Mathews was not there. So they drove across country to Oakamoor Prison near Stoke-on-Trent, where Meehan wanted to visit a woman prisoner by the name of Lil Connolly, whom he had met in London at the time of the abortive raid on the Edmonton Co-op. Meehan bought her a plant and a bunch of flowers, and while he was visiting her, Griffiths sat in the car outside. For Meehan, inside, it must have been quite like old times. Then they started back to Glasgow. The whole enterprise was typical of the amateurish way they often acted, setting off somewhere almost on impulse, never bothering to inquire whether people would be in or out.

At a Forte's café on the M6 Paddy telephoned Betty to say when he would be back. She told him the Police had been up at the flat; also that the television that day had carried the news that one of Mrs Ross's killers might be called Pat.

Meehan got home about nine, and Betty told him that two police officers had been up about 5 p.m. and one of them was Detective Constable Baxter. Meehan rang the Central Police Station straightaway. He was told Baxter had gone home, got the number and rang him there. Baxter said he was making routine inquiries into the Ayr murder and wanted Meehan to make a statement accounting for his movements over the weekend. He asked Meehan when he could come to the police station and Meehan suggested the next morning.

Although Meehan realized he was only one of many Glasgow villains being questioned by the Police, he appreciated the danger of his position; for not only were the Police looking for a Pat, and he was called Pat, not only had the money been taken from a safe, and he had a long record as regards safes, but his alibi was that he was in the company of a wanted criminal, doing things he shouldn't be doing, and at one point not far from the scene of the crime.

However as that *was* his alibi, he had no alternative but to give it, and when Griffiths rang a few minutes later he told him what had happened, and that he would have to give an account of their journey to Stranraer. Inevitably this would include a description of the car, and Meehan advised Griffiths to get rid of it at once. (At this time of course Meehan had no idea that the name of the other man the police were looking for was Jim.)

Griffiths, when he put down the phone, also realized the seriousness of his position. Not only as a wanted man would he be unable to come forward to support Meehan's story, but as soon as Meehan had made his statement, there would be a massive search for him and the car. He could take care of himself; but the discovery of the car, with his fingerprints all over it, would be enough in itself to send him down for several more years. So he must put it where no policeman would ever find it, where he had put other cars in the past, deep into the peaty waters of Loch Awe.

Griffiths lost no time. Stopping only long enough to ring Irene at her home and say that he would see her the following night, he got into the Triumph for the last time and headed north. In the dusk he sped up Loch Lomondside, over the hill to Crianlarich and Tyndrum, down the river to Dalmally and Loch Awe. And there in the middle of the night, with not a soul to see him, Griffiths sent Mr Moir's turquoise-blue Triumph plunging into deep water to join the other dead vehicles in his private graveyard of stolen cars. Then, on foot and in pouring rain, he set out for Oban to see about getting transport back.

It was 5.45 in the morning that a Mr William Maclaughlan, driving south from Oban to Glasgow Airport, saw a soaked, bedraggled figure by the side of the road, carrying a paper parcel. He stopped and asked Griffiths if he wanted a lift, which Griffiths gratefully accepted. As they drove south Griffiths explained that *his* Triumph 2000 (he still couldn't resist boasting about it) had broken down the day before, that he had been unable to hire another car because of the holiday season, and so was having to hitchhike to Glasgow for an important business appointment. Mr Maclaughlan noted his marked English accent, and later how very quiet he was (he had reason to be, having had virtually no sleep for 48 hours). He dropped him off on the outskirts of Glasgow at Anniesland Cross. Griffiths proffered a note to help pay for the petrol, but Mr Maclaughlan refused.

At 9.30 next morning, Friday July 11th, Detective Constable Baxter rang Meehan to cancel the interview, as there was no need for him to come after all. That day, however, the Police were questioning other villains. These included William Macintyre, who told them of having spent part of the night with Andrew Dick. During the day Meehan took to the Clydesdale Bank £150 of the £180 cash he had brought back from the abortive Scunthorpe trip, and opened a current account there. In the evening Irene Cameron visited Griffiths, and noticed the Triumph was not at the front door. She asked him where it was and he replied, 'Oh, I got fed up with it, I got rid of it.' She also noticed that his car coat and a pair of shoes beside the fire were sopping wet.

It was the following day, Saturday July 12th, that the Police finally got around to interviewing Meehan. At 9.30 a.m. two police officers, Detective Sergeant Smith and Detective Constable Lawtie, turned up at Old Rutherglen Road. On Thursday Smith had been given a list of twenty to thirty possible suspects to interview, and now he was nearing the end of them. He asked Meehan if he would give him an account of his movements the previous weekend, and Meehan said he would be happy to. He could have refused to do so without his solicitor being present (and had he been guilty he certainly would have done); but as he had nothing to hide except casing the motor taxation office and waiting outside the Lochryanhall Hotel, he saw no reason to. His attitude, said Smith, was very co-operative.

This is the statement that Meehan gave to Detective Sergeant Smith:

> About 4 p.m. on Saturday the 5th of July, 1969, along with an English friend of mine called Jim Griffiths, we left Glasgow in Jim's car, a blue Triumph 2000, which he had a loan of from a friend in England to go to Stranraer to see a motor car which was for sale in a garage near Stranraer Police Station. After we left Glasgow I don't know the road we took but we arrived in Stranraer about 7 o'clock. When we arrived there we went to the garage where we spoke to an old man who was in charge of the petrol pumps. He could not tell us anything about the car we were interested in so we left the garage. I then went with Griffiths to a tearoom where we had high tea. We stayed in the tearoom for about an hour and a half. After we left the tearoom Jim said he was going to the car to fix the indicator handle which had broken. He said it would take a while as he had to remove a part of the dashboard. I told him I would just go

for a walk round the town. I walked down to the harbour where I had a drink in a pub. I left the pub and stood watching the car ferry being loaded. After that I went to a different pub where I stayed till closing time. After I left the pub I walked about for a while. As I was passing the station a girl spoke to me and asked if I knew the time of the bus to a local village, I can't remember the name of it. I spoke to someone or it could have been a driver, and asked the time of the bus and then told the girl. I walked back to where Jim was sorting. When I got there he told me he hadn't managed to fix it. A while later, I think it would be midnight, both of us left to go back to Glasgow, I don't know the way we came back but I remember seeing the airport at Prestwick. Further along the road, near Kilmarnock, I saw a girl standing on the road. She was distraught. Jim stopped the car and then reversed it to where the girl was standing. I asked her what happened and she told us that her and her friend had got a lift from Prestwick from two boys in an old white-coloured car. One of the boys tried to get funny with her and she didn't like it, and that he had put her out of the car. I asked her when this had happened and she told me four or five seconds ago. I told her to get into the back of our car. Jim then drove off towards Kilmarnock after the white car. I won't tell you what speed we were doing. About a mile or so along the road we overtook the car which she said was the car which she had been given the lift in. I signalled the driver to stop by waving my hand out of the window. The car stopped. I then told the girl we had in our car to go and tell her pal to come out of this car and come with her in ours. She did this. After that we drove off. I don't know what kind of car it was but would say it was a dirty white colour with the front of it badly rusted. I would say the bloke in the back seat was tall and thin. One of the girls we took in the car said her name was Irene Burns. We drove both girls into Kilmarnock and dropped one of them near a roundabout. I don't know where we dropped the other one but it was in Kilmarnock somewhere. We then drove back to Glasgow getting there I think about 5 a.m. When I got up on the Sunday I phoned Stranraer Police to get the name of the garage where I was making enquiries the day before about a Morris 1100. I then, I think either Tuesday or Wednesday this week, saw in the papers that a woman had been murdered in Ayr at the weekend. I then told my wife about the girls we had given a lift on the Sunday morning. She told me I better report it to the police. I didn't want to report it as I didn't like getting involved with the police. My daughter said I would be better to report it. On Wednesday I telephoned the police at Ayr and told them about the girls we had picked up. When I phoned I could not remember any of the girls' names. I did not say who I was when I phoned. A short time later I remembered one of the girl's names as Irene Burns. I then phoned the police at Ayr again and told them the girl's name. I did not give them my name.

In this statement Meehan leaves out entirely any reference to his two unlawful acts, inspecting the motor taxation office with a view to breaking into it – the real object of the trip to Stranraer – and waiting outside the Lochryanhall Hotel to pinch things from the cars there. At this stage the first omission did not much matter. The second was more serious, for it meant there was a long time-lag in the middle of the night, that by his own reckoning he had taken five hours to travel the eighty-six miles from Stranraer to Glasgow. But worse than what he had left out was what unknowingly he had put in – the name of Jim Griffiths. The Police were looking for two men who called each other Pat and Jim. Now Pat and Jim had been served up to them on a plate.

On that Saturday too Irene Cameron went round to Holyrood Crescent. She told Griffiths she wanted to go out and buy some clothes, and he opened his wallet and offered her a £10 note. She noticed that it was the only note in the wallet, but he made her take it. Closing the wallet, he said, 'I could be doing with another £10. I'm skint.'

Over the weekend Meehan too seems to have been short

of ready cash. On the Sunday morning, as he was going out, he asked Betty if she could lend him £1; he had spent all his loose cash the night before on whisky for a party they had been unexpectedly invited to. Betty had a fiver, but knew if she let Paddy have it, she'd be unlikely to see any of it back. But her neighbour, Mrs Dobbie from across the landing, was in the flat, so Betty borrowed £1 for Paddy from her, and later when Paddy had gone out, she found some change and paid Mrs Dobbie back.

For the Police, Meehan's statement to Detective Sergeant Smith was like an unexpected legacy. For the past week they had been under great pressure to produce results, well aware how passionately both public and press wanted Mrs Ross's murderers to be brought to book, yet not having a clue who they might be.[4] Now, out of the blue their identity had been revealed; and that morning, as soon as senior police officers had read over Meehan's statement, they applied for a warrant. It was for two things; a search of Meehan's flat where they might find blood-stained clothing, cash from Mr Ross's safe and other evidence that would associate Meehan with the crime; and for Meehan to take part in an Identification parade where, hopefully, witnesses might recognise him.

But they did not execute the warrant immediately. The reason, said Detective Superintendent Struthers, in charge of the case, was that he wanted to supervise a massive operation involving roadblocks that were to be set up on roads leading into Ayr between midnight on Saturday and 6 a.m. on Monday; and he was billed to address some 100 officers who were going to make further house to house inquiries on Sunday. Time was also needed to organise the Identification parade.

[4] Dr David Bremner writes: 'Ayr CID were in and out of Ayr County Hospital a lot during the week after the crime and interviewed me, I think, three times. They became more intense and nervous as the week progressed, and it was very obvious that they were under considerable pressure to make some progress in the case.' (Letter to the author, March 26th, 1976.)

There could be other reasons why the warrant was not executed at once. It may well be that some police officers asked themselves why, if Meehan was the man they were looking for, he had acted so strangely out of character. How was it possible for a man who had committed such a murder only six days before to be so relaxed and friendly with Detective Sergeant Smith? Why, when on every past occasion Meehan had robbed a safe and had disappeared for days, sometimes weeks, had he not done so this time? Was it likely that a man with a 25-year record for blowing safes, who had never entered a dwelling-house unlawfully nor ever participated in robbery with violence, should suddenly do these things now? And most extraordinary of all, would two professional criminals like Meehan and Griffiths be quite so wet as deliberately to toss each other's real names to and fro in the course of the crime ('Get this cunt off me, *Pat*!' – 'They're not here yet, *Jim*!'), so that those they were robbing would hear?

But these could have been no more than passing thoughts. The Rosses had been attacked by two men. Meehan now admitted to being with another man. The Rosses had been attacked in the middle of the night. Meehan had admitted to passing that way in the middle of the night. Meehan in telephoning Ayr police to throw suspicion on the two youths had pretended he had not been there himself: now in his statement he admitted he had. And finally, and most devastating was the fact that Mr Ross had heard the two men call each other Pat and Jim or Jimmy, and Meehan and Griffiths were Pat and Jim – this surely was beyond the bounds of coincidence? It must have seemed then to the police officers in charge of the case, as it would have done to any of us had we been in their shoes, that their search for Mrs Ross's murderers had ended.

They came to Old Rutherglen Road at 8 a.m. on Monday morning, July 14th, Detective Superintendent Struthers and Detective Inspector Derrick Macallister of the Ayrshire CID, and Detective Chief Inspector Sam Macalister of the Glasgow Police, and Detective Sergeant Crisp of the

Regional Crime Squad, all in plain clothes. 'The way they hammered at the door,' said Liz, 'put the fear of God into me.' Betty let them in. She and Liz were both dressed but Paddy was in bed. The officers went into the bedroom and Meehan, in his pyjamas, said 'What's this for?' Derrick Macallister told him to get up and, as Meehan was getting dressed, he cautioned him, and read out the warrant. Meehan listened to it aghast. 'You are making the biggest mistake of your life,' he said when Macallister had finished, 'I can prove I was in Stranraer that night.' Then he said, 'What do I have to go to an ID Parade for? There's only the two girls I picked up?'

The Police started searching. According to Betty they searched everywhere, in the cupboards, under the carpets, beneath floorboards and mattresses, even in the bathroom and kitchen. She asked them if they would search methodically, so it would be easier to put things back. She asked what they were looking for, was it something large or small, but, she says, they wouldn't say. As Liz went out of the flat to go to work, they made her empty the contents of her handbag, and she was so upset she never went to the office. They asked Betty for two cases and they put into them all Meehan's clothes, apart from what he was wearing, his tools, his papers. For Meehan, watching it all in silence and knowing there was nothing they would find, the search must have had a kind of mad, surrealistic quality, like an early Chaplin two-reeler.

Now it was time for Meehan to attend the Identification parade, and before the search of his flat was over, two officers took him away across the river to Glasgow Central Police Station.

For the Police the Identification parade was going to be a gamble. Those called as witnesses were a Mrs Mathieson from Cumnock, who had been in Ayr during a day previous to the crime (though she couldn't remember which day) and had been approached by two men in Barnes Crescent who had asked the way to Blackburn Road; a Mr Falconer who on the afternoon of the robbery saw two men in a lane opposite the Rosses' house (possibly Waddell and Mc-

Guinness), and heard one saying something about the backs of the houses; Mr Haxton, the petrol-pump attendant at Stranraer; the two girls, Irene Burns and Isobel Smith; and of course Abraham Ross.

The Police knew that the chances of a successful identification were slim. The two girls and possibly Thomas Haxton would probably pick Meehan out, but they were nowhere near the scene of the crime, and he had freely admitted to having seen them. Mr Falconer and Mrs Mathieson would be unlikely to make an identification from their fleeting glimpses of two men. This left Mr Ross; but Mr Ross had never seen one of the men, and the other, whom he had only caught sight of briefly during their struggle, was wearing a hooded mask. So the only possible identification Mr Ross could make would be by voice – and all from a few words said in a Glasgow accent by a stranger in the dark a week before. Clearly it was going to be a very long shot – some might say a totally impossible shot. Mr Ross was going to need all the help he could get.

But the Police pinned their faith on Mr Ross. They knew if he didn't turn up trumps, that if he, or Mr Falconer, failed to make a positive identification, they would have little option but to let Meehan go; for although they believed in their bones he was the man they wanted, they also knew there was not a scrap of direct evidence against him.

Identification parades at Glasgow Central Police Station usually take place in the Identification Parade Room in the basement. But, because it was unavailable that day, the parade was to take place instead in the Detective Constable's room on the ground floor. The witnesses would assemble in the Detective Sergeant's room, along the corridor, and be called in turn to view the parade. After viewing the parade each witness would leave by a door at the other end to which he entered, be ushered down another corridor parallel with the first, and shown into a small room known as the Interview Room. Here he would join the witnesses who had already viewed the parade, and they would remain together until the proceedings were over. Rules for Identification parades are very strict. Witnesses are not allowed to talk to each other about the case before viewing the parade, and an officer is supposed to be on hand to see that this rule is carried out.

At about 11.30 on this morning of July 14th 1969 – according to everyone a scorching hot day – the parade assembled in the Detective Constable's room. It consisted of Meehan and eight other men, picked off the street at random and matching roughly Meehan's height and build. Meehan however was different from the others in that he was wearing a blue pin-stripe suit and a green tie. Also present were Meehan's solicitor, Peter McCann, and his colleague Cornelius McMahon, Detective Sergeant Inglis of the Ayrshire Police in charge of the parade – an astute independent minded officer, Detective Superintendent Struthers, Chief Inspector Macalister and Inspector Macallister. On the floor in front of each man on the parade were big printed numbers by which witnesses were expected to identify them.

Meanwhile along the passage the witnesses were waiting to be called. Mr Falconer, Mr Haxton and Mrs Mathieson had been brought to the station by police car. On arrival they were not taken direct to the Detective Sergeant's room, but upstairs to what Mr Falconer and Mr Haxton describe as 'a room where there were a number of typists'. They waited here a little, and were then taken down to the Detective Sergeant's room, where they found Mr Ross with a nurse, and the two girls from Kilmarnock. What conversation Mr Ross may have already had with the only two people who would almost certainly identify the suspect is not known; but Mr Haxton states that after his party had joined the others, 'Mr Ross was asking everyone what they knew of the incident, and if they thought they could identify anyone on the parade.' Mr Ross's zeal to discover some clue as to the man the police believed was his wife's murderer was perfectly understandable; although such a conversation was in contravention of Identification parade rules.

The police usher outside called for the first witness. This was Mr Ross. He and the nurse went out of the room, and the five left behind were under the impression that he was going to view the parade. This is what he should have done, but it seems didn't do. He and the nurse were ushered into the Interview Room and there asked to wait until called for again. It is unlikely that Mr Ross, who had had no previous experience of Identification parades, saw anything odd in this.

The other witnesses were called in turn, made their way down the corridor to the Detective Constable's room and viewed the parade. Mr Falconer was the first to view the parade: he started with the man opposite him as he entered, No 7, and worked his way up to No 1. He was unable to identify anyone either then or when he asked to look at the men's profiles. He was ushered out of the room by the door at the far end, then went down the corridor to the Interview Room. Here he saw Mr Ross and the nurse, and naturally assumed that Mr Ross had already viewed the parade.

The next witnesses were Mrs Mathieson and Mr Haxton. Like Mr Falconer they stared at No 7 and walked up to No 1; but they too were unable to identify anyone and joined Mr Falconer and Mr Ross in the Interview Room. Then came Irene Burns, who picked out Meehan as one of the two men who gave her a lift, and after her Isobel Smith. Isobel Smith too recognised Meehan, but was in such a nervous state that she seemed hesitant to pick him out. Meehan, seeing her distress and having nothing to fear, said, 'Don't worry, pet, everything will be all right.' She too then went to the Interview Room.

What happened in the Interview Room is best described by Irene Burns. 'The old man asked me if I had picked out anyone. I told him I had ... Isobel came in and together we discussed the parade and I described Mr Meehan to Isobel. The old man was sitting near us as we were talking. Isobel and I both agreed we had picked out the same person.'

Other witnesses confirm this. 'I remember one of the girls discussing the fact that she had picked out someone in the parade,' said Mr Haxton, and Mr Falconer remembers both girls talking about having identified someone. 'Mr Ross asked them if they had identified anyone, and one of them nodded, Yes.' In addition, said Mr Falconer, Mr Ross asked him if he had identified anyone.

By now Mr Ross must have had a fair idea in his mind of the man the girls had recognized, and whom the police believed, had broken into his home and murdered his wife. It must have been a dreadful moment for Mr Ross, as he was helped along the corridor, to think that in a few moments he was going to meet the man again face to face. The door was opened and they went in. The parade faced them. Meehan, who had changed his position once or twice, as he was entitled to, was now in position number one, at the far end. He expected Mr Ross to start inspecting the parade from the other end as all the previous witnesses had done, but instead Ross was assisted by an officer to where Meehan stood in the No 1 position. Meehan, looking at Mr Ross, noticed he had his hands to his head 'and looked rather excited'.

According to his agreed instructions Mr Ross then asked Detective Sergeant Inglis for the men to say, 'Shut up, shut up, we'll send an ambulance.' Inglis repeated the phrase and asked Meehan, at No 1, to say it first. Had Meehan been Mrs Ross's murderer, he might well have tried to disguise his voice. Having nothing to lose he spoke the words firmly and clearly: 'Shut up, shut up, we'll send an ambulance.'

The effect on Mr Ross was catastrophic. These were the words which, only a week before, his wife's murderer had said in answer to her pathetic pleas to send an ambulance. Now here was the murderer in the flesh saying them once again. He staggered back, visibly shaken, and exclaimed, 'That's the voice, I know it, I know it. I don't have to go any further.' Meehan, appalled said, 'You're mistaken, laddie.' 'Oh, that's him, that's him,' said Mr Ross, collapsing. Meehan said, with some heat, 'Sir, you have got the wrong man, honest.'

No one else on the parade was asked to say the words, although they too had Glasgow accents. The parade broke up, the witnesses were sent home; and Meehan was taken by Superintendent Struthers to the Bar of the Central Police Station to be charged with robbery and murder. This took place at noon. Superintendent Struthers read out the charges, and Meehan, feeling caught up in some never-ending nightmare, again vehemently protested his innocence. 'You are making a horrible mistake. I know absolutely nothing about it.'

By this time Betty Meehan had arrived at the police station to see Paddy and bring him some cigarettes. She was sitting on a bench near a door when Paddy came by on his way down to the cells. 'He was chalk-white,' said Betty, 'and he said to me, "That old man *picked me out.*" He couldn't understand it.'

Presently Detective Chief Superintendent Tom Goodall, the head of Glasgow CID, came to see Paddy and said to him, 'We know the two men at Ayr had Glasgow accents, so Griffiths couldn't have been with you. Who were you with then?' Paddy repeated that he had been with Griffiths that evening, and that neither of them had been in Ayr. 'Well, in that case,' said Goodall, 'the sooner you can get Griffiths to come in and clear you, the better.' On the way up Tom Goodall passed Mrs Meehan, and she said to him, 'This is a terrible mistake.' He repeated what he had said to Paddy: 'Get hold of Griffiths, and we'll get it straightened out.'

Betty was taken to see Paddy in a cell. She found him very shaken. But he told her what Goodall had said about the men having Glasgow accents, and asked her to get Griffiths to come in and clear him as soon as possible. And he kept repeating, 'How *did* that old man pick me out?'

In Ayr and Glasgow and elsewhere, there was much relief and satisfaction that only a week after the crime the Police had arrested a man for Mrs Ross's murder. They had done, everyone thought, a splendidly prompt job. But forty miles away in Edinburgh there was one man puzzled by Meehan's arrest. He was Stanley Bowen, the Crown Agent, head of the office, like that of the Director of Public Prosecutions in England, that prepares criminal prosecutions for the Crown and briefs Counsel for the trial. His office had prosecuted Meehan many times in the past, and if Crown Counsel found the evidence sufficient, would soon be prosecuting him again.

After a lifetime in the Crown Office Stanley Bowen probably knew Meehan's professional career better than anybody. Yet when Meehan was charged with murder he was very surprised. 'At the time of the Ayr robbery,' he remarked, 'I said to my wife, "That looks like the work of X." It never for a moment occurred to me it might be Meehan.'

Hardly had Betty got home than the telephone rang. It was Jim Griffiths, knowing nothing of the morning's happenings, and wanting Paddy. Uncertain if the telephone was being tapped, Betty said she had something urgent to tell him and would meet him as soon as possible in the basement of Lewis's store in Argyle Street. They met as arranged, and then walked to St Enoch's car-park. There Betty told Griffiths of how Paddy had been picked out in an Identification parade and charged with murder. 'That's ridiculous,' said Griffiths, 'the Police haven't got a thing on Paddy, and they know it. But they've arrested him so as to get at me.' Betty told him what Tom Goodall had said about the men having Glasgow accents. 'Paddy says you must go down to the station, and clear both of you.' Griffiths said, 'If I go to the station, they'll release Paddy, and for the things I'm wanted for I'll get ten years. What am I to do?'

Presently Griffiths remembered that Paddy knew a couple of reporters on the *News of the World*, Jim Cassels and Ron Belbin, and he said he would telephone them to tell them the true story. So he and Betty took a taxi to West Campbell Street, away from the city centre, and Griffiths called up the *News of the World* from a public call box. But neither reporter was there; Monday was the paper's day off. Griffiths told the speaker that his inquiry concerned the Ayr murder, and could he have Belbin's home number? He was given it, rang it, and there was no reply.

By this time Betty was exhausted, for it was very hot and

she hadn't eaten all day. So she told Griffiths she would go home, try and locate Cassels or Belbin during the afternoon, and arrange for one of them to meet Griffiths in the Botanic Gardens at 7 p.m. Griffiths said that if neither showed up, he would get his girl-friend, Irene Cameron, to telephone Betty at the flat, and if she would give Irene the last four digits of the telephone number of the public call box below the flat (he knew the area code was 429), he would telephone there five minutes later to find out what had happened. Before leaving him, Betty implored him to telephone Detective Chief Superintendent Goodall, and clear Paddy.

At about 4 p.m. Detective Chief Superintendent Goodall was sitting in his office with Detective Superintendent Elphinstone Dalglish, when the telephone rang. Goodall answered it, then, putting his hand on the mouthpiece, said to Dalglish, 'It's Griffiths.' At the other end Griffiths told Goodall that Meehan had nothing to do with the Ayr murder, and that the two of them had been together in Stranraer. (Whether he told Goodall about having heard that the two men had Glasgow accents, and drew attention to his own, is not known.) Goodall then said to Griffiths, 'If you are so sure of Meehan's innocence, you should give yourself up and make a statement that would cover the innocence of Meehan, and account for the movements of both of you.' Griffiths replied that he could not give himself up.

Half-an-hour later Griffiths rang again, again to emphasise Meehan's innocence. He and Meehan, he assured Goodall, had been together until 2.15 a.m. (he meant presumably in the neighbourhood of Stranraer). Goodall again urged him to give himself up, and left his home number in case he wanted to get in touch later. Then, rather abruptly, Griffiths rang off.

Griffiths went back to his flat in Holyrood Crescent, and Irene Cameron arrived after work. Griffiths said, 'Pat's been arrested.' She thought he was joking. He said, 'No, I'm serious, he's been arrested for the Ayr murder. And I'm the other man they're looking for.' Irene looked stunned, and asked him point-blank if he had had anything to do with it. 'I swear,' said Griffiths angrily, 'I had nothing to do with it at all.' Irene had never seen him angry before, and by the way he answered knew he was speaking the truth.

Griffiths then told Irene the true story of the Triumph, how he had dumped it near Oban. He had to do this, he said, because of people seeing it who shouldn't. She realised he was in deep trouble but didn't ask for more information than he wanted to give. She suggested he go to England to get away from it all, and indeed he had every opportunity to do so. With his new passport, recently sent to Marywood Square and now in his possession, he could even have gone abroad, and had he committed the robbery, and got his share of the money from Mr Ross's safe, he assuredly would have done, as he had in the past. But he felt a responsibility for Pat. 'I can clear Pat because of my accent,' he told Irene. But just *how* was he to do it, how to gain Meehan's liberty without losing his own?

He went to the Botanic Gardens at 7 p.m. but no one was there, and he returned to the flat very depressed. He asked Irene to ring Betty and say the reporters hadn't shown up, and that she would ring later to get the phone number in the call box below the Meehans' flat. He also asked Irene to tell Betty that he was 'thinking of going in himself'.

He may have been thinking about it, but he knew he could never do it, never voluntarily make out his own ticket to further years behind bars in Parkhurst and Wandsworth and Gartree. At 8.30 he rang Tom Goodall for the third time, this time at his home. Once again he reiterated Meehan's innocence, but said categorically that he would not give himself up. Then he added, with a touch of bravado, he knew who the two men were. Who were they, asked Goodall? Of course Griffiths couldn't say. But, he added, in a fury of frustration, if they knew what was good for them they'd better give themselves up.

At about 10 p.m. Griffiths and Irene went down to the telephone box at the corner. Irene telephoned Betty and got the number of the phone box below Meehans' flat. Five minutes later Griffiths rang this number and Betty answered it. She said she had rung Belbin's number just before 7 p.m., but there was no answer. She had been told that Cassels was staying with his granny in Carluke, but no one knew the granny's name or number. Griffiths told her not to worry, he said he believed he knew who were responsible, and in his frustration and anger he bragged that he would get at them, just as he had bragged to Goodall.

But when he came out of the phone box, the stuffing had gone out of him. 'He was that worried-looking,' said Irene, 'he was on the verge of tears.' They went back to the flat, and Griffiths said, 'I've *got* to get Pat out somehow. He has a wife, and children in good jobs, and they'll suffer through this. It's so unfair.'

Next morning Meehan was due to appear to answer charges of murder and robbery in the Sheriff Court at Ayr. Before leaving he was told about Griffiths telling Mr Goodall that he definitely wasn't going to give himself up. Until now Meehan had refused to divulge Griffiths' address, observing a certain honour among thieves. But now, if the robbery and murder charge was to be lifted from him, he had no alternative but give it.

Give it he did; and after he had left for Ayr orders went out for detectives to go to 14 Holyrood Crescent and bring Griffiths in.

* * *

Because of a conflict of interests, Peter McCann, who had been Meehan's solicitor at the Identification parade, was unable to act for him thereafter. His new solicitor was Mr Joseph Beltrami, of the firm of Beltrami, Dunn and Co., one of the most experienced and knowledgeable of Glasgow criminal law solicitors, who had acted in the past for many of the city's Neds. He had first interviewed Meehan in the Central Police Station on the evening of the Identification parade, and was impressed, as Peter McCann had been earlier in the day, by Meehan's vehement protestations of innocence. He remembers in particular Meehan saying, 'If you don't believe me, I don't want you to take my case.'

When, on the morning of Tuesday July 15th, Meehan

arrived in a police car at Ayr Sheriff Court, there was a big, hostile crowd surrounding the entrance to the court. They reckoned that as Meehan had been charged with murder he must be guilty, and they wanted to show their detestation of the man who had committed so disgusting a crime. As Meehan got out of the police car, with a blanket over his head and guided by Detective Sergeant Richie, the crowd broke into a chant of hatred; there were cries of 'Hang him!', 'Get a gun!', and Shoot the sod'. Inside the court Mr Beltrami was waiting; and in his presence Meehan grabbed one of the detectives by the lapels and said with anger, 'For fucks sake, do your job! Go to Stranraer, check my alibi and get the bastards who did this.' Mr Beltrami, observing it, said later, 'It was a completely spontaneous outburst, it simply couldn't have been put on.'

Before going into court Meehan was asked if he would agree to a medical examination: the Police wanted to take fingernail scrapings in case they contained flakes of paint or other evidence from 2 Blackburn Place, and also for him to be examined generally for signs of a possible struggle. Meehan said he had no objections, and invited the police doctor, Dr Campbell (who was also the Rosses' doctor), to examine him thoroughly. During the examination, the doctor noticed a small cut on Meehan's finger and some marks on his back. Meehan said the first had been caused by a nail in his kitchen, and the second by himself in the cells the night before, having a good scratch. The doctor accepted these explanations; but the Police solemnly took photographs of both marks.

Then Meehan appeared in private (as is usual in Scotland) before Sheriff George Reid. The hearing lasted only a few minutes; the charge was read, but no plea asked for or taken; and Meehan was remanded in custody pending further inquiries.[5]

Outside the court, the crowd began catcalling again. One demonstrator kicked Meehan on the shin. Protesting loudly,

[5] At his second appearance at Ayr a week later, Meehan, though not asked to plead, made a judicial declaration of innocence – a most unusual event.

he was bundled into the car and, all the way back to Glasgow, in Sergeant Richie's words, 'kept saying he was innocent'.

Meehan was taken to the remand wing of Barlinnie Prison. There, in the early afternoon, he was told by the Police that his alibi, Griffiths, had committed suicide.[6] In fact he had been shot dead by the police.

* * *

Griffiths must have known that sooner or later Meehan would divulge his address, and that sooner or later the police would come for him, so why he didn't leave Holyrood Crescent is a mystery. It is true he no longer had a car, and he may not have had the money to go south, or any roof to shelter him if he got there; but he had the lease of Marywood Square for another ten days, and could have holed up there for a while with Irene Cameron to attend to him.

Perhaps he had considered this and rejected it; perhaps he was fed up living on the run and had decided to meet his fate, whatever it might be. At any rate when they came for him on the morning of July 15th, he was ready with a dusty answer. In bright sunshine (it was as hot a day as the one before) a squad car drew up outside 14 Holyrood Crescent. No less than five men got out, for Griffiths had a reputation as a man of violence and they were taking no chances. They mounted the stairs until they came to the attic landing. On the other side of Griffiths' door they heard a radio playing. They knocked loudly, and the radio was switched off. They knocked again, saying who they were. Again there was no answer. Then one of the officers pushed the door in, and there was a bang and they saw Griffiths coming at them with a shotgun.

Being unarmed, they turned and started hastily down the stairs. Griffiths came after them and from the landing

[6] Letter of July 15th from Meehan to Mr Beltrami. Presumably the police told this lie to convince Meehan that Griffiths had realised the game was up, and thus persuade him to make a full confession.

fired again at their retreating figures. He wounded the last man down, Detective Sergeant Walker, with seventeen pellets.

The policemen retired to what they thought was the safety of their car, but now Griffiths opened the front attic window and began firing at them from there. Two of them crouched down behind the car with the wounded Walker, and another ran off to raise the alarm. Meanwhile with the shotgun and a rifle with telescopic sight, Griffiths continued firing, not only at the Police and their car, but at everybody and anything that moved. It was as though he was releasing in one great destructive flood all the pent-up rage he had felt as a result of being hunted for a crime of which – for once in his life – he was innocent; as though he knew somehow that the game was up at last, and if he had to go down, then he would take as many with him as possible.[7] He injured several passers-by, men and women, then pinned down a police van that had arrived with two tracker dogs, sending bullets whistling into its roof.

He also shot into the windows of houses nearby. In one he narrowly missed Detective Chief Inspector Binnie who had just arrived, and in another there was a narrow shave for a Mrs Maria Pantlich, who was wallpapering her sitting-room. 'I was decorating with my eleven-year-old grandson,' she said, 'when there was a sudden crack and a hole appeared in the window. . . . I threw myself on the floor, put my arms round my grandson, and just lay there terrified for what seemed ages.'

After half an hour Holyrood Crescent was like a battlefield. Griffiths had shot down six or seven people, and ambulance men were busy picking them up. Two police marksmen had arrived and were taking up position in a house in Great Western Road. The dogs and their handlers were still pinned down in their van. A call had been put

[7] In an interview broadcast in Granada Television's 'World in Action' later that year and called *The Life and Death of James Griffiths,* his old Scunthorpe friend Wally Gow said of him: 'He used to say it often enough – when I go, I'm going to take everyone with me that I hate. I won't go on my own, you know.'

through to the Army to help and they were preparing a Ferret Scout car. The press had arrived in strength and one reporter noticed that Griffiths had shot out both headlights of a police Land-Rover, and punctured the radiator. 'Sometimes between shots,' he wrote, 'the hissing of hot water from the damaged radiator was the only sound.'

Then, abruptly, there was silence. While everyone's attention concentrated on the front of 14 Holyrood Crescent, Griffiths, armed with his two guns and two belts of ammunition, crept down the stairs, out of a back window, and into the road at the back. He ran down two or three roads and then, outside a pub called the Grapes Bar, he saw a blue Ford Anglia. At the wheel was a 57-year-old commercial traveller called Jim Kerr, who had just finished making a visit. Griffiths fired at him through the passenger window, ran round and pulled his bleeding body on to the pavement, got in himself and drove off.

By now the Police had realised he had given them the slip, and with every available police car on the move, and the city's radio-controlled taxis working for them, they set off in chase. Their dilemma was that they did not know for certain which way Griffiths had gone. For ten minutes there was no news of him, then he resolved their dilemma for them. He had crashed the Anglia at a place called the Round Toll, and gone into the Round Toll Bar. For Griffiths to do this was extraordinary; he seldom drank, and he knew that the whole of the city's police force was after him; it shows how demented he had become.

There were about half a dozen customers having a quiet noonday drink in the Bar; in the intense heat the atmosphere in the pub was somnolent. Then the door burst open and in came Griffiths with his guns and ammunition, like something out of a cowboy film – perhaps that is how he saw himself too, Big Jim Griffiths, toting gunman from the west. In good John Wayne style he fired two shots into the ceiling, then marched up to the bar. 'Don't mess me about,' he said to the landlord, John Connolly, and his wife. 'I've already shot some people this morning. Nobody moves or they've had it.' He called for a bottle of brandy and took a large swig from the neck. Then one of the customers, William Hughes, an elderly newsvendor, reached for his glass and Griffiths, misinterpreting the move, shot him.

The Police were nearing the Round Toll Bar when Griffiths left as suddenly as he came. Pursued by Mr Connolly, at whom he fired a couple of shots, he made for a stationary lorry, got in and drove off. Presently an alert policeman spotted him, commanded a passing taxi, and set off in chase. At speed Griffiths drove the lorry up Keppochill Road into the Springburn area, past the huge Sighthill Cemetery on the right and crumbling tenement houses on the left, and along into Springburn Road. Here some traffic lights were against him, so he turned sharp left into Kay Street. To his horror he saw that a hundred yards ahead the road ended; he had entered a cul-de-sac.

He jumped out of the lorry and ran up the stairs of the last tenement building on the right, a two-storey house in poor repair. The door of the top flat was locked, the tenant Mrs Gaul having just gone out. Griffiths shot away the lock and went in. There was an open space and playground on the other side of Kay Street, and Griffiths put up his rifle and, continuing to act out the fantasies with which he had lived for so long, started shooting at people there.

The Police arrived in force soon after. Some cleared people from Springburn Road where it entered Kay Street (for Griffiths had had a few pot-shots there), while others went round and took up positions in the playground. While these were attracting Griffiths' attention, two officers with revolvers, Chief Superintendent Callum Finlayson, head of the Maryhill Division, and Sergeant Ian Smith crept up the side of Kay Street, and into the area of No 28.

The two officers went up the stairs and reached the landing outside Mrs Gaul's door. There was a letter-box in the door and Mr Finlayson lifted the flap and peered through. At this moment Griffiths was crossing from one side of the flat to the other; he was carrying the rifle and shotgun. He saw Finlayson's eyes looking at him through the letter-box and made towards him.

'It was either Griffiths or myself,' said Finlayson. 'I took my revolver and aimed it, through the letter-box, at his shoulder and fired. We pushed the door open and sprang at him. He fired at us but missed, and slumped to his knees. We grappled with him and took the guns from him.'

Seconds later Griffiths, his blood welling on to Mrs Gaul's landing, died. The man who had hoped to retire to South America and buy a yacht, had met his end with a police bullet in his heart in a Glasgow slum. In an hour and a half he had killed one person and wounded thirteen. Glasgow had never seen anything like it.

* * *

No one now, the police least of all, doubted that justice had swiftly caught up with one of Mrs Ross's murderers. Would any man behave as Griffiths had behaved if he were not wanted on a capital charge? They did not know that Griffiths had behaved as he had because that was how he said he would behave: 'If–a policeman charges at me shouting out, Stop, stop, stop . . . if I had a gun in my possession, I would use it. In fact I *would* use it.'

So certain were the authorities that Griffiths was the man they wanted that the very next day, without one single piece of evidence against Griffiths, with nothing to connect him with the Ayr murder at all, on no other grounds except that Meehan said they were together that night, the Crown Office issued this unprecedented statement:

> With the death of Griffiths and the apprehension of Patrick Meehan, the police are no longer looking for any other person suspected of implication in the incident concerning Mr and Mrs Ross at Ayr.

It would be difficult to think of any statement more calculated to prejudice Meehan's case. When Mr Beltrami heard of it, he was outraged. He wrote at once to the Crown Office to protest and also issued a statement (author's italics):

> It will now be near impossible for my client to have a fair trial before an unbiased jury.

The Crown Office statement with regard to the finality of the police inquiries perturbs me.

This would appear to mean that the police are satisfied that they can exclude any possibility of error or mistake.

In my opinion, *in the particular circumstances of this case, there might well be a possibility of a mistake. I am far from satisfied that this possibility can be excluded.*

My client is entitled to a presumption of innocence. Following the Crown Office statement it might well appear to some that he is now required to prove his innocence, whereas Scots law requires the prosecution to prove his guilt.

I therefore feel that my client's case has been prejudiced....

And as if that were not enough, the authorities now compounded the prejudice by two further actions. First they 'leaked' to the press Griffiths' criminal record. Had Griffiths been only wounded instead of killed, and had he survived to stand trial, his record could not have been published either in the press or at the trial for fear of prejudicing the jury. For the same reason Meehan's record would not be introduced at his own trial. Yet his defence was that he was with Griffiths that night, and as the jury would now know that Griffiths was a man with a long record, it would be reasonable to assume that Meehan had one too, and was therefore more disposed to have committed the crime than not.

Secondly, because the Police were very anxious to trace the Triumph (for evidence to connect Griffiths and Meehan with the Ayr murder), they inserted in the Police Gazette an announcement that it was now *known* – not believed or thought or assumed, but *known* – that the car that had taken part in the Ayr robbery was a turquoise blue Triumph, Registered No MAV 810 G.

By their actions the authorities were irrevocably committed to the case against Griffiths and Meehan. There could be no going back from it. Griffiths was dead; but for

Meehan, alive and in Barlinnie Jail, his case had been lost before it had begun.

* * *

So now the Police set about looking for evidence that would consolidate the case against Meehan (and, though he was dead, Griffiths).

On July 8th, the day after the discovery of the crime, Detective Inspector George Cook of the Glasgow Police Forensic Department, in company with Detective Superintendent Cowie of the Ayr Police, visited 2 Blackburn Place. Cook is a big powerfully built dark-haired man, ex-Navy, with long experience of his job and a reputation for being 'straight down the line'. Cowie is an officer of not very great imagination who, his colleagues say, 'does everything by the book'. Their object was to take samples, traces of which might eventually be found on the person or clothing of the two intruders. These included paintwork from the window that had been forced and entered, soil from an upturned bowl in the bedroom, small stones from the roof of the next-door garage from which the intruders had cut the telephone wires, a portion of the wire that had been cut. In addition the whole house was examined carefully for fingerprints; this included Mr Ross's safe, which had been examined by Cowie the day before, and found to be empty; it was taken to Ayr Police Headquarters.

Next, on the day that Griffiths died, officers went to 14 Holyrood Crescent, and made a thorough search of Griffiths' flat. They were looking in the first instance for cash from Mr Ross's safe, just as they had done in Meehan's flat, and to their surprise they found nothing. But both there, and in Griffiths' lock-up garage in Shawhill Road, they found some stolen goods, 'mostly junk' said one police officer – but including several of the things taken from Mr Moir's Triumph – the MAV 810 G number plates, the dress material, picnic chairs, a map, a torch, a knife. These and Griffiths' clothes, including his anorak-type car coat, were carefully labelled, and anything relevant was sent along to Detective Inspector Cook at the forensic department.

By now Inspector Cook had received all the clothes, tools, etc, that had been taken from Meehan's flat, and he set about examining them for traces of any of the samples he had taken from Blackburn Place. He could have had no idea what an uphill task he had been set; but as he went along he found out. There was no trace of any blood on the clothing of Griffiths or Meehan (apart from a tiny stain in one of Meehan's trouser pockets); there was no trace of any soil on the clothing of Griffiths or Meehan; there was no trace of any paintwork in Meehan's nailscrapings or Griffiths' nails; there were no indications the telephone wire had been cut by any of Meehan's tools. It was true that some of the stones from the garage roof were similar to stones found in the soles of a pair of Meehan's shoes, but similar stones could be found in the shoes of thousands of others. Finally there was not a single fingerprint of either Griffiths or Meehan anywhere in Blackburn Place.

Elsewhere an intensive search had been going on for Mr Moir's Triumph. The Police had been looking for it everywhere, even bringing in naval divers to plumb the depths of Loch Awe. It was not surprising that in that peaty water they found nothing (though it says much for Griffiths' ingenuity that he had disposed of it so completely). On August 14th they ceased operations at Loch Awe and transferred their operations to water near Connel Ferry. This was equally unsuccessful and a day or two later they called off the search.

It was now over a month since the arrest of Meehan, and the Police had no more evidence against him than when they started. Soon they would have to prepare papers for the case for the Ayr Procurator Fiscal, and at present all they had got was the Pat and Jim coincidence, Meehan's unsatisfactory statement and Mr Ross's voice identification, obtained in such unorthodox circumstances. Taken together, this was hardly sufficient evidence for the Crown Office to proceed – let alone for any jury to convict. Where else might evidence against Meehan be found?

On August 18th Detective Superintendent Cowie of the Ayrshire Police, who with Mr Struthers was in charge of the case, came back from leave. He was told about the search for the Triumph being called off, that Meehan's and Griffiths' clothing had revealed virtually nothing, indeed that no progress in the case at all had been made since he went away. He and Mr Struthers had a talk, and after the talk two things happened. Firstly, Detective Sergeant Inglis, who had been in charge of the Identification parade, was told to travel to Barlinnie, take away the suit that Meehan was wearing and see if anything was to be found in that. Secondly, Mr Struthers telephoned Detective Inspector Cook at the forensic department in Glasgow. But what Mr Struthers said, and what resulted from what he said, and what later Mr Cowie and Mr Cook did, was something that Meehan was not to know about until much later.[8]

* * *

When Meehan heard that Inglis was coming to take away his suit, he was immediately suspicious: the police could have looked at his suit weeks ago, when the rest of his clothing was taken. As a professional criminal Meehan knew that when police evidence against a man whom they believe guilty is not strong enough to convict, they sometimes 'bend the rules' – by 'fixing' Identification parades, falsifying records, putting words into a suspect's or accused's mouth, planting incriminating material on him – in order to make their case stronger. In this way they feel that justice is being done: it is an understandable practice, though never excusable. There have been many examples of it in recent years, particularly in England, and Meehan himself had experienced one incident of 'planted' evidence earlier in his criminal career.

Only the day before, Meehan had read in the papers of the search for the Triumph being abandoned. He knew that if the police had found it, they could not have found anything in it to connect him with the Ayr murder, and so might

[8] Readers who do not like being kept in suspense may turn to pages 155–9.

have been tempted to plant something. Now this opportunity had been denied them, why did they want his suit unless to plant something in that?

Meehan was sufficiently worried by this possibility to express his fears to two prison officers, Mr Deans and Mr Gaitens. Mr Deans, in Meehan's words, 'assured me that they would take good care to examine the suit before handing it over'. After Detective Sergeant Inglis and another officer had collected the suit, said Meehan, 'I was informed by Prison Officer Deans that the suit had been examined, pockets turned out, etc., in the presence of the detectives before it was handed to them. And Officer Deans told me, "If they plant something, it will have to be something that will only show up under a microscope".'

* * *

At the beginning of August Ian Waddell decided to get out of Glasgow for a while, and went down to London where a friend got him a job at a block of flats in Emperor's Gate. By September 10th he was 'fed up', returned to Glasgow and moved back to Andrew Dick's house. Presently he was arrested by the police on charges of housebreaking, and sent to Barlinnie to await trial. William Macintyre was already there.

* * *

Mr Beltrami meanwhile was preparing Meehan's defence. He had seen him a number of times in Barlinnie, and now had no doubts about his innocence. 'I have acted for literally scores of Glasgow criminals,' he said, 'and I get to know when they are lying and telling the truth. Some, when guilty, say they are innocent to begin with, but it never lasts long. Meehan has never wavered in his assertions of innocence, from the time of his arrest to the present day.'

Mr Beltrami pointed out to Meehan that in view of what had happened to Griffiths together with the Crown Office statement, his defence that he and Griffiths were casing the motor taxation office in Stranraer that night was not a strong one. Meehan said maybe not, but it was the truth, and he asked Mr Beltrami to go to Stranraer and obtain evidence there and at the Lochryanhall Hotel, that would confirm that he had been in the area until late on the Saturday night. Mr Beltrami got his brother Mr Raymond Beltrami, a photographer on the Scottish *Daily Express*, to take a photograph of Meehan, and with this Mr Beltrami's office manager, Mr Macdonald, left for Stranraer.

A few days later Meehan wrote privately to Mr Beltrami:

Dear Mr Beltrami,

I trust that your visit to Stranraer and to the hotel there in particular has brought some results.

I find it very difficult not to worry over the position I find myself in. It has been a terrible experience for my wife and grown-up family.

It helps a little to know that you, as my solicitor, are aware that I am innocent of the crime. I wish to God the Police realised this too.

I trust you will visit me in the near future and let me know what has developed.

* * *

Between now and his trial nearly three months later hardly a day went by without Meehan writing Mr Beltrami at least one letter, and sometimes two or three, with observations and suggestions that might be useful in his defence. Many of them were extremely to the point.

As you know the Police have not produced one witness to say I was in Ayr. It is a fact that I did not set foot in Ayr. The evidence as it stands is (1) a voice (2) my name is Pat (3) I passed through the area in a car. Since I was never involved in the crime I cannot imagine what else the Police could have. If the Crown really intend to take me to trial then I very much fear that I can't be getting a clean trial. In view of the Crown Office Statement the Police will be determined to get a conviction. The Crown Office may have had an assurance from Mr Struthers that the guilty men were Griffiths and Meehan and this resulted in the Crown Office Statement. Mr Struthers may now feel that his reputation is at stake and is now prepared to go to any length to gain a conviction. The general public are convinced that Griffiths and I are guilty and the Police know that if the case gets to a jury I will be convicted out of hand.

The prejudice against him caused by the Crown Office statement was seldom out of his mind.

Dear Mr Beltrami,

I am becoming more and more concerned about the prejudice created by the Crown Office Statement. The evidence against me is practically non-existent and yet I don't feel I have any chance of a fair trial. Now the Crown intend to put a string of other charges against me on the same Indictment as the Capital Charge. I don't feel I am being tried – I'm being railroaded – and for a crime I did not commit. It's a case of 'Trial by Press' and 'Crown Office Statements'. To talk about giving me a fair trial is complete hypocrisy. I don't know what the law is on The Crown Office Statement but common sense tells me that it is contrary to the whole concept of justice.

Talking to prisoners and staff I have come to grasp the extent of the damage done by the Crown Office Statement. *The prison doctor actually assumed from it that I had confessed to the crime.* Can you not raise an action in the High Court before my trial date is set, and argue that the Crown Office have forfeited their right to put me on trial? After all it was a shocking statement to make while the case is sub-judice.

But the thought that worried him most was that because of lack of evidence against him the police would have to 'plant' false evidence.

That the old chap Ross made a mistake when he identified my voice goes without saying. Having played no part in the crime I cannot see what other evidence the police could have. If I am being given a clean trial by the police then I have every confidence that I will be cleared of the crime. The possibility that one of the policemen in the case might manufacture evidence is ever in my mind. This could only be done by tampering with the clothing removed from my house at the time of my arrest. I think, Mr Beltrami, you should argue about this clothing, I shouldn't think the police would manufacture evidence in a murder trial but anything is possible – after the Crown Office Statement.

The paint samples and stone samples listed as productions are worrying me. Is this some sort of plant? As an innocent man I can't see what evidence there can be except planted evidence. It's the only way the police could get the case to reach a jury. Please let me know what these paint and stone samples are. It occurs to me that my wife and I painted the bedrooms a couple of weeks before my arrest. Could this be paint taken from our house?

Will you please let me know which pair of shoes this bitumen was found on?

After I saw you at Court on 22nd July, Mr Beltrami, I was taken to Ayr Police Station. Det. Inspector Macallister and another detective came into the cell to speak with me. I asked him if he had verified that I had been in Stranraer and that cars were damaged in the hotel car park. He avoided my question and I could tell by the look on his face that he had verified that cars had been damaged and that what he had found out wasn't to his liking, i.e. didn't suit the police case. He went into a temper and said that Griffiths and I must be guilty when Griffiths tried to shoot his way out. I told him again that I was innocent and the other detective said: 'We've got evidence you don't know about yet. You'd be surprised at what the backroom boys can do.' I said 'What's that supposed to mean?' and he replied 'You'll find out.'

First evidence that the backroom boys had been active came when he heard from Mr Beltrami that the Police were claiming to have found pieces of paper in the pocket of Griffiths' car coat that matched similar paper found in the Rosses' house. Quite apart from the falsity of this evidence, asked Meehan, what had bits of paper in Griffiths' pocket to do with him?

> I have tied myself to Griffiths. The Crown are arguing that my statement is a denial that Griffiths was involved in the crime. The Crown are therefore going to point to the paper in the pocket of Griffiths as evidence against me, the Crown case being that evidence against one is evidence against both. The Crown argue 'association'. But the 'Associate' is not present to explain the paper in his pocket to the jury. I don't think the nature of the evidence justifies the Crown demanding from me an explanation for what is in the pockets of Griffiths. The Crown are trying to use evidence against one accused to corroborate evidence on the other. Am I to sit in the dock with a ghost who can't communicate with Court, counsel or jury? Can we apply to the High Court to have a spiritualist medium in the dock, just in case Griffiths decides to get in touch!!

In another letter Meehan showed how inconsistent with having committed the Ayr murder was Griffiths' behaviour.

> Griffiths knew I had been arrested but he made no attempt to leave Glasgow. Had Griffiths been involved in the crime at Ayr then he would have left Glasgow.
>
> It was *I* who gave the Police the address at which Griffiths was living. I wanted Griffiths brought in so that I could prove that we were in Stranraer together. The old man who was assaulted made a mistake about my voice but as soon as he heard Griffiths speak, he – the old man – would have been able to say that Griffiths definitely was not involved. Knowing that Griffiths was not involved in the crime any more than I was, I decided

that it was in my interest to have Griffiths brought in. Had Griffiths and I been involved in the crime then it certainly wouldn't be in my interest to have him brought in. The fact that Griffiths resisted arrest had nothing to do with the crime at Ayr.

Meehan thought a lot about the Identification parade, and the extraordinary way in which Mr Ross had 'identified' his voice. He described to Mr Beltrami what he called 'one rather peculiar aspect' of the parade.

Why did Mr Ross say he would like to hear the parade say 'Shut up, we'll send an ambulance'? *Why that particular sentence?* We know now that these words were spoken by the man whose name may be Pat. And that I was the man suspected. Why did Mr Ross choose the words that the particular suspect on the parade was believed to have used? Did the police tell Mr Ross that the suspect was named Pat and that he, Mr Ross, when asked, should ask to hear the words 'Shut up, etc.' spoken. I mean, why didn't Mr Ross ask the Parade to say 'Get this c . . . off me, Pat'. Was it because the police told him that the man suspected of saying these words wasn't on the Parade? This aspect of the Parade suggests that Mr Ross was prompted previous to the parade.

Meehan realised early on that there were two sides to his defence. The first clearly was the bringing of evidence to show that he himself had not committed the murder. But almost as important was to find out who did. If any one place was likely to furnish this information it was Barlinnie. From the very beginning Meehan started making intensive inquiries. A string of names were brought up and discarded. Then only a couple of weeks after being charged, Meehan struck lucky.

July 30th
I have just been told by a prisoner that Ian Waddel and another man were responsible for the crime. It appears

that Waddel told a man named John McKew that he (Waddel) had done the crime. John McKew is known to the police and I suggest you get the police to interview him.

* * *

At this time Meehan had never heard of Waddell, and, as will have been noticed, misspelt his name. But from now on the evidence against Waddell began to build up.

I have it from a prisoner that the police came up to see Waddel and asked him if he paid a large sum of money to a Solicitor. I am given to understand that Waddel denied it. Waddel asked the prisoner if the police could force a solicitor to disclose how much he was paid. The Detective who questioned Waddel was Det. Chief Inspector Macalister of The Crime Squad.

I have it from McCusker that Waddel is in a sweat in case his girl-friend makes a statement to the police implicating him in the Ayr murder. McCusker says there was an incident when Waddel and his friends were in a pub. Two men entered and looked like detectives. Waddel slipped a roll of notes to 'Big Skip' behind the bar. (I assume 'Big Skip' is a barman.) The two men left and Waddel got the roll back from 'Big Skip'.[9]

When Waddel was interviewed by the police he had a solicitor present.[10] The solicitor received quite a large sum of money for being present and the money was paid to the solicitor by this 'Big Skip'. McCusker thinks the solicitor's name is Quinn. It appears that 'Big Skip' is a close friend of Waddels. I don't know the name of the pub where 'Big Skip' works behind the bar. I assume it is in Bridgeton.

Information as to how much money Waddel paid to a solicitor would have to be declared in Income-Tax Re-

[9] John Skivington of the Club Bar.
[10] Mr William Carlin.

turns. It can hardly be classified as confidential between client and solicitor. My information is that the £200 was paid by Skivington on behalf of Waddel. But if Mr Carlin says Waddel paid it then it must have been Waddel.

I am now convinced that Waddel was directly involved in the crime. What of his alibi? It must be false. Waddel's alibi for the hours 11 PM till 2 AM should be checked again. Whoever alibis him for those hours is lying.

I think Detective Chief Inspector Macalister of the Crime Squad is the one who rechecked Waddel's alibi. Macalister, in my opinion, is prejudiced against me and may not have made a good job of the recheck. Is it not possible to have a recheck made by some senior Detective not already involved in the case?

Having seen Waddel, I am now convinced that his drawing attention to himself through talking has nothing to do with a preconceived plan to keep suspicion from someone else. Waddel looks what he is – a big-mouthed Ned.

I have just been told by Macintyre that the car used by Waddel was a hire car.

I am convinced that Waddel played a direct part in the crime.

And then, quite unknowingly, Meehan struck gold:

I have it from a prisoner that Waddel is very worried because we have impeached [*the man who at this time the defence believed was Waddell's accomplice*]. To-day McCusker said to me, 'Wee McGuinness left the house at 5.30 am to go for the car and was pulled up by the coppers'. McCusker said this to me in the presence of another prisoner who comes from Bridgeton and is a friend of Waddel's. McCusker dropped this name 'Wee McGuinness' as if it was a slip of the tongue. It may have been a slip of the tongue but I'm inclined to think there's a plot afoot to cover up for. 'Wee McGuinness' is William McGuiness. He is known to me and goes in for tie-ups. His description 5′ 3″, sandy hair, thin built, about 42 years old is nothing like that of.

On receipt of this letter Mr Beltrami wrote to the Chief Constable of Ayr asking if anyone had been picked up by the police in the early hours of the morning and taken to the bus-station. He received an unsatisfactory reply, so telephoned the Chief Constable's office and was told by an officer there that nothing was known of such an incident. Mr Beltrami therefore assumed, as Meehan had done, that the information was false and an attempt to protect, to whom the defence had tied themselves as Waddell's accomplice.

Finally in mid-Ocober and only a few days before the trial was due to begin, Meehan got some evidence direct from the horse's mouth.

Tuesday evening October 14th
Dear Mr Beltrami,

This evening I cornered Waddel and I told him it was important to my Defence to know if the old man had been blindfolded. Waddel is most emphatic that the old man was neither blindfolded nor gagged. Waddel says a blanket was thrown over the old man and several times the old man knocked it off and it had to be replaced.[11] Waddel says the old man is definitely lying if he says he was blindfolded. Waddel says the old man must have known it was daylight when they left as the house lights were turned off by Waddel at dawn, and they didn't leave until 6 AM.

Assume that Mr Ross was covered by a blanket and heard the men leaving the house. Having heard the men leaving Mr Ross would naturally knock the blanket off immedi-

[11] Confirmed by Mr Ross.

ately if he knew the men had left. There wouldn't be any point just lying there. If Mr Ross says it took him 10 minutes to get the blanket off and he noticed it was daylight then, this would be proof positive that it couldn't have been Griffiths and I.

Waddel says that the names 'Pat and Jimmy' were used during the attack. I always called Griffiths 'Jim' never Jimmy. It seems that it really was a coincidence.

Dear Mr Beltrami,

I have tried a little experiment. I lay on the floor ... with a sheet over my head and the cell light out. It was day and even with my face to the floor I could still tell it was daylight outside. I tried the experiment with a blanket and I could still tell it was daylight. I could see daylight through the weave of the blanket. I think it would be a good idea to question Mr Ross on this.

If Counsel can get Mr Ross to agree that the attackers left at daylight then it couldn't have been Griffiths and I because Griffiths and I were with the two girls at Prestwick when it was still dark.

I have again sent to Waddel and he is very emphatic that the old man was not blindfolded and must know it was daylight when they left the house. Waddel agrees that the names Pat and Jimmy were used. But never 'Jim'.

With the names Pat and Jimmy being used it is no wonder the police were convinced that Griffiths and I were responsible.

If you can get Mr Ross to admit that the name used wasn't Jim but Jimmy, it should help.[12]

[12] Waddell's disclosure to Meehan that he and his accomplice had used the name 'Jimmy' confirms Mr Ross's first statement to the police that 'Jim *or Jimmy*' was used. Neither of these facts (that Waddell used the name 'Jimmy' and that Ross heard the name 'Jimmy') have been revealed before.

By this time the whole prison knew of Waddell's guilt, and when it was clear that nevertheless Meehan was going to have to stand trial, one prisoner resolved to speak up for him. This was William Macintyre. On October 8th he wrote to Mr Beltrami saying he could be of assistance in a case he was handling, and when Mr Beltrami visited him next day, he told him of Andrew Dick's proposal in May for him to join Waddell in a tie-up job at Ayr and his refusing; of his being Dick's alibi on the night of the robbery; and of Dick paying him the money he owed, plus alibi money, the day after; of his borrowing £10 from Waddell later to tax his car, and Waddell saying he wouldn't have need of the loan if he had been on that job with him.

On October 10th Meehan was taken to Ayr to attend his Pleading Diet and to answer the Indictment.[13] In addition to a plea of Not Guilty, he put in two Special Defences, one of Alibi, the other, thanks to Macintyre, of Incrimination against Ian Waddell.

And then that very afternoon a second incident occurred to strengthen Meehan's Impeachment of Ian Waddell. A prisoner called Robert McCafferty, who was also on remand in Barlinnie, was exercising with others in C Hall exercise yard. They were discussing what sentences they might get, if found guilty, and one said, 'We think we're bad off, but just look at Pat Meehan there, he's in for a murder he never committed.' Whereupon, said Macintyre, he heard Waddell's voice behind them saying, 'How do you think I feel? It was me that done it.' McCafferty asked if he was joking and Waddell said No, he wasn't, adding, 'But what can I do if the police make a bloomer?' McCafferty asked why he had left the Rosses tied up all weekend without telephoning the police, and Waddell said that the man with him *had* telephoned but only to the exchange operator. McCafferty told Waddell what he thought of him, and like Macintyre, also wrote to Beltrami.

Meehan was delighted at this turn of events. 'Although prisoners normally stick together,' he wrote to Beltrami, 'it is well known that they don't take kindly to men who beat

[13] See note on page 267.

up people and murder old ladies. This can be pointed out to a jury, and I don't think it harms me having prisoners to support the impeachment.' And he added, 'If we brought forward *everyone* to whom Waddel has stated guilt, then there would be a couple of hundred witnesses for the Defence'!

In one endeavour, though, Meehan and Mr Beltrami were disappointed – the application for Meehan to undergo interrogation under a truth drug. For some time Mr Beltrami had been concerned that Meehan's trial was going to require the defence to prove his innocence rather than the prosecution to prove his guilt; so that when he read in the paper that the truth drug had been used in the Sharon Tate case in California, to clear a houseboy of complicity in murder, he saw the possibilities for Meehan.

That evening in Barlinnie he told Meehan about the truth drug; that it was a compound of sodium pentothal and methedrine that induced a semi-conscious state in which it would be difficult to lie. If he agreed to be interrogated while under its influence, police officers would have to be present and be permitted to use as evidence at his trial anything he might say. Meehan accepted at once. 'I have nothing to fear from the truth,' he told Mr Beltrami. 'Please let me have it as soon as it can be arranged.'

A day or two later Mr Beltrami travelled to London to see the psychiatrist Dr William Sargant who had been an expert witness on the truth drug in the case of the Boston strangler. Having heard the details of the Meehan case, Dr Sargant agreed to travel to Glasgow and administer the drug to Meehan without fee.

In Glasgow, however, Mr Beltrami received a setback. The governor of Barlinnie would not allow the drug to be given in the prison, and when Mr Beltrami applied to the High Court, three judges also turned him down. 'This Court has a duty,' said Lord Cameron, 'to protect an accused person against the folly of his legal advisers.'

'Had I had the slightest doubts about Meehan's innocence,' said Mr Beltrami afterwards, 'it would indeed have been folly. But as I had no doubts, it was not folly at all.'

Meanwhile the Prosecution, as they completed their preparations, were not too happy about their own chances of success. The Crown Agent, Stanley Bowen, having read all the papers forwarded by the Procurator Fiscal in Ayr thought the Crown case 'thin' and added, 'I wouldn't have bet a humble shilling on the chance of a conviction.' But there were other reasons for going ahead. 'In some cases we prosecute to allay the public. Often we have to accept a loser.' The trial was fixed to begin in the High Court at Edinburgh (where Mr Beltrami had asked for it to be transferred because of the prejudice against Meehan in Ayr) on October 20th.

PART III

The Trial

The High Court of Justiciary in Edinburgh, No 3 Court in the old Parliament Buildings, has in its 140 years' history, seen many celebrated trials. Here in June 1857 the famous Madeleine Smith, daughter of a respected Glasgow citizen, stood in the dock that Meehan was to occupy to answer charges of murdering her lover, Pierre L'Angelier, by poisoning. Here the notorious Dr Pritchard was convicted of the double murder of his wife and mother, to be subsequently hanged at the last public execution in Scotland. And here too in 1910 came poor Oscar Slater who, like Meehan, was indicted primarily as a result of wrongful identification; was sentenced to death, reprieved, and served nineteen years in Peterhead prison before the mistake was acknowledged and he was freed.

All court-rooms are small, and No 3 Court in Edinburgh is smaller than some, 46 feet by 36 feet (the same width but only three-fifths the length of a standard tennis court), but with a high, lofty ceiling, making it almost as tall as it is long. The bench is covered in red felt with tassels, and at either end, set in alcoves, are Victorian fireplaces that warmed the judges of another age. Below the bench are three high-backed chairs for the Clerk of the Court and his assistants, and in front of them the table for counsel and solicitors, Crown counsel on the judge's right, defence counsel on his left. Behind Crown counsel are three rows of seats for the fifteen-man jury, and behind defence counsel at the opposite side of the table, the witness stand, with its curved oak sounding-board to prevent whispered replies from drifting uncaptured to the roof.

In the well of the court, facing the judge across counsel's table, is the long, narrow dock, and between it and the table a trapdoor, now rarely used, concealing a flight of steps that leads down to the cells. Behind the dock ten rows of seats, panelled in light oak and stretching the width of the room, rise steeply to the back of the court. Here sit the curious and anxious; the press, low down near the accused, members of the public come to hear detailed accounts of what man can do to man; and the parents, wives and children of the accused waiting for the painful moment, which may affect their lives for years, when fifteen men and women decide their loved one's fate.

By 10 a.m. on the morning of October 20th 1969 the court, less the jury, had assembled. Counsel for the Crown was the Solicitor-General of Scotland, Mr Ewan Stewart, Q.C.[1] Mr Stewart, in his forties, had won an M.C. in the war, and in 1970 had stood unsuccessfully as a Labour candidate. He was a skilful and experienced advocate, quiet, but pertinacious, with many years of practice behind him. In 1968, at Aberdeen, he had won much praise for his handling of the Crown case at the notorious Sheila Garvie trial in which the wife of an Aberdeen farmer, and her lover, were convicted of murdering her husband.

Counsel for the defence was an altogether different figure, the flamboyant Nicholas Fairbairn, son of an Edinburgh psychiatrist, married to a daughter of Lord Reay and living in a castle on the north shore of the Firth of Forth, which he had helped to restore himself. He was, and is, a man of great talents and industry, a Conservative politician,[2] an accomplished artist, a witty speaker and the most successful criminal defence lawyer in Scotland (he had appeared against Mr Stewart in three previous murder trials and won them all); but his dandified dress and desire to shock had never endeared him to the more conventional members of his profession. Since being retained for the defence, he had had many talks with Meehan, asked him many searching questions and was now as convinced of his innocence as Mr Beltrami.

And sitting in the dock, dapper as usual in the sports jacket and casual trousers he had worn on the trip to Stranraer, was the prisoner at the bar, Patrick Connolly Meehan. In his time he had appeared in most of the principal courts

[1] Now Lord Stewart.

[2] Now M.P. for Kinross and West Perthshire.

in Scotland, but this was new to him. As he observed the panoply and bustle around him, as he waited for the judge to enter and the curtain to go up on what he knew to be a gigantic charade, yet for him might well end in personal tragedy, one wonders what his thoughts were.

He was where he was for a variety of reasons: because of the coincidence of Pat and Jim; because of the unsatisfactory statement he had given the Police; because of Mr Ross's wrongful identification; because of Griffiths' gun-battle and death; but he was also there because he was a man with a record that went back into the mists of time. Had he had no record, been a man of good character, then the Pat and Jim coincidence would not have been a coincidence, for it was about the past as much as the present; Mr Ross would not have made, or even been asked to make, the voice identification; indeed Meehan himself would never have been questioned, let alone arrested. Now, if ever in his life Meehan had cause to regret his criminal past, this moment was it.

The door at the back of the bench opened, and in came the Macer carrying the Mace. 'Court!' he called, and everyone stood up. Behind him walked the tall, formidable figure of the Lord Justice-Clerk, Lord Grant, the second most senior judge in Scotland. In his red and cream silk robes with their big red crosses and small red diamonds, wig, and linen fall at the throat, he was an imposing sight; and for the next five days his presence was to dominate the court. Once he had been Conservative M.P. for the Woodside Division of Glasgow, and as such had been appointed Lord Advocate, equivalent to the office of Attorney General in England. He had subsequently been appointed Lord Justice-Clerk.

In private Lord Grant was said to be a shy man, though companionable when you got to know him. He liked golf and shooting, supported the Edinburgh Festival, and was a member of the Royal Company of Archers, the Queen's Bodyguard for Scotland. He had a clear, forceful mind, and his opinions were always cogently expressed, though, since a recent throat operation, he could sometimes in court be extremely testy. His comments, as the Meehan trial progressed, showed a marked bias in favour of the prosecution.

'Call the Diet,' said the Clerk of the Court, 'Her Majesty's Advocate against Patrick Connolly Meehan'; and Mr Fairbairn rose to move that the charges on the Indictment be separated. There were three charges against Meehan: acting along with James Griffiths in that he did (1) steal Mr Moir's car and its contents, (2) assault and rob the Rosses and murder Mrs Ross, and (3) make a false application for Griffiths' passport. It would be very unfair to Meehan, said Mr Fairbairn, to lump these three together; the first charge had taken place some time before the main charge, and the third charge some time after it, and they were not connected as regards place or form. Furthermore, said Mr Fairbairn, he was under the great disadvantage that, as Griffiths was dead, he could not cross-examine any evidence relating to him.

Mr Stewart then argued that in his view it was highly relevant to keep the charges together; and past cases showed it was usual to do so. Lord Grant said that if the charges were separated, relevant evidence on the main charge of robbery and murder would be excluded, 'and the interests of justice would be subverted.' And he added: '... this court has to keep in mind not only the interests of the Accused but the interests of the public ... That has been laid down more than once recently and is possibly putting an end to a trend by certain judges in the past who tended to give greater weight to the Accused's interests than was justified, to the detriment of the public itself and to the administration of justice. I will refuse the motion.' For Meehan and his counsel it was not the most favourable start.

Lord Grant asked Mr Fairbairn how his client pleaded, and he answered Not Guilty on the first charge, Not Guilty on the second charge and Guilty on the third charge. Mr Stewart said he would not accept the guilty plea on the third charge (because he wanted the jury to hear evidence relating to it); Lord Grant said he didn't think he would. Mr Fairbairn put in his two Special Defences.

The eight men and seven women of the jury were called

and took their seats, the Indictment was read to them. Then the Clerk of the Court gave them the oath. 'Do you fifteen swear by Almighty God, and as you shall answer to God at the great day of judgment, that you will the truth say, and no truth conceal, so far as you shall pass in this assize?' They said they would, and the Special Defences were read to them.

In Scottish criminal law there are no opening speeches by counsel, as in England, to tell the jury what they hope their witnesses will say (and in the event often fail to say). The Scots believe in the simpler method of letting the story unfold through the mouths of the witnesses direct.

'Call Abraham Ross.'

He was shown into the witness-box, small and frail, the wound above his right eye visible for all to see, the object throughout the court of sympathy and compassion. Lord Grant rose to his full six foot two, magnificent in his robes, and faced the tiny man below him.

'Raise your right hand and say after me —'

Ross raised his right hand.

'I swear by Almighty God —'

'I swear by Almighty God —'

'And as I shall answer to God at the great day of judgment —'

'And as I shall answer to God at the great day of judgment —'

'That I will tell the truth, the whole truth and nothing but the truth.'

'That I will tell the truth, the whole truth and nothing but the truth.'

The judge sat down and Mr Stewart rose. In answer to his questions Mr Ross described the layout of his house, then the movements of himself and his wife that evening, finally the attack.

> 'You were asleep? What is the next thing you remember that night?'
>
> 'The next thing I remember that night was something just coming at me. I didn't even see him coming at me,

but somebody dived right on top of me. . . . It was like a nightmare.'

He described the rest of his terrible ordeal, how he was covered with a blanket and hit if he tried to move it, the two men calling each other Pat and Jim, their asking where the wall safe was, and hitting him whenever he told them he didn't have a wall safe, how eventually he gave them the keys of the safe and they took the money. It was clear from what he said that the two men were in the house a considerable time.

For both prosecution and defence the matter of the voices of the two intruders was going to be crucial, and when questioned on this, Mr Ross was much less certain that he had been at the Identification parade. He was asked if he knew at the time of the attack which of the two men had said 'Shut up, shut up, we'll send an ambulance.'

'Well, at this stage, I mean, I didn't know whose voice it was. I didn't know whose voice it was at that stage.'

'The voice that said these words – is that a voice you have heard subsequently?'

'I have heard it at an Identification parade.'

'The voice that said the words, "Shut up —" '

'Shut up, shut up. We'll send an ambulance. He didn't finish the word "ambulance" . . . he kind of stuttered at the word "ambulance".'

The judge asked if this was the voice Mr Ross picked out at the Identification parade, and his answer was less than sure.

'When I heard this voice at that time, I mean it was fresh in my memory at that time, and I more or less knew that was the voice – at that particular time.'

And he was just as hesitant when Mr Stewart returned to the matter later. How sure was Mr Ross, he asked, that the voice of the Identification parade was the voice he had heard in the bedroom?

'Well, at this time I was kind of sure, but I think it must be difficult to recognise a voice.'

'At the time you were kind of sure?'

'At the time because it was fresh in my mind, anyway, that was all.'

'And indeed were you very upset?'

'Yes, I was very upset. It sounded so *like* the voice.'

Then it was Mr Fairbairn's turn. He asked about the various things the intruders had said, and then, knowing of Griffiths' distinctive North Country voice, he asked:

'Were these voices both similar?'

'I would say so, yes.'

'Were they both Scottish voices?'

'Yes.'

'Were they both Glasgow voices?'

'Yes.'

'You are sure of that?'

'Yes, I think.'

'Are you sure they were both Scottish voices?'

'Yes.'

'Do you think they were both Glasgow voices?'

'They sounded to me both like Glasgow voices, yes.'

Mr Fairbairn asked if he had described his attacker to the police as 'in the thirties, round about five foot eight inches, medium build, wearing what you took to be tight-fitting dark trousers and no jacket?'

'That is right.'

'And did you say that his accent you took to be Glasgow?'

'Yes.'

'So Jim the intruder was a man with a Glasgow accent as was the other man?'

'Yes.'

'Was it Jim or Jimmy,' Mr Fairbairn asked, and Mr Ross replied, 'Jim.'

Mr Fairbairn asked if the man who spoke at the Identification parade had spoken in a Glasgow accent, and Mr Ross agreed he had.

'You said yourself it sounded like the voice at the time – "I was kind of sure but it is very difficult to say with a voice" – is that your evidence now?'

'Yes.'

'Was it merely because it was a Glasgow accent?'

'No, I think it was because at that time it was fresh in my memory.'

'There were only six words?'

'Yes.'

'You had not heard those words spoken in a Glasgow voice since the appalling incidents in your house with these intruders?'

'That is right.'

'And at that time you were still considerably injured and under sedation?'

'I don't know if I was under sedation, but I was considerably injured, yes.'

'And you were still in hospital?'

'Still in hospital, yes.'

'Did you hear any of the other voices of the men in the parade to see whether they could have been either of the men?'

'No, I did not.'

'Do you think you could recognise either of the voices now?'

'I don't think so.'

Mr Fairbairn had a surprise waiting in the wings, a rabbit to be pulled from a hat, and now he was ready to produce it.

'I wonder if I could have a witness brought into court to read words which we have been told this man said. The witness is named in the Impeachment?'

The Solicitor-General had no objections, the judge approved. Mr Fairbairn turned to Mr Ross.

'I propose to get this man to read something, he will then be taken out of court and I will ask you some questions. He will then be brought back in again to read something else. Do you understand?'

'Yes.'

'The things which I propose to ask the witness to read are, "Shut up, shut up, we'll send an ambulance". "Pat, get this cunt off me". "They are not yet here, Jim"; and "They have not arrived yet, Jim".'

Lord Grant said, 'We'd better hear the name of the witness' and Mr Fairbairn said, 'The witness is Ian Waddell.'

He came into the court and faced the man whose house he had burgled and ransacked.

How did he feel, seeing Mr Ross for the first time since he had helped to tie him up in his own bedroom and then left him there, awash in his own blood? Much later he was asked about this, and all he could say, obscurely, was: 'It was nae bother.'

Waddell read from the paper the words he had uttered in the Rosses' bedroom three months before. 'Shut up, shut up, we'll send an ambulance.' Mr Ross made no reaction; but had Waddell, rather than Meehan, been the police suspect, and said these words at the Identification parade, one wonders what his reaction would have been. Waddell was led out.

'Was that like the voice of either of the men?' asked Mr Fairbairn.

'It was *like* the voice, yes,' said Mr Ross.

'The one who said, "Shut up, shut up, we'll send an ambulance"?'

'Yes.'

'Could you say if it *was* the voice?'

'I wouldn't say for sure, no.'

'Is it as like the voice as the one you heard in the Police Station at the Identification parade?'

'It's very difficult to remember how the voice of the other fellow spoke, but that also *sounds something similar*.'

Seeing which way the wind was blowing Lord Grant intervened:

'Is your recollection as clear now, three months later, as it was when you went to the Identification parade?'

'No,' said Mr Ross, gratefully, 'it is not as clear now as it was at that time. At that time it was fresh.'

Mr Fairbairn endeavoured to retrieve the position.

'I want to ask you this. Could that voice you have just heard have belonged to either of the two men who were the intruders?'

Mr Ross thought carefully.

'It is possible,' he said.

Now Waddell was brought back into court, read the other

things on the piece of paper, and went out. Mr Fairbairn asked Mr Ross if he could say anything more about the voice, and at first Mr Ross said no, he couldn't, he didn't now think that that was the voice, and then later that it could have been. 'It is guesswork now on my part,' he said, 'if I try to remember voices.'

Mr Stewart, like a good advocate, picked up the point Lord Grant had made, when he came to re-examine.

'Do I take it then, that your memory is not so clear after three months —?'

'No, that is right.'

'Whereas on the 14th July, you were quite certain of the accused's voice?'

'At that time, yes,' said Mr Ross.

There were two other points made by Mr Ross on the witness-stand, which were going to prove important later. This was one:

Mr Fairbairn: 'You told us that shortly after the men, the intruders, left your house, it was then daylight?'

Mr Ross: 'Yes.'

'Was it full daylight at that time?'

'Yes, it was quite full daylight.'

'How long after the intruders left did you shake off the blanket and see that it was quite full daylight?'

'Oh, it couldn't have been very long, about five or ten minutes. My wife said, "I think they are gone."'

'And was it on your realising they had gone that you shook off the blanket?'

'That's right.'

'And indeed they had gone?'

'Yes.'

And this was the other point.

Mr Stewart: 'The safe, did it have some drawers in it, shelves?'

Mr Ross: 'Yes, drawers.'

'Were those drawers covered with some kind of shelving paper or some sort of paper?'

Mr Ross had no shelving paper in the drawers of his safe,

but he didn't want to seem unhelpful.

'I couldn't tell you that,' he said, 'I don't remember that.'

'Do you know if there was *any* paper in the safe?' asked Mr Stewart.

Mr Ross thought. What paper was Mr Stewart talking about? He certainly didn't remember any.

'I don't think so,' he said.

'But you can't remember?'

'I can't remember, no.'

For Meehan the full significance of this exchange was not to become apparent until later.

After Mr Ross came a succession of minor witnesses – Mrs Grant, the Rosses' daily, who told of her discovery of the crime; Mrs Adamson from the house opposite, to whom Mrs Grant had run for help, and who had noticed the Rosses' curtains drawn all Sunday; the Rosses' gardener who identified the weeding tool and steps from the garage; Mrs Ross's two brothers who had identified her body at the mortuary; the doctors at Ayr County Hospital who had examined the Rosses on arrival, and conducted the post-mortem on Mrs Ross.[3] And Dr Campbell told of his examination of Meehan at Ayr Police Station on July 15th, and of Meehan's willingness to be examined all over. ('And when you did look all over him, there was absolutely nothing which was consistent with having indulged in a fight or fracas with another person some ten days before?' – 'No, there wasn't.')

[3] Among these was Dr David Bremner, who later wrote: 'I have had the misfortune to be involved in several court proceedings (including two attempted murders) during a relatively short career, and have always found the court staff and police to be very relaxed and off-hand, almost casual. During the Meehan trial, however, the policemen were very agitated and up-tight, and they spent the morning that I was there scurrying around, having whispered, nervous conversations in the corridors. The atmosphere in the witness-room (which held the various police officers involved as well as the main witnesses) was electric, almost unbearable. I was mistakenly ushered into the wrong room when I arrived and this contained two prisoner witnesses (presumably Waddell, etc.) and conversely here the atmosphere was relaxed and easy!'

Then came the two girls, Irene Burns and Isobel Smith both in crimson mini-skirts. Irene described her evening with Isobel and later with the two youths whom they had met at the airport; how she was put out at the lay-by, how Meehan and Griffiths had picked her up, and how Meehan, although calm, did appear to be talking fast and had large staring eyes, as though he had taken drugs. It has already been said that Meehan is a voluble talker, and that his eyes were larger than usual because he was scared of the speed Griffiths was driving and asked him to go slower. Mr Fairbairn, in cross-examination, took the matter further.

'You were asked by the learned Solicitor-General about whether you noticed anything odd or strange about the mood or mannerisms of this man here, and you said that he was calm but that he was talking fast and his eyes were large, kind of staring, as if he had been taking drugs.'

'Yes.'

'Have you ever seen anybody who has taken drugs?'

'No.'

'It was just what you imagine a person who has taken drugs looks like, from what you have read or heard on television and so on?'

'Yes.'

'At any rate, apart from that, which you attributed to having taken drugs, were the two men behaving perfectly normally like two men just travelling along the road?'

'Yes.'

'Did they seem agitated in any way?'

'No.'

'Did they seem frightened?'

'No.'

'Did they seem frightened of seeing you?'

'No.'

'Did they hide their faces?'

'No.'

'Did they have any disguises?'

'No.'

'Were they wearing gloves?'

'I didn't notice.'

'Did they have nylon masks on them?'

'No.'

'Did they appear to you to be two perfectly ordinary, normal people driving along the road?'

'Yes.'

'Did you see any signs of travellers cheques, money, notes – anything of that kind?'

'No.'

'Perhaps I could ask you this. Once it had overtaken the white car with the boys in it, was the remainder of your journey to your homes carried out at a perfectly normal speed?'

'Yes.'

'Do you see policemen walking about in Kilmarnock in the early hours of the morning from time to time?'

'Yes.'

'Did these men appear in any way to be afraid that they might be seen by a policeman?'

'No.'

'Did they ever do anything which you regarded as underhand, suspicious?'

'No.'

'Did they behave in any way like two men who had just carried out a robbery in which they had beaten old people up and tied them up?'

'No.'

It was a view which Isobel Smith confirmed when she gave evidence. Mr Stewart asked her what state the two men were in.

'They were all right to me.'

'What do you mean, all right?'

'They seemed to be all right, they talked all right and that.'

When Mr Fairbairn cross-examined, he referred to some object covered with a coat which Isobel had earlier told Mr Stewart she had seen lying on the back seat. It was probably Griffiths' thermos-flask.

'You saw something in the back seat?'

'Yes.'

'And Irene Burns sat next to it?'
'Yes.'
'The men didn't try to stop you looking to see what the object was?'
'No.'
'Or interfering with it in the back?'
'No.'
'They were unconcerned when you got in beside it? Is that right?'
'Yes.'

Another aspect of the girls' evidence concerned the times that they met Griffiths and Meehan, and whether it was dark or light; for even if Meehan's Cairnryan alibi succeeded, the prosecution were going to try and prove that between leaving Cairnryan and picking up Irene, Griffiths and Meehan had time to nip into Blackburn Place and assault and rob the Rosses. The consensus of opinion among the two girls and (later) the two boys was that Irene had been dumped at the lay-by and picked up by Meehan and Griffiths about 3.30 a.m. or just after. If the prosecution accepted that Meehan and Griffiths were at Cairnryan until about 2 a.m., that would leave a maximum of 90 minutes for them to motor the 52 miles from Cairnryan to the lay-by *and* make a diversion to Blackburn Place to break into the Rosses' house and assault and rob them. It looked as though the prosecution were going to have a very uphill job.

The visibility was another crucial factor. Bell in evidence said it was 'still dark' when the Triumph overtook him in Kilmarnock and his friend Mackie said it was 'still very dark'. (Irene Burns said she thought it was quite light by then as she could see the colour of the Triumph, but, as Mr Mackie said, this was because of the street lights – a fact which didn't stop Lord Grant from wrongly stating that Irene had said it was 'daylight'.) Now Mr Ross had said in evidence that five or ten minutes after the intruders had left, it was 'full daylight'. So how, as Mr Fairbairn was to ask later, could Meehan and Griffiths have been in the Rosses' house five or ten minutes before Mr Ross noted 'full daylight', and yet be on the edge of Kilmarnock twelve miles away when it was still dark?

The next witnesses were Jo Cassidy of Jo's coffee stall in Ayr, who told of times of closing, and Detective Constable Scott, who gave evidence of Meehan's anonymous telephone calls about Irene saying Mackie and Bell were 'doped up', and about the possibility they might therefore have done the crime. Detective Constable Little gave evidence of making a drawing of 2 Blackburn Place, and the court rose for the day.

* * *

Next morning Detective Sergeant Inglis, the officer who had been in charge of the Identification parade, went into the witness-box, faced Lord Grant, and swore that as he would answer to God at the great day of judgment, he would tell the truth the whole truth and nothing but the truth. Mr Stewart rose to examine.

'On Monday 14th July last, you conducted an Identification parade at the Central Police Station, Glasgow?'

'I did.'

'Was the present accused, Patrick Connolly Meehan, on that parade?'

'He was.'

'Along with six other men?'

'He was.'

'I think his solicitor was present.'

'That is correct.'

'Were also Superintendent Struthers, Detective Chief Inspector Macalister and Detective Inspector Derrick Macallister present?'

'They were.'

'I think that certain witnesses viewed the parade, and *the first witness* was Mr Abraham Ross?'

'That is correct.'

Meehan thought he must have heard wrong; Ross was not the first witness, but last. He waited. Mr Stewart went on.

'Would you look, please, at Production No 17? Is that a schedule of the parade, and is that written by you and signed by you?'

Sergeant Inglis was handed the schedule, on which he had written that Ross had viewed the parade first.

'It is.'

'And is that a correct account of the parade.'

'That is a correct account.'

'The accused elected to stand in Position 1 for the first witness? Is that right?'

'He did.'

'For the first one, that is Abraham Ross?'

'Yes.'

Now Meehan realised his ears had not betrayed him. He leaned forward from the dock to Mr Beltrami and said, so clearly that David Scott of the BBC could hear. 'Ross *wasn't* first, he was *last*.' Mr Beltrami passed this on to Mr Fairbairn, but Mr Fairbairn naturally did not think it of any importance. What did it matter if Ross had gone first or last? He, no more than Mr Beltrami or Meehan himself, knew of the circumstances in which Mr Ross was meant, and by the other witnesses *thought* to have gone first, but in fact went last.

Later, Sergeant Inglis compounded his error. After speaking of Mr Ross's voice identification he was asked by Mr Stewart: 'And I think *after that* various other people viewed the parade?'

He answered, 'That is correct.'

Detective Superintendent Struthers, when he came to give evidence, also compounded the error:

'I think you were present later that day when Meehan was on an Identification parade?'

'I was.'

'And did you see *the first witness who viewed the parade, Mr Abraham Ross*, viewing the parade?'

'I did.'

As the former Lord Justice Devlin observes in his book, *The Criminal Prosecution in England*, 'It is the general habit of the police not to admit to the slightest departure from correctness.'[4]

[4] See note on page 268.

But for Meehan that was a small surprise, compared with what awaited him. After a couple of officers had given evidence about taking photographs of exhibits and Sergeant Ritchie had told about arriving at Blackburn Place after the 999 call, and of accompanying Meehan to the Sheriff Court at Ayr, Detective Superintendent John Cowie took the stand; and this is the evidence that Meehan heard him give.

Mr Stewart: 'Now I think you were on leave at the beginning of August?'

'That is true.'

'And did you report back on duty on the 18th August?'

'Yes.'

'Did you understand when you came back, did you hear about some fragments of old paper having been found in a car coat?'

'In the course of discussion with my colleague Mr Struthers.'

'... Now because you heard about this, did you recollect having seen something similar?'

'That is true.'

'Where had you seen something similar?'

'In the drawers of the safe in the house at 2 Blackburn Place.'

This was the safe examined by Mr Cowie on July 7th and by Detective Inspector Cook on July 8th, and found to be empty.

'Is that the safe just next you, Label No 2?'

'That is the safe, yes.'

'And was this information passed to Detective Inspector Cook?'

'By way of the Crime Squad, yes ...'

'And on Thursday 21st August, did you and he together look at the safe?'

'That is true.' (Mr Cowie, it will have been noted, preferred three words when one would do.)

'And was the safe by that time in Glasgow or was it still at Ayr?'

'It was at our office, at Headquarters.'

'And when you examined this along with him on the 21st August ... did you see brown-coloured paper, Label No 80?'

'That is right.'

'Now, where did that come from?'

'From one of the drawers in the safe.'

'... And did you also see in the right-hand drawer of the safe a piece of paper from a diary?'

'A small page of a diary, yes.'

Cowie was shown a piece of paper, Label 81, and said yes, that was it.

'Now the first piece of brown-coloured paper, Label 80, which drawer had that come from of the safe?'

Mr Cowie said the right-hand drawer too.

'Was there also a piece of paper taken possession of from the left-hand drawer?'

'There was,' said Mr Cowie and agreed that was Label No 82.

Finally, asked Mr Stewart, had Mr Cowie accompanied Inspector Cook to Blackburn Place, and seen him take possession of pieces of brown paper on the floor of the cupboard where the safe had been? Mr Cowie said, 'That is true,' and on being shown the paper, Label 83, said, 'That is right.'

Meehan had listened to this extraordinary story appalled. What Mr Cowie was suggesting was that pieces of old paper from Griffiths' car-coat matched no less than four similar pieces of paper in Mr Ross's safe or in the recess containing the safe, and the clear inference for the jury was that Griffiths had inadvertently taken away these pieces when robbing the safe. It was a fantastic theory, and Meehan knew that as neither he nor Griffiths had been near Blackburn Place that night, there was not a word of truth in it. But its full import and implications were not to be revealed until Detective Inspector Cook took the stand in the afternoon.

Inspector Cook began by describing his visit to 2 Blackburn Place on July 8th, and the many samples he had taken there. These included tarry stones from the garage roof which were similar to tarry stones found in the heels of a pair of Meehan's shoes – but as was admitted later, these were to be found in many places. Then Inspector Cook was asked about the car-coat that had been sent him from Holyrood Crescent, and of the fragments of old paper that on July 31st he had found in the right-hand pocket.

'Can you tell us something about those fragments of paper?'

'Some of them were brown in colour and one piece which is now in two pieces, I see, was white in colour.[5] All the paper appeared to be old because it disintegrated fairly easily, as if it had been lying about for some considerable time, and in addition on the white paper I did notice some printing in a dark blue-coloured ink.'

'... On the 21st August did you go and examine a safe in the Police Station at Ayr ... which you understood had come from Blackburn Place, Ayr?'

'Yes, I did.'

He was asked to look at the safe, which was on the bench near him, and agreed it had a right-hand drawer.

'And on that day did you find something in that drawer?'

'Yes, I found paper in the drawer. It had been used – some brown paper in the drawer had been used as a lining for the drawer, and I also found a piece of paper which looked like a diary page.'

Meehan wondered why he hadn't taken samples of these bits of paper when he made his comprehensive examination on July 8th – nearly six weeks earlier![6]

Inspector Cook then confirmed what Mr Cowie had said, and elaborated on it. The brown piece of paper from the car-coat was similar to both pieces of brown paper in each of the two safe drawers, and to the brown paper on the floor of the safe cupboard.

'Similar in all respects?'

'Similar in all respects – microscopically – and in addition they were all old, obviously old, as they disintegrated easily.'

[5] Later Mr Cook described this as being 'about one quarter inch diameter', i.e. the size of a shirt button.

[6] See note on page 269.

'And they matched in colour and shade?'

'Matched in colour and also in microscopic appearance.'

As regards the piece of white paper from the car-coat, said Mr Cook, it was similar in colour and in age to the piece of the diary from the right-hand drawer of the safe, and in addition the lettering on it, the blue-coloured ink of the lettering, was similar to the blue-coloured ink of the lettering in the page of the diary.

'Was that examined microscopically?'

'Well, we did a chemical examination of the dyestuff from the printing.'

'So that in every possible respect these items matched exactly?'

'Yes—' said Inspector Cook, and spelt out item by item, exactly how much they did match.

Mr Stewart was now ready for the kill.

'Were you able to draw any conclusions about the origins of these samples?'

'Well, from this examination,' said Inspector Cook, *'I am of the opinion that they have a common origin.'*[7]

Now to any layman this could only mean, and to the jury sitting in judgment on Meehan it did mean, one thing: that the bits of paper in the car-coat and the bits of paper in the safe had originally been one piece. But Mr Stewart wanted them to be in no doubts.

'Do I take it from your evidence that not only does each brown match the other, and each white match the other, but brown and white came both from the car-coat and from the safe?'

'They are identical both from the car-coat and from the safe?'

'And there were some brown and some white in the car-coat and some brown and some white in the safe?'

'Yes, that is correct.'

Later Mr Cook's assistant, Detective Constable Beaton, confirmed everything Mr Cook had said about the similarity of the bits of paper, and added something of his own. The blue printing on the white piece of paper, he said, was

[7] See note on page 270.

identical to the printing on the diary page found in the safe.

'Could you tell me please in what respect was the printing identical?'

'The constituent colours of the ink, they were examined by a technique known as chromatography and it was found to have identical constituents.'

'And what about the shape of the letters themselves?'

'The size and shape of the letters also corresponded.'

After this, could the jury have had any doubts about Griffiths' participation in the crime, and therefore Meehan's too? Until now, most of the evidence had been circumstantial, but here was proof positive of Griffiths' presence in Mr Ross's house, as convincing and irrefutable as if he had left his fingerprints. Meehan was quite stunned; he had considered himself pretty smart in foiling any schemes to plant things in his blue suit, but he had not bargained for this. Because of this evidence of incriminating things having been found in Griffiths' coat rather than his own, the Crown case appeared virtually unassailable; for Griffiths, being dead, could not give his version of the story. For this reason Mr Fairbairn, when he came to cross-examine, hardly touched on the subject. 'There was nothing I could usefully do,' he said, 'for I had no rebuttal to it.' He did not know – and neither did the jury – that the safe had been examined by police officers on July 7th and 8th and found to be empty.

Until now Meehan had been reasonably optimistic about his chances of acquittal. But now for the first time he felt a chill wind blowing across the court-room, the shades of the prison house near.[8]

* * *

After Mr Cowie came Mr Robert Scott of 2 Blackburn Road, Ayr (adjoining 2 Blackburn Place), who had found McGuinness's bloodstained gloves in his lupins on the Thursday after the murder, and then Mr Ronald Allan, a Met officer from Prestwick Airport, who said that between 4 a.m. and 4.30 a.m. on the night of the crime, it would be as

[8] See note on page 272.

light as it would get before the sun came up. Detective Sergeant Smith and Detective Constable Lawtie told of interviewing Meehan on July 12th and taking the statement from him (which was read out in court), and then came Sergeant David Louden of the Ayrshire Constabulary Traffic Department.

Sergeant Louden, together with Constable Jess, had made various journeys in a Triumph 2000 between Glasgow, Ayr and Stranraer, and now gave the court the results of them. First he had taken Irene Burns on the route between Prestwick and Kilmarnock and she had pointed out where she had been dumped, where Griffiths and Meehan had overtaken the white Anglia, where they had dropped Isobel and her off. Next he described a drive on a Saturday afternoon, in which they had left Old Rutherglen Road at around 4 p.m., and arrived at Stranraer 86 miles away, 2 hours 28 minutes later. They had stayed in Stranraer for the evening, as Griffiths and Meehan had done, and then left at midnight (the time Meehan said in his statement that they had left) for Ayr: they did the 52-mile journey in 1 hour 27 minutes, at an average speed of 35·17 mph. The further 7 miles to the spot where Griffiths and Meehan had picked Irene up took another 12 minutes, making a total time of 1 hour 39 minutes for the journey from Stranraer to the lay-by. Louden and Jess had continued on to Kilmarnock, passed the places where the girls had been put down at 1.50 and 1.52, and got back to Old Rutherglen Road at 2.31 a.m., or only three minutes more than it had taken them on the journey down. On another occasion they took an alternative route from Stranraer to Ayr, but the distance and time taken were almost the same.

Now by this evidence the prosecution sought to show that there was a missing two hours between the 1.39 a.m. when the police Triumph arrived at the lay-by and the time of around 3.30 a.m. when it was agreed that Meehan and Griffiths had picked Irene up. But this premise was based on the information in Meehan's statement that he had left Stranraer at midnight. If he could bring witnesses from the Lochryanhall Hotel to show that he and Griffiths had been in the vicinity until 2 a.m., then the Crown's argument regarding times fell through, and that really was the end of their case.

* * *

Next came the petrol-pump attendant at Reid and Adams, Mr Haxton, who thought Meehan and Griffiths had arrived at the garage later than Meehan said, but remembered them well enough; Police Cadet Pirrie who had answered Meehan's call to Stranraer Police Station on Sunday 6th to remind him of the name of the garage; Allan Burgess, son of the foreman of Reid and Adams, and also his father Andrew, to confirm Meehan's telephone inquiries about the Morris 1100 on the same day; Mr Martin Johnston, a partner of the Chequered Flag Garage, to explain the circumstances of Meehan buying a Ford Corsair and then on July 4th having to turn it in and being given a cheque for £156; and Detective Constable Macphie who had taken Griffiths' fingerprints in the mortuary and Meehan's in Barlinnie Prison.

Then came the officer in charge of the case, Detective Superintendent Struthers, who described the circumstances of Meehan's arrest, the Identification parade and Meehan being charged, also the fruitless search for the Triumph ... Unfortunately for Meehan he was not asked to elaborate on his statement to the press on July 8th that the intruders had been in the Rosses' house for several hours. He was followed by two blood experts, Dr Grogan and Mr William Muir. Mr Muir stated that the blood on various bloodstained articles found in the Rosses' bedroom, pyjamas, sheets, etc., was Blood Group O, that the stain in the pocket of Meehan's trousers was also O, that half the population was O, but that he hadn't made any further subdivisions. Dr Grogan said that at the request of the defence he had analysed a sample of Meehan's blood a few days earlier and found it to be B Rhesus Negative (which as a blood donor Meehan knew). Lord Grant asked Dr Grogan what proportion of the public would be B Rhesus Negative, and Dr Grogan said about 5 per cent.

Next came Detective Inspector Derrick Macallister of the Ayrshire Police, one of the officers who had searched Meehan's flat on July 14th. His evidence related only to Charge 1, Meehan having acted along with Griffiths in stealing Mr Moir's car and its contents. He said he had found in Meehan's flat a suitcase and a tie; and later Mr Moir in evidence claimed they were his. When Mrs Meehan came to take the stand, she said that Griffiths had brought the suitcase to the flat at the end of June, when returning some blankets she had lent him: the matter of the tie was never wholly cleared up.

After Detective Sergeant Brown had given evidence about searching Griffiths' flat, and Detective Inspector Cook had talked about the pieces of paper, Irene Cameron appeared, 'the wee girl with a blonde beehive wig and spectacles' Betty Meehan had spoken of. She told of her visits to Griffiths' flat, and what they had done and discussed, and then when Mr Fairbairn cross-examined, he asked:

'How did he speak, what sort of accent?'

'An English accent.'

'Was it a particular English accent?'

'It was very English.'

'Was it particularly obvious whenever he opened his mouth that he came from England?'

'Yes.'

'Could anyone on this earth have ever thought he had a Scottish accent?'

'No.'

'Could anybody have thought that he had a Glasgow accent?'

'Definitely not.'

'The very first time you met him and were introduced to him, did you realise from what he said that he was English?'

'Yes.'

Later Mr Fairbairn turned to the Sunday when she had gone to Griffiths' flat after his trip to Stranraer – the same day, according to the Crown, on which he had robbed and assaulted the Rosses.

'Did you notice anything peculiar or strange about his

behaviour when you saw him on that day?'

'No.'

'Did he appear agitated on that day?'

'No.'

'Did he appear to try and hide anything from you in the house?'

'No. I mean, I could go about the house as freely as I liked, I could go in anywhere but there was nothing.'

'Did you notice if the clothing he had been wearing the previous day was still in the house?'

'Oh, it was still in the house.'

'I mean, can you tell us that it hadn't been destroyed?'

Irene doubted if it had been destroyed, because she saw it lying over a chair in the corner. Did Griffiths, she was asked, continue to drive about in his car for a considerable number of days after the Ayr murder?

'Yes.'

'In the public streets?'

'Yes.'

'With you?'

'Yes.'

'Did he go anywhere with you in particular in those days?'

'No, nowhere particular, except when he drove me home, he did go through the town.'

'And did you pass policemen?'

'Oh, yes, going by Gorbals Cross, there are usually plenty of policemen standing about there.'

'Did he ever say anything like, "I hope those policemen won't see this car." or anything like that?'

'No.'

'So that for several days after it was known that murder had been committed in Ayr, he drove about the public streets in this vehicle?'

'Yes.'

'Did you see any alteration in his behaviour following the days that he had been to Stranraer?'

'No.'

Even Mr Stewart could not shake her on this when he came to re-examine.

'You said to Mr Fairbairn – or rather he put it to you – that Griffiths was driving round the public streets days after this incident not attempting to hide the car from anybody – do you remember – and you agreed that was so?'

'Yes.'

'And you said there was no alteration in Griffiths' behaviour following the days he had been to Stranraer?'

'That is right.'

'That is not really right, is it?'

'Yes.'

Earlier Irene had admitted to Mr Stewart that she had wondered whether there was any connection between the arrest of Meehan for the Ayr murder and Griffiths dumping the Triumph, but had not liked to question him about it.

'Were you afraid what you might hear?' asked Mr Stewart, and she had answered, 'Yes.'

But in the end she finally did pluck up courage to ask him if he had anything to do with the murder.

'How did he react?' asked Mr Fairbairn.

'Well, he said – I have never seen him violent or angry, but he said to me in an angry voice, "I swear I have nothing to do with it." '

'And did you believe him?'

'Yes.'

'Were you satisfied from his reactions that he was telling the truth?'

'Oh, the way he said it to me, I never seen him angry before, I took it that was the truth.'

* * *

On Wednesday morning the first witness was Lil Connolly, the woman whom Meehan had met in London when planning the Edmonton Co-op job, and had visited at Oakamoor Prison, near Stoke-on-Trent, when he and Griffiths had made their abortive trip to see the fence at Scunthorpe five days after the Ayr murder. The prosecution had called her so it could be shown that she was another who knew Meehan as 'Pat' – she had received a letter from him signed 'Pat' after the visit – and also presumably to show that Meehan was still associating with people in his criminal past. But it gave Nicholas Fairbairn the opportunity of some useful cross-examination.

'Did he appear just his normal self?'

'Yes.'

'Did he appear agitated or anxious in any way?'

'No, no different.'

'No different?'

'No different at all.'

'And you at that time were in prison, is that right?'

'Yes.'

'And in order to gain admission to see you, did he have to go through Prison Officers who were in charge of the prison?'

'Yes, there was an officer with us all the time.'

'And did he have to obtain permission and give his name in order to see you?'

'Yes.'

'And that was on the 10th July, five days after the incident we are investigating?'

'Yes.'

After Mrs Connolly came a Miss Leary from Carnie's Car Hire to confirm they had hired a car to Meehan on June 19th, two police handwriting experts, a woman from the Passport Office to give evidence about the false passport for Griffiths which Meehan had counter-signed in another name, and then pretty little Mrs Murray from Appleby. It was during Mrs Murray's examination-in-chief that Crown and Defence counsel had one of those brushes that so delight laymen.

Mrs Murray had told Mr Stewart that Griffiths had 'not much of an accent but you could tell he was Lancashire'.

'Not much of an accent but slightly Lancashire,' said Mr Stewart.

Mr Fairbairn got up. 'I think the witness was saying, "But you could tell he was Lancashire", and the learned Solicitor-General inadvertently interrupted her.'

Mr Stewart turned to Mrs Murray.

'You could tell he was Lancashire if you knew Lancashire?'

Mr Fairbairn got up again. 'Well, with respect, that was not what the witness was going to say, and she should be allowed to say what she was going to say.'

'Well,' said Mr Stewart, 'I think the witness probably knows better what she was going to say than Mr Fairbairn.'

Mrs Murray described Griffiths' and Meehan's various visits, including the occasion when they were driving the Boyles home after the accident at Scotch Corner. And once again Mr Fairbairn took the opportunity of showing how different were Meehan's and Griffiths' accents.

'Was it obvious when he spoke that Jim was an Englishman?'

'Yes.'

'What sort of voice did Pat speak in, was it Scottish or English?'

'Scottish.'

'Was it obvious when they spoke that one was a Scotsman and one was an Englishman?'

'Yes.'

Mrs Murray was followed by Mrs Boyle who told how Meehan had given assistance at the time of the Scotch Corner accident. She also told Mr Stewart that it was possible that when Meehan was feeling her bleeding knee, some of the blood might have got on to his hands. This was helpful to Meehan as one explanation of the tiny bloodstain found in one of his trouser pockets. (He himself had no idea how it had got there.) Mr Fairbairn brought up again the question of Griffiths' accent, and Mrs Boyle described it as 'definitely English'.

Mr Moir came next, related how he found the Triumph gone when he woke up in the motel at Gretna Green and later had identified various articles from the car that had been found in Griffiths' flat or lock-up. Mr Thomas Hamilton told of the circumstances of Griffiths taking the flat at Marywood Square in the name of Francis Macneil, and also of seeing an envelope from the Passport Office in the letter rack there.

And then, as the defence had put in the Special Defence of Incrimination against Ian Waddell, the Crown called Waddell's alibi, Donald Carmichael. Carmichael, who described himself as a lorry-driver, was a short, stocky man with dark hair that was thinning on top. It will be recalled that Waddell and McGuinness had left Glasgow in the early afternoon of the Saturday in question, and Waddell had not arrived at Carmichael's house until early on the Sunday morning. But when examined by Mr Stewart, Carmichael told a different story.

'Do you remember Saturday 5th July last?'

'Yes.'

'Were you with your wife at Mac's Bar in the Gallowgate, Glasgow?'

'Yes.'

'And I think you later went on from that bar to the Noggin public house?'

'Yes.'

'And did you then go to the Waverley Bar in Gallowgate?'

'Yes.'

'And did you leave there about 9.15 and go home, go back to your home, and on the way I think you bought fish suppers?'

'Yes.'

'Do you remember somebody coming to your house about midnight?'

'Yes.'

'Who was it who came?'

'Ian Waddell.'

'What state was he in?'

'He had had a drink.'

'And did he have with him a carry-out?'

'Yes.'

'Did he have with him some whisky and wine and beer?'

'Whisky and wine.'

'And did you and he and your wife have some drinks together?'

'I had a couple of drinks with him.'

'Where did Waddell spend the night?'
'He spent the night on my couch.'
'I think you invited him just to stay the night.'
'No.'
'Well, your wife did?'
'He asked to stay.'
'Did you see him in the morning?'
'Yes.'
'About what time?'
'About ten o'clock.'
'Was that when you woke?'
'Yes.'
'Was he there when you went to sleep?'
'Yes.'
'Can you remember roughly when you went to sleep that night?'
'After twelve I think it was.'
'I think you were questioned, weren't you, by the police, shortly after the Ayr murder?'
'Yes.'
'And you were asked about Waddell's movements?'
'Yes.'
'And did you give this account, you have given just now?'
'Yes.'

It sounded a good watertight story that absolved Waddell from the crime completely. Now it was up to Mr Fairbairn to pick what holes he could in it; and in his first question he found a chink in Carmichael's armour.

'How do you know that Ian Waddell, as you tell us, stayed in your house on the night of the 5th July?'

'*I didn't say I knew he stayed the night*. He fell asleep there.'

Further questioning revealed how confused and contradictory Carmichael's replies were. He had first met Waddell at school, he said, but after that had not met him again until they were both in prison. And had he never seen Waddell, he was asked, from the time of prison until July 5th?

'I have passed him once or twice in the Gallowgate.'
'But you have never spoken to him?'

'No.'

No?

'And he has never stayed in your house before?'

Once in February, said Carmichael, and the reason he stayed was the same as on July 5th – 'he was arguing with whoever he was staying with, wherever he was staying, and he didn't want to go home and he was drunk.'

Asked why Waddell should have gone to Carmichael's house, as he wasn't a friend, Carmichael said he didn't know; and then, 'He was a friend but I didn't want to associate with him', which sounded odd.

Mr Fairbairn turned to the Police interest in Carmichael after the Ayr murder. They had been to interview him once to check Waddell's alibi, and then because they were not satisfied, they got in touch again and asked him to come down to the station. When he heard this, he was worried enough to ring his solicitor, Mr Beltrami, even though it was near midnight. Mr Beltrami told him to come and see him next day, but before this, the Police called to say they now didn't want to see him again after all (by this time they had arrested Meehan).

Mr Fairbairn put the question that was in everyone's mind in court.

'... isn't the reason you telephoned the solicitor because you knew your story was false, and you were frightened of getting involved?'

'No.'

'What was your reason for phoning a solicitor?'

'Well, sir, any time I have ever been in trouble with the Police, I have always phoned my solicitor.'

'But you weren't in trouble with the Police? You were, according to you, giving a perfectly genuine alibi to Ian Waddell?'

'Yes.'

'Well, how on earth, if you are telling the truth that Ian Waddell could not have done the Ayr murder – how on earth could you be in trouble with the Police for telling them the truth about that?'

'I couldn't have been in trouble with them.'

'Well, you told us the reason you phoned your solicitor again that if Carmichael was not in trouble with the Police, you had phoned your solicitor.'

'That's right.'

'Did you regard yourself on this occasion as being in trouble with the Police?'

'No.'

'Well, will you give the jury the reason why you telephoned the solicitor?'

'Well, as I have said already, before, any time I have been in trouble with the Police, I have always asked for legal advice if I can possibly manage it.'

This dialogue was beginning to get an Alice in Wonderland flavour; and before Mr Fairbairn could point out yet again that if Carmichael was not in trouble with the Police, there was no reason to phone his solicitor, Lord Grant came to Carmichael's rescue.

'You have been in trouble several times, I gather?'

'Yes.'

'And I imagine you realise that whether you are guilty of an offence or not, a person who is summoned to the police office is always wise to consult his solicitor, and that solicitors always advise their clients to that effect – if they are reputable and able solicitors, and the courts have said frequently that it is always desirable that a solicitor should be present if anybody is summoned to the police office in order to make a statement. Do you realise that?'

'Yes,' said Carmichael (and he might have added, 'and thank you very much!').

But Mr Fairbairn was not going to be put off.

'Now, will you please tell the jury why you considered on this occasion you were in trouble with the Police?'

But he got no further than before. Carmichael made a rambling reply, about having read in the papers that Mr Beltrami had stated that the man the Police had [i.e. Meehan] was innocent, and he didn't see what reason the Police wanted him down.

Mr Fairbairn made one final shot.

'So you thought, did you, that in alibi-ing Waddell you

were in sufficient trouble with the Police to consult a solicitor?'

'No.'

'Well then, why did you consult him?'

Carmichael launched again into the story he had read in the papers about Mr Beltrami stating there was a man that didn't do the murder, 'and I says, "Well I am getting pulled in on this", or "I am getting taken down and questioned again about this murder", and I had nothing to do with it.'

Mr Fairbairn gave up.

'Your alibi of Waddell is completely false, isn't it?'

'No.'

Mr Stewart made little headway either, though right at the end he gave the defence an unexpected bonus. Remembering that Carmichael had said that when Waddell arrived at his house, he was drunk, Mr Stewart asked, 'Was he in the sort of condition in which he could go out and commit a crime?'

'I presume if he wanted to, yes.'

'And if he had gone out, how would he have got back?'

'Well, I stay in a low-down house and it is only an ordinary lock that is on the door. When you are going out, you can put the sneck up on it.'

Mr Stewart said that his next witness was to have been Mrs Carmichael, but that there was a medical certificate saying she couldn't come. After Detective Chief Superintendent Elphinstone Dalglish had given evidence of Mr Goodall's three telephone conversations with Griffiths (Mr Goodall would have given evidence himself, but had died ten days before), Mr Stewart told Lord Grant that there was a soul and conscience certificate in relation to Mrs Carmichael; this meant that a doctor had sworn on his soul and conscience that she was unfit to attend the court. Whereupon Mr Fairbairn, whose case was to discount Carmichael's alibi, said that he would very much like to examine Mrs Carmichael himself; and from the certificate he would have thought there was every likelihood of her becoming available during the course of the trial.

Lord Grant said if that was so, then he could call her

but he would have to make his own inquiries; and Mr Stewart said that that closed the case for the Crown.

* * *

It had originally been the intention of the prosecution to call Waddell as a Crown witness to spike the defence's guns. They had hoped that his evidence, and Carmichael's, that Waddell had been in Carmichael's house on the night of the murder, would blow the defence's impeachment of Waddell sky-high. But now they had got cold feet about Waddell. For a start Carmichael's evidence had been less than satisfactory. Then Ross in evidence had been far less sure about the Identification parade than he had at the time. Having heard Waddell's voice, he had said that it sounded 'something similar' to the one he had heard in the bedroom, and indeed that it was 'possible' that it was the voice. Furthermore, if by chance Waddell was involved in the Ayr crime and gave evidence for the Crown against Meehan, he would himself be immune to further prosecution. So just before the prosecution case ended, the Crown informed the defence that they did not propose to call Waddell.

This meant that the defence could now call him themselves; and as soon as Mr Beltrami heard the news, he sent his office manager, Mr McDonald, down to the cells to interview Waddell to see if he could get a precognition (i.e. written statement) from him, as is usual with all witnesses before they are called. Waddell asked McDonald what his position would be if, during his evidence, he admitted to the crime. Mr McDonald said that as he was now a defence witness, he could be prosecuted. Waddell said that in that case he had nothing to say.

* * *

'Call Patrick Meehan.'

He was ushered out of the dock and across the carpeted well of the court to the witness-box, went through the great day of judgment routine, and swore that he would tell nothing but the truth. This time, whatever he might have said or failed to say in the past, he meant it: indeed his whole future depended on it.

'Do you wish to give evidence in this case?' asked Mr Fairbairn.

'Yes, I do.'

'Have you always wished to give evidence?'

'Yes, I have.'

'Had you anything whatever to do with the robbery and murder in Ayr on the night of the 7th July?'

'I was never at any time involved in that murder, robbery, and I never set eyes on that man Ross until I saw him on the Identification parade.'

It was said with a force and conviction that held the attention of the court.

Mr Fairbairn then took Meehan through all his movements with Griffiths from the time of their leaving Old Rutherglen Road on the afternoon of Saturday July 5th: the drive to Stranraer, inspecting the Morris 1100 at Reid and Adams, casing the motor taxation office, having a meal in Spencer's Hotel, driving to Cairnryan and waiting outside the hotel until about 2 a.m.; then picking up Irene Burns between Prestwick and Kilmarnock, chasing the other car and rescuing Isobel Smith, taking both girls home, and the drive to Glasgow. Meehan described also his telephoning Stranraer the next day for the name of the garage where the 1100 was, and of ringing the Ayr police at his daughter's insistence about the two men in the white Anglia. But why, asked Mr Fairbairn, had Meehan told the Police that 'two friends' of his had picked Irene up, and not himself?

'Well,' said Meehan, 'I was in a very delicate position for the simple reason that James Griffiths was a man for whom the Police had been searching high and low for the past five or six months; there had been an intensive search for James Griffiths.'

'And had you anything to fear from giving your name?'

'Not from giving my name, but I couldn't very well give my name and not tell them who I was with.'

It was a pity that Meehan did not add that Superintendent Struthers had said publicly he would welcome anonymous information.

'Taking it for the moment from me,' said Mr Fairbairn, 'that you and Griffiths were the men who committed the Ayr murder ... does that mean that you made a telephone call ... disclosing the names of two girls who could probably identify you?'

Meehan would have been better to reply, 'Yes, it does', enforcing Mr Fairbairn's good question. Instead he said, 'Well, the reason I made the phone call was, like everyone else, I was thoroughly disgusted at this crime. I thought it was a filthy crime.'

It was, and there is no doubt that Meehan thought so; yet pots are unconvincing when calling kettles black.

Meehan went on to describe the trip with Griffiths to Scunthorpe and Oakamoor Prison to see Lily Connolly, the return to Glasgow and telephone conversation with Detective Constable Baxter, and finally on July 12th the making of a statement to Detective Sergeant Smith.

Mr Fairbairn took Meehan through the statement, which the court had already heard; and he put two questions that must have been in the front of the jury's minds.

'Does that say that you left Glasgow ... to go to Stranraer to see a motor car which was for sale in a garage near Stranraer Police Office?'

'Yes.'

'Now, what in fact was the purpose of your visit?'

'To look over the motor taxation office.'

'And does the account you gave say that at any stage you looked at the motor taxation office?'

'Well, obviously not.'

'Why not?'

'Well, you don't tell the Police these things when they come to ask you.'

And again:

'Now, did you leave Stranraer at midnight?'

'No.'

'You say that you left, you think it would be near midnight?'

'Yes, but obviously I couldn't tell the Police that I was standing on a Ministry of Defence yard watching an hotel, that is one thing I couldn't tell them.'

'Yes,' intervened Lord Grant, presently, 'but you had invented a reason for going to Stranraer, why didn't you invent a reason for staying on in Stranraer until 2 o'clock – or was that beyond your powers of invention?'[9]

Meehan said that during the trip when there was an accident at Scotch Corner, he was wearing the suit in which the bloodstain had been found in a trouser pocket; and he was asked if he could have got blood on his hand from Mrs Boyle's cut knee.

'I distinctly remember the blood on her knee was dark-coloured, it was not like a scratch, red, and I took out my handkerchief and dabbed it, but I only done it to see if the cut was deep, and it was not a serious cut.'

He spoke about Griffiths stealing Mr Moir's car on the way back to Glasgow, and helping Griffiths with a false passport application, and being picked out at the Identification parade, and telling Griffiths to get rid of the Triumph, and the stones found in his shoes being similar to stones on roofing material sold at Lewis's when he worked there, and what he did with the money from the Chequered Flag Garage, and Griffiths having an 'unmistakably English' accent.

'And have you throughout the inquiries on each occasion when you were entitled to, such as when you were cautioned and charged, protested your innocence?'

'Yes, I have.'

'And are you innocent?'

'I am innocent.'

'Is there any question whatever of your being involved?'

'I was never at any time involved, never, and neither was James Griffiths.'

* * *

Mr Stewart's cross-examination of Meehan lasted for about two and a half hours – or three-quarters of an hour longer than Mr Fairbairn's examination-in-chief. Throughout his questioning his attitude to Meehan was consistently

[9] Meehan wrote in the margin of his copy of the trial transcript, 'A very unfair comment'.

hostile and disbelieving, often sarcastic, as the attitudes of prosecuting counsel inevitably are: they hope by throwing doubt on what the accused says to break down his defences and so arrive at the truth. Such tactics are admirable when, as is usual, the accused is guilty; but when he is innocent, as Meehan was, the questioning often makes uncomfortable reading. Mr Stewart knew he had in front of him one of Scotland's most hardened criminals, a man he also believed to be the murderer of Mrs Ross; but he knew as well as Stanley Bowen, the Crown Agent, beside him that the evidence was thin. He would be doing less than his duty if he did not use all his forensic skill to propagate convincingly the Crown's case.

'Is the evidence you have given us today the whole truth?'

'Yes, it is the whole truth.'

'And how long have you been telling the truth about this matter?'

'Since I came into the witness-box I have been telling the truth.'

Mr Stewart paused. 'Since you came into the witness-box? You lied before that, didn't you?'

'I lied only by omission. I couldn't explain to the Police about the two hours outside the hotel – one or two minor things.'

'Were you protesting your innocence about the passport matter until quite recently?'

'I was not aware that I was charged with the passport until I read it on my indictment ...'

'And then you appeared in court to answer to your indictment ten days ago?'

'Yes, that is correct.'

'And how did you plead to the passport charge?'

'I pleaded not guilty.'

'And now you say you are guilty.'

'Yes.'

In a few deft strokes Mr Stewart had given further proof of Meehan's capacities for lying – and invited the jury to think that if he had lied in his pleading to one of the charges, he was just as likely to be lying about the others.

Next Mr Stewart turned to the various car trips Meehan had made with Griffiths.

'. . . at night you would run about England with Griffiths?'

'No, I was with Griffiths on several occasions, but I wasn't with him every day.'

'You were with him almost constantly, weren't you?'

'No, I wasn't.'

'You used to go about with him very frequently on long journeys?'

'I went on three or four trips with him, I was not in the man's company every day.'

'What about the night, though, you were with him every night?'

'No, I wasn't.'

'And you knew well what sort of a man he was?'

'I knew the man, what he was doing, I knew that.'

Mr Stewart held out a sheet of paper.

'Look at that Production, the Police Gazette of the 15th of July. Do you see that?'

'Yes, dated 15th of July.'

'Convictions for larceny, taking a motor vehicle without consent, conspiracy and robbery etc, you knew about that, didn't you?'

'No, I didn't.'

'Surely you asked the man what his record was?'

'I didn't. I knew the man had a record but I didn't know what his record involved.'

'Did you not know very well that he had been convicted for robbery with violence?'

'I did not.'

'You went out on your own admission with Griffiths on a criminal enterprise on the 5th of July?'

'Yes, yes.'

'Surely you knew what sort of a man you were going out with?'

'I knew he was a criminal.'

'... And a criminal who had been convicted of robbery with violence?'

'I was not aware of that.'

'... Oh, come, come, surely a man with whom you are associating frequently and running about in motor-cars with and going on a criminal enterprise with, you want to know surely what his criminal record is?'

'No,' said Meehan, 'these questions are not asked.'

And, oddly, he was right; unlike golfers and Lotharios, criminals are not in the habit of swapping track records.

'I take it you were genuine when you said that you regarded the crime here as something that you detested?'

'Yes.'

'I think you called it a filthy crime?'

'It *was* a filthy crime.'

'Did you know that Griffiths had been guilty of such a crime, namely robbery with violence?'

This brought Mr Fairbairn to his feet. 'I think that is a most improper question. I have allowed my friend to go this far, but your Lordship will appreciate that Griffiths, though dead, stands as a co-accused.'

What Mr Fairbairn meant was that had Griffiths been alongside Meehan in the dock, the Solicitor-General would not have been allowed to mention Griffiths' record, for fear of prejudicing the jury. But what of the prejudice to Meehan? Why should the rule be waived just because Griffiths was dead?

Mr Stewart said the defence themselves had raised the question of Griffiths' record, firstly as a man who had stolen many cars and for whom the Police were searching high and low, and secondly as a man who had a number of false passports. Therefore he was entitled to go further into Griffiths' record in cross-examination. Lord Grant agreed: unfortunately for Meehan this was the law.

Mr Stewart asked Meehan about Griffiths stealing Mr Moir's Triumph at Gretna Green and got him to admit that he had 'travelled in this car thereafter, well knowing it to have been stolen'. He came to the time of Meehan's return to Glasgow on July 10th after seeing Lily Connolly at Oakamoor; and Meehan agreed it was that evening he learnt the Police were looking for a man called Pat in con-

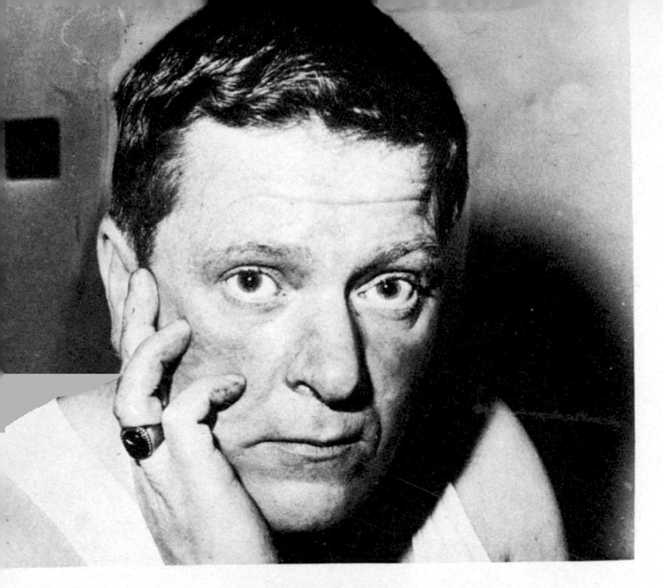

Photograph of Patrick Meehan in Barlinnie Prison shortly after his arrest. It was taken by Mr Raymond Beltrami, brother of Meehan's solicitor, for showing to people in Stranraer to verify Meehan's presence there.

'. . . a wife of exceptional courage and character who has never wavered in her efforts to get her husband's case reviewed': Betty Meehan.

'. . . drifted into crime in 1964 and since has had several convictions in Glasgow for theft, housebreaking and carrying an offensive weapon': Ian Waddell.

'. . . if in the course of my going on a job, it means either I get caught and put in prison, or I whack somebody over the head and they die, that's their hard luck': James Griffiths.

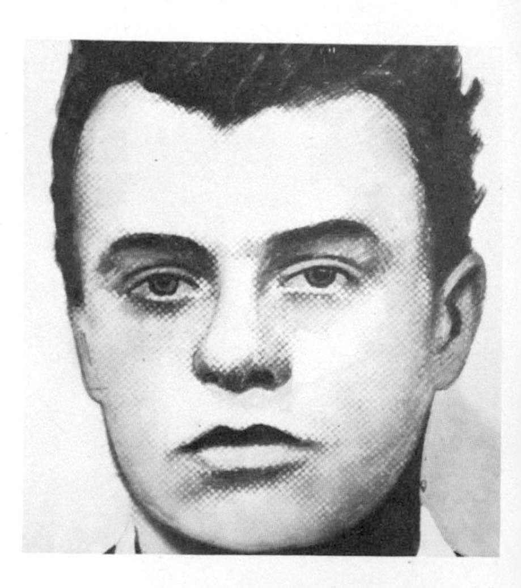

'. . . soft-spoken, shrewd, extremely conservative . . . gambled modestly on the pools and horses, and also fond of cigars': Abraham Ross shortly before Meehan's trial.

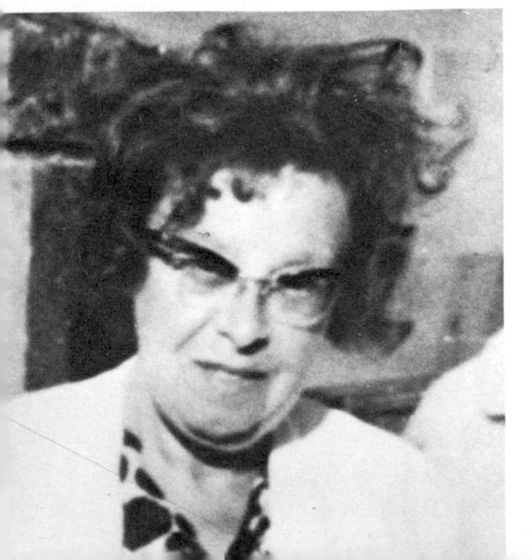

'. . . a great reader and much interested in politics . . . her own views were very left-wing': Rachel Ross.

William (Tank) McGuinness.

'A bungalow situated in a quiet residential area of Ayr.' No 2 Blackburn Place. On the left of the picture is the garage which contained the stepladder and weeding tool, and to the left of the front door the bedroom window through which the intruders entered. The window at the extreme right is that of the Rosses' bedroom in which the crime was committed.

Patrick Meehan leaving Ayr Sheriff Court on 15th July 1969, after being charged with the murder of Mrs Rachel Ross.

Ian Waddell leaving Glasgow Sheriff Court on 6th August 1976, after being charged with the murder of Mrs Rachel Ross.

'. . . with the shotgun and rifle Griffiths continued firing at everybody and anything that moved': Griffiths at the attic window of Holyrood Crescent.

'In an hour and a half he had killed one person and wounded thirteen': A police marksman shelters behind a car during the siege of 14 Holyrood Crescent.

'. . . a skilful and experienced advocate . . . won an MC in the war and stood in 1970 as a Labour candidate': the then Solicitor-General of Scotland, Mr Ewan, now Lord, Stewart.

Left: '. . . one of the most experienced and knowledgeable of Glasgow criminal law solicitors': Mr Joseph Beltrami, Meehan's trial solicitor.
Right: '. . . a Conservative politician and accomplished artist . . . the most successful criminal defence lawyer in Scotland': Mr Nicholas Fairbairn, now QC, MP.

Elizabeth R

ELIZABETH THE SECOND, by the Grace of God of the United Kingdom of Great Britain and Northern Ireland and of Our other Realms and Territories QUEEN, Head of the Commonwealth, Defender of the Faith, to all to whom these Presents shall come,

GREETING!

WHEREAS Patrick Connolly Meehan was at the High Court holden at Edinburgh on the twenty-fourth day of October 1969 convicted of murder and sentenced to life imprisonment;

NOW KNOW YE that We in consideration of some circumstances humbly represented unto Us and of Our Prerogative Royal, Proper Motion, and Royal Clemency are graciously pleased to extend Our Grace and Mercy to the said Patrick Connolly Meehan and to grant him Our Free Pardon in respect of the said conviction thereby pardoning, remitting and releasing unto him all pains, penalties and punishments whatsoever that from the said conviction may come.

Given at Our Court at St James
the 19th day of May 1976
in the Twenty-fifth Year of Our Reign.

BY HER MAJESTY'S COMMAND
(SIGNED) BRUCE MILLAN

CERTIFIED A TRUE COPY D.W. Boyce

The Royal Pardon.

nection with the Ayr murder. (It was also, it will be recalled, the day that Detective Sergeant Baxter had called at Old Rutherglen Road to interview Meehan about his movements on the night of the murder.)

'... You knew that day that the name of Pat must have been given by somebody?'

'Oh, yes.'

'And that was the first time you knew it, because if that paper is correct, the announcement had only been released by the Police the previous night?'

'Well, I believe that was the first time I knew.'

'And of course you are an innocent man?'

'That is right.'

'Of course you are. You are an innocent man.' Mr Stewart was preparing the ground well.

'Yes, I am innocent.'

'But your name is Pat?'

'Yes.'

'And you read in the paper that the killer's name may be Pat, and you are an innocent man. And what do you do? What *did* you do?'

'What did I do? I didn't do anything.'

'You told your friend James Griffiths to get rid of a Triumph 2000?'

'I told him to get rid of it because the Police had been to my house.'

'Yes. But you were innocent?'

'Of course. I *am* innocent.'

What Meehan should have said was that he was innocent of the Ayr murder, but he was not innocent of riding in a stolen car with a man who was wanted by the Police.

'If you were innocent, why did you tell your friend to get rid of a motor car in which you had been driving through Ayr on the previous Saturday night?' (No evidence had been given that Meehan had driven through Ayr, and Mr Fairbairn might well have risen to say so.)

'Simply because Griffiths was on the run from the Police.'

'For what?'

'For several things, and I told him so, I said, "The police

have been wanting to see me. Now I can't tell any lies about this matter. I have to tell them I was with you. I have to tell them you have a Triumph 2000. So you are on the run, the Police will be looking for you with a Triumph 2000. Get rid of it."'

'... you wanted to protect Griffiths?'

'Exactly. That's it exactly.'

'And you thought if he didn't have a Triumph 2000, they wouldn't be able to find him?'

'Well, there was less likelihood of him being found.'

Mr Stewart turned to the forged passport application form, and inferred that Griffiths had got this false passport at this time in order to flee the country after the Ayr murder. But as Griffiths had received the passport before Meehan's arrest, and had every opportunity (except shortage of funds) to flee the country after it, yet had not done so, this trail led to a dead end.

Nor was Mr Stewart any more successful when he tried to show that there was something sinister in Meehan having opened a bank account on July 11th with £150 of the Chequered Flag money which he had brought back from the abortive trip to Scunthorpe.

'... the 11th. That was then six days after this murder, for the first time in your life you opened a bank account?'

'No, not for the first time in my life.'

'I thought you told Mr Fairbairn that you didn't have a bank account?'

'I didn't, but this doesn't mean to say I never had a bank account.'

'You didn't have a bank account before 5th July?'

'No.'

'And six days later you opened a bank account?'

'Yes, that's correct.'

'Why?'

Meehan explained at length about the money from the Chequered Flag originally going into Betty's account, and her not being able to draw it until the Wednesday, and then taking it to England.

'... So it is just a coincidence that it is six days after the murder that you open a bank account that you haven't had previously?'

'It is,' replied Meehan, 'just as you say, a coincidence.'

But like the passport, it wasn't much of a coincidence. Had there been evidence of Meehan paying into the account several hundred pounds in new notes, it would have been a different matter. In fact he had openly paid the £150 in the day after he had heard from Detective Constable Baxter that the Police might want to interview him.

Next Mr Stewart turned to the business of identification of the murderers, and Meehan impressed the court by the nature and forcefulness of his replies. Mr Stewart's questions were clearly based on the premise that the accused was guilty. But were Meehan's replies the replies of a guilty man?

'Now you were innocent, as you have told us, of this murder?'

'I am innocent of this murder.'

'And you don't know who witnessed or who might have witnessed the crime – or rather you didn't know that in the week after the murder?'

'How could I know it?' asked Meehan.

'How could you know, precisely? You didn't know who might have seen the perpetrators, you didn't know whether somebody might have seen a car in the vicinity?'

'I didn't know anything about it.'

'You knew nothing of these things?'

'No.'

'And Griffiths, equally, you say, would be entirely ignorant of these matters because he was innocent too?'

'Griffiths had absolutely nothing to do with it.'

Mr Stewart turned to the Identification parade on July 14th, and asked Meehan if he would agree that the purpose of such a parade was for people who might have seen something significant at the place of the crime, to view people and say 'Oh, yes, I saw that man in such and such a place.'

'Yes,' said Meehan.

'And as you are innocent, you were, I think on the 14th

July, not in a position to say what witnesses had seen what?'

'No,' said Meehan, 'I wouldn't know at all.'

'There might, for all you know, have been people who had seen a couple of men or more than two men leaving this house in Ayr?'

Meehan wondered what Mr Stewart was driving at. 'Well, I wouldn't know,' he said.

'And therefore you had no knowledge of what witnesses might be produced to look at suspects on the parade?'

'How could I?'

'How could you, and what was it you said when you were told you were going on an Identification parade?'

What had he said? He couldn't remember.

'You said, "Why have I to go on an Identification parade, there is only the two girls I picked up?"'

'I may have said something like that.'

Now at last the line of Mr Stewart's questioning was becoming clear. As Meehan had committed the murder, how could he be so sure that people had not seen him and Griffiths in the vicinity of Blackburn Place?

'We have evidence,' Mr Stewart went on, 'that that is what you said, from Superintendent Struthers. "There is only the two girls I picked up."'

'This is as far as *I* am concerned,' said Meehan with some heat. 'I never set foot in Ayr that night, so how could *anybody* say I was in Ayr? There were only the two girls I picked up, so how could anybody say I was in Ayr? I was never in Ayr.'

'You thought that nobody had seen you at the house?'

'I thought *nothing*.' Meehan was almost shouting now. 'I never *set foot* in Ayr.'

'And you were right, nobody had seen you coming in or out?'

'I am an innocent man,' bawled Meehan.

But Mr Stewart was not to be put off.

'You are an innocent man, how did you know that somebody had not seen the perpetrator of the crime?'

'How *can* I know?' said Meehan, and then in exasperation, 'I don't get the point of this.'

'Did you suppose that the only people to view the parade would be the two girls?'

Meehan took a deep breath and tried to explain.

'I could only see things as I saw them. All I knew was that I had picked up two girls, and I had been charged, or a charge was mentioned about a Mr and Mrs Ross in Ayr, and I didn't have a clue. I said, "What's it all about, all I done was picking up two girls, why am I getting an I.D. parade?"'

'Did you know by then that the assailants had had their features obscured in some way?'

'How could I know anything?'

'You could read the papers?'

'Yes, I read the papers.'

'I thought you said you were very interested in this, you said you were shocked by it?'

'I was shocked.'

'You could know quite a lot of things —'

'But how do I know what has happened in a house,' said Meehan angrily, 'if I have never been in that house?'

Were these replies, the jury asked themselves, those of an innocent or guilty man?

Next Mr Stewart attempted to throw suspicion on various times Meehan had given in his statements to the Police, and which were afterwards proved to be wrong. But these times were only approximate as Meehan then had no reason for knowing, or indeed caring, what the exact time was.

First Mr Stewart referred to Meehan's anonymous telephone call to the Ayr police on July 9th, when he said that his 'friends' picked up the two girls at 4.30 a.m. Meehan now agreed that it was not 4.30 a.m. but sometime earlier.

'You didn't point that out when you were shown that before.'

'At the time I phoned, I was not interested in conveying the exact times, I was only interested in conveying that two girls were involved in this incident, and there was a white car involved . . .'

'. . . But your memory has improved since then, and you

have put the time about an hour earlier, or more than an hour earlier?'

'I have actually had to sit down,' said Meehan, 'and think it all out.'

'I am sure you have,' said Mr Stewart.

'And my wife has assisted me in this.'

'Your wife has assisted you to think it out, has she?'

'I said, "What time did I come in, half four or half five?" and my daughter remembered me coming in.'

'So you have sat down with your wife and daughter and worked out a time schedule?'

'Oh, no.'

'Did you do all this working out before the police saw you?'

'Oh, no, I have done it in prison, I have been doing it ever since I was charged.'

'But before you were charged?' suggested Mr Stewart.

'*No*,' said Meehan forcefully, 'the *last* thing I ever *thought* of was being charged with this crime.'

It was difficult to see where this line of questioning was leading. Meehan in his anonymous call to the Ayr police had said that his 'friends' had picked up a girl at 4.30 a.m. He had subsequently telephoned the Ayr police again to say the girl's name was Irene Burns, so they could if they wanted check the time from her. They had, and she had suggested the time was nearer 3.45 a.m. than 4.30. So what?

Mr Stewart found fault with other of Meehan's times. Meehan had said that they had arrived in Stranraer 'about seven o'clock', but the petrol-pump attendant suggested it was much later. Meehan had stated they had left Glasgow at 4 p.m. Was that correct?

'No,' said Meehan, 'it was after 4 p.m., it was about 4.30.'

'But you were trying to tell the truth,' said Mr Stewart, 'apart from certain facts you were concealing?'

'Yes,' said Meehan, 'but when someone asks you a question, you don't give it too much thought, but if someone charges you with murder, then you have good reason to think . . . "Oh God, what time was it?"'

Next, remembering Mr Ross's cut telephone wire and the general circumstances of the break-in at Blackburn Place, Mr Stewart wanted to find out if Meehan had a burglar's kit with him. Meehan agreed the real object of the trip to Stranraer was not to buy a car but to look over the motor taxation office with a view to later breaking in.

'You agreed you were going to break into it?'

'That was the intention, but we went down to look it over.'

'And did you take with you such tools as pliers?'

'No.'

'And torches?'

'No.'

'And some quiet footwear?'

'No.'

'And you were going to break in then?'

'We didn't go to actually specifically break in that night. We went to look over it.'

Meehan agreed that he had looked over it but hadn't fancied it.

'But if the place had been of a different nature, you might have fancied it . . . ?'

'Well, I could have, yes.'

'And therefore you would have carried on with the break-in?'

'Not that particular night.'

'Why not?'

'Because we only went there for the purpose of looking at it.'

Next there arose an unfortunate misunderstanding between Mr Stewart and Meehan about Meehan's telephone inquiries to Reid and Adams concerning the Morris 1100. It will be recalled that on the Sunday evening of July 6th Meehan had spoken to Allan Burgess, son of the foreman of Reid and Adams, to inquire about the car, and that Allan had said his father was out and to ring later. Meehan had not rung Mr Burgess later (he had gone out that evening with Jo McLean to sort out the deaf mutes) but in the morning he had telephoned the garage and spoken to Mr

Downie the sales manager who had told him the Morris was going for £465 but that he had another for less. But Meehan was under the impression when speaking to Mr Downie, that he was speaking to the father of the boy he had spoken to the night before, Mr Burgess. And Mr Burgess's evidence had been that no one had rung him back.

So Mr Stewart, not knowing about Mr Downie either, said, '... I am putting to you that you weren't interested in the car at that time?'

'Oh, yes, I was.'

'Well, why did you not persist in your inquiries?'

'Well, when I phoned the chap and he said the car cost £400 odd, I said, "Well, this is an funny price ..." It wasn't a sort of modern car, it was three or four or five years old. In fact it was a "C" registration.'

'You see,' said Mr Stewart, 'this is a complete lie, isn't it?'

'What is?'

'What you are telling us about what the chap said on the phone?'

'No. I am telling you the man told me the price was £400 odd, and I said "Are you kidding?" Then he said, "Wait a minute, hold on, I have another one", and he said it was £295.'

'You see,' said Mr Stewart, 'we have had both these people, the father and the son, in the witness-box, and they were never asked about this. Did you tell your solicitors this story?'

'What story?'

'About the man telling you it was £400 or something and then telling you it was £295?'

'I'm not sure. Possibly I did. I'm not sure. But that in fact did happen.' And then, thinking that Burgess was Downie, 'You can call the man back in and ask him.'

But Mr Stewart was not to be deflected, and went on hammering away at the same point, emphasising that, as Mr Burgess had not rung Meehan back and Meehan himself had not rung again, Meehan's story about being quoted prices for the two cars was 'a parcel of lies'. Ten minutes later he was still at it.

'Mr Burgess said he never rang you back on the Sunday night?'

'I never said he did.'

'But he said there was no further inquiry about the car?'

'Further to what?'

'Further to the inquiry that had been handed to him by his son?'

Meehan made a last attempt to be understood.

'I phoned his son, and after I phoned his son I phoned again, and whether it was Mr Burgess I spoke to – I can't be sure about that, I spoke to someone – it was a girl who answered the phone first, and a man came on the phone after it.'

A chink of daylight had now appeared, but before it could be opened up, Mr Stewart suddenly shifted his line of questioning.

'Why were you so keen to do all this?'

Because, said Meehan, he wanted to know the price of the car; that is why he had rung the police station to get the name of the garage.

'You rang the police station, didn't you?' said Mr Stewart, 'so that they would remember you ringing?'

'No,' said Meehan, 'that is utter nonsense.'

'Why ring the Police? The Police don't sell cars? ...'

'No, but the police station was adjoining the garage....'

'And you knew that a police station was somewhere where a call would be remembered?'

'No,' said Meehan, shaking his head, 'I'm afraid I can't agree with you there.'

Again it was difficult to see where this questioning was leading. Meehan was not making out that he had been in Stranraer at the time of the robbery and murder, but several hours before it. What did it matter whether he had rung the police station or not?[10]

After this the court rose for the day, and Mr Beltrami, realizing that Meehan must have spoken to someone at Reid

[10] See note on page 273.

and Adams other than Mr Burgess telephoned the garage to find out. He discovered that Mr Downie was the man in question, and that he would be available to travel to Edinburgh next day to give evidence.

In the morning Mr Stewart, having heard about Mr Downie, resumed his line of reasoning of the previous night.

'The whole car business was just a blind to draw attention to yourself, wasn't it?'

'I'm afraid that is not the case.'

'It is not the case? When you had made according to you three long-distance telephone calls to Stranraer, did you think you had drawn attention to yourself sufficiently for your purpose?'

'There was no intent to draw attention to myself, I was making normal inquiries about the car.'

'And you knew that you had no genuine alibi for this murder?'

Exasperated Meehan replied, 'How would I know I had no genuine alibi for murder?'

'Did you not know that on the Sunday?'

A guilty man would surely have answered with a monosyllabic 'No', and left it at that. Meehan said, 'On the Sunday? You mean the Sunday I came back from Stranraer? I didn't even know there'd *been* a murder.'

Mr Stewart asked Meehan what his alibi was between midnight and 3.30 a.m., and he told about being outside the Lochryanhall Hotel with Griffiths; that around 1.30 a.m. a woman [Sheila Prestlie] had come out of the hotel, walked down the road and entered a house nearby; and that around 2 a.m. the lights had gone out, and Griffiths had broken into the van. But who had seen him and Griffiths, asked Mr Stewart, between about 11 p.m. in Stranraer and 3.30 a.m. north of Prestwick, and of course Meehan had to admit nobody.

There was a moment of comedy when Mr Stewart asked Meehan if he had tried to leave some impression on the people in Stranraer that he had spoken to – a suggestion that Meehan denied.

'Did you use bad language to the lavatory attendant?'

'Not that I recall.'

'Did you say, indicating the public house, "I have a good mind to cut his fucking throat. He wouldn't give me a pint of fucking beer"?'

Meehan smiled. 'I don't drink beer,' he said, 'he has got the wrong man.'

'Would it be Griffiths then?'

'Griffiths doesn't drink beer as far as I know.'

Mr Stewart cleverly retrieved the situation.

'What is your drink? Is it whisky?'

'Normally I take whisky, yes.'

'Which you mix with lemonade?'

'American dry ginger.'

'And lemonade when you can't get it, I take it?' said Mr Stewart, thinking of the empty lemonade bottle in Mr Ross's house.

'Well, lemonade,' said Meehan.

'Lemonade and whisky is a drink you take frequently?'

'It is a drink that many people take frequently,' said Meehan.

And he was right. It is a drink which half of Scotland takes.

Surprisingly Mr Stewart seems to have accepted that Meehan could have been at Cairnryan until 1.30 a.m. ('You could have seen everything you needed to see ... by about 1.15 or 1.30?') and it was established that he was at the lay-by north of Prestwick by 3.30 a.m. As Meehan had already said that the car was capable of 110 mph, could it not have done the 45 miles to Ayr in an hour? Meehan agreed it was possible (though on that winding road, in the dark, and with rain falling for part of the journey, it would have been quite incredible). But – though Mr Stewart didn't pursue it – this would have still left only about 45 minutes for Meehan and Griffiths to have broken into the Rosses' house, assault them, rob them and tie them up before leaving to be at the lay-by seven miles away by 3.30; and on Mr Ross's evidence alone it was clear that the raiders had been in the house much longer.

Mr Stewart went on prodding away at Meehan's defence, casting doubt on almost everything he said.

'Your idea in your evidence is to mix up something false with something true, isn't it?'

'That is not my idea at all.'

'Isn't this the whole technique that you have been adopting since that week-end?'

'Sir,' said Meehan, goaded beyond endurance, 'You are constantly calling me a liar.'

'You are a self-confessed liar, aren't you?'

'Yes,' said Meehan, 'I have asked some months ago to be given a truth drug and interrogated under the truth drug.'

Here Lord Grant intervened. 'Can't you tell the truth without having a truth drug?' It was a most cruel and unjust remark; for Meehan's object in offering to take the truth drug in the presence of police officers was not so that he could tell truths he would not have told otherwise, but to give himself a better chance of being believed.

Mr Stewart was now nearly at the end.

'Have you gone in for every possible gimmick in presenting your defence?'

'I have not.'

'You wanted to attract attention to other persons as possible perpetrators of this crime, didn't you?'

'That's not true.'

'Wasn't it?' asked Mr Stewart. Had he not first suggested that the two men in the white Anglia had done it, then that Waddell and an accomplice had done it, even that Andrew Dick had done it.

'I am quite convinced in my mind,' said Meehan '... that Waddell did commit this crime.'

Well, suggested Mr Stewart, had Waddell and his accomplice been using the names Pat and Jim just to frame Meehan, was that it?

'No,' said Meehan, 'not to frame me.'

'Well,' said Mr Stewart, 'is it then just a very unfortunate coincidence that the names of the two criminals were apparently Pat and Jim?'

'It is very unfortunate these two men choose to call each other Pat and Jim.'

'And it is a very unfortunate coincidence that you were near the scene of the crime about the time of the crime?'

'Well, I was there, and I later stated I was in the area.'

'And it is just a very unfortunate coincidence that Jim Griffiths had apparently got into his coat pocket fragments of paper exactly matching paper in the Ross safe?'

'Well, I can't answer for what was in Jim Griffiths' pocket.'

'... Was it a very unfortunate coincidence that you had material on your shoes similar to that from the garage roof on which one of the murderers must have climbed?'

'Well, it was.'

And isn't the most unfortunate coincidence of all that you don't have Griffiths to support your story here today with further corroboration?'

'Yes, that is very unfortunate.'

Mr Stewart was ready for the final thrust. 'Griffiths apparently tried to shoot his way out of his predicament?'

'I believe this,' said Meehan (though not, he might have added, a predicament that had anything to do with the Ayr murder).

'And you are trying to lie your way out of yours?'

'I am not.'

Mr Stewart had done a masterly job with very thin material; and by the time he sat down, there can have been few members of the jury who had doubts about Meehan's guilt.

* * *

Mr Fairbairn did what he could to salvage the position, but he had little to work on. There was no comment Meehan could make about the bits of paper allegedly found in Griffiths' coat pocket, and as Mr Stewart hadn't referred at the close of his cross-examination to the evidence of the voice identification (perhaps not thinking it strong enough?), Mr Fairbairn thought it wiser to abstain too.

However there were one or two telling points he could make.

'Now, if Griffiths was a man who committed the Ayr murder ... he must therefore have known that he ... was wanted?'

'Yes.'

'He had a passport?'

'Yes.'

'But he apparently made no attempt to leave the country?'

'None at all.'

And again:

'... since you didn't commit the Ayr murder you knew that the only two people who saw you between Stranraer and Glasgow were two girls and Griffiths?'

'Yes.'

'So that is why you could say to the Police that you knew nobody could have seen you except these two girls?'

'Yes.'

And even more telling:

'Were you the person who brought the existence of these girls to the knowledge of the Police?'

'I was.'

'So the position is this, is it, that having committed the Ayr murder, you rang the Police in order to oblige them by telling them that you were within seven miles of that house about the time the murder was committed.'

'It is ridiculous,' said Meehan.

And finally:

'Can you imagine using your proper name if you were doing a robbery of this kind?'.

'No, no man doing a robbery like that – you don't commit a crime and leave your calling card.'

'Take the names Ian and Samuel, which are the Christian names of the men who are named in the Impeachment, can you imagine them going in and saying, "Ian, give me a hand with this" – "O.K. Sam."'[11]

'No.'

Mr Fairbairn also elicited from Meehan that his daughter Liz (who by urging him to ring the Police about the men in

[11] The man whom the defence thought then was Waddell's accomplice.

the Anglia had helped to land him where he was) had since had a nervous breakdown, and was now in Leverndale Hospital: and he told the Court that if the doctors allowed it, she would give evidence later in the day.

Mr Downie, the Sales Manager of Reid and Adams, took the stand, and soon demolished Mr Stewart's suggestions to Meehan that his ringing the garage and being quoted a price was 'a parcel of lies' and an attempt to draw attention to himself. Meehan had rung up on Monday July 7th, and there had been a discussion about the 1100, and another car.

But Mr Stewart was still not satisfied that Meehan had not been trying to draw attention on to himself.

'It is somewhat unusual to get someone from Glasgow interested in your cars?'

'Well, yes, to a point.'

The judge tried taking the point further.

'Have you ever before had a telephone call from Glasgow out of the blue like that?'

'Yes, I have.'

'Somebody who has seen a car in your garage?'

'Yes,' said Mr Downie.

Mr Stewart, thinking that Meehan had given his name to Mr Downie, said:

'If people ring up and ask the price of a car, is it of any interest to you at that stage what their name is?'

'Yes,' said Mr Downie.

'And do you ask for their name?' said Mr Stewart.

'Yes,' said Mr Downie. It is a fact, which Mr Stewart may not have known, that car salesmen do ask for potential buyers' names in order to get them hooked.

'Now, did you ask for this man's name?'

'Yes.'

'And he gave it as Meehan?'

'Yes.'

It was a good lead for Mr Fairbairn when he came to re-examine.

'And if it hadn't been for the fact that you asked the man

for his name, you would never have known who telephoned?'

'No.'

* * *

Then came Mrs Harkness and her niece, Miss Pollock, of Spencer's Hotel, Stranraer, who spoke of seeing Meehan and Griffiths having a meal there, and Mr Ambrose Stanyer, proprietor of the Lochryanhall Hotel, who confirmed everything Meehan had said about the time the band stopped playing, the time his sitting-room light went out, the habits of his German shepherd dog, and his having discovered after July 6th that the door lock of his van was broken and the interior light was not working. Mr Stanyer was quite definite that on a Saturday night everyone would be off the premises by 1.30 a.m. though he and the band might discuss the programme for the following week until not later than 2 a.m.; and that during this time his sitting-room light would be on. Furthermore he kept his van in front of the sitting-room window so he could keep an eye on it. By the time he had finished, and his barmaid, Sheila Prestlie, had corroborated Meehan's account of a woman coming out of the hotel and walking down the road to a house 100 yards away, the jury must have been convinced that wherever Meehan and Griffiths had been that night, they were outside the Lochryanhall Hotel until at least 1.30 and possibly until 2 a.m.

And then there came to the witness-box the small but sturdy figure of Betty Meehan, who despite her husband's appalling life of crime, had stuck faithfully by him, in marriage and out, and largely without his help had brought up four children and seen the first three (Garry was still only eight) grow into responsible and self-respecting citizens. After she had taken the oath, she glanced at him sitting in the dock a few feet away, and he gave her a smile of encouragement; yet had she known on that bright April day in 1945 that twenty-four years later she would be in this situation, one wonders if she would still have married him?

She didn't really have much to say. She was shown Mr Moir's suitcase, which the Police had said they found in the flat, and she thought it might have been the one that Griffiths brought his dirty blankets in; she couldn't help identify Paddy's ties as he had dozens; she had put the Chequered Flag money into her own account because then Paddy didn't have one.

But she was quite definite when it came to the important things. On Wednesday July 9th, after the family had heard that Mrs Ross had died,

'... my daughter asked her Dad to phone the Police because she thought that the two chaps that had originally lifted the girls may have been the chaps involved, and Paddy phoned the Regional Squad about four o'clock, and I made him put the telephone down, and it was after I went out and came back I learned my daughter had told him to phone the Police.'

'Well, when you made him put the receiver down ... did you not want him to telephone?'

'Well, I didn't want him to telephone because I knew he would have to say he had been with Jim Griffiths, and I knew the Police had been looking for Jim Griffiths ...'

And this was fully confirmed when a little later that day Liz Meehan, pale and nervous, was brought into court from the Leverndale Hospital.

'On the Sunday my father told me of the two young girls being picked up by boys that were under drugs, and whenever we found out that there had been a murder in Ayr, I said to my father, "Phone up the Police", and my mother said, "Well, you wouldn't expect them to pick up two girls having committed a murder", and I said, "But my Daddy said they were under drugs, so phone the Police".'

'You suggested it first on the Monday evening.'

'Yes, whenever it came out that the old couple had been attacked, and then *I pleaded with him* whenever I found out that the old lady had died.'

Betty was equally definite about Paddy not having any money on the Sunday a week after the murder. On the Saturday night Paddy had asked her if she had any money to buy drinks for a party. She had a £5 note but was saving it for the planned holiday to Germany, so said she hadn't any and with what money he had Paddy bought half a bottle of whisky and a bottle of lemonade.

'So on the Sunday morning he asked me if I had any money, and I said, "No", because I couldn't say I had it on the Sunday if I didn't have it on the Saturday. So when my next-door neighbour came in on the Sunday about 11 o'clock ... I said [to her], "I will borrow £1 for Paddy and you give it to him and let him think you are giving it to him, and when Paddy goes out, I will give you the £1 back." '

And according to the neighbour, Mrs Josie Dobbie, who was the next witness, this is exactly what happened.

'I was in Mrs Meehan's house.'

'What time?'

'In the morning, at 11 o'clock.'

'What happened?'

'Mr Meehan was waiting to go out, he was in the house at the time, and she, Mrs Meehan, said, "There, Josie will give you a loan of £1." '

'And did you give him a loan of £1?'

'Yes.'

'How did you get your £1 back?'

'I got it back off Mrs Meehan.'

Was this the behaviour of a man, the jury asked themselves, who only a week before had stolen hundreds of pounds from Mr Ross's safe? Was he just pretending to his wife and Mrs Dobbie that he was short of cash when he wasn't? Had he involved them both in a conspiracy to lie? Or alternatively, was he short of cash because he had never been to the Rosses' house at all?

The next witness was William Macintyre, whom Mr Fairbairn had called to tell how Andrew Dick had approached him with an invitation from Waddell to join him in a robbery in Ayr. Here Mr Fairbairn was in a difficulty. Ideally he would have liked to get what Dick had said to Macintyre direct from Dick, but although the Police said they had searched for Dick all over the city, he was not to be found.

So Mr Fairbairn had no alternative but to find out from Macintyre what Dick had said, and as soon as he did so, Mr Stewart was on his feet to protest: this was hearsay evidence and therefore not permissible. Mr Fairbairn explained about Dick not being available, and said that in his view it was perfectly competent for a witness to say what somebody said 'in order to prove that it was said, but not to set up the truth of what was said'.

After further objections from the Solicitor-General, Lord Grant said he would allow the question under reservation; and so Macintyre told the court of the details of Dick's proposition, how Macintyre had agreed to it, and bought a car in Ballachulish and blue paint to alter its colour. Then Mr Fairbairn brought Macintyre to his meeting with Waddell in Dick's house.

'What occurred on that occasion?'

'Waddell gave me what we term a run-through on what was to happen —'

Mr Stewart was on his feet again: unlike Dick who couldn't be found, Waddell was outside the court waiting to give evidence, 'and this is obviously a most blatant and deliberate attempt to elicit quite improper and inadmissible hearsay, and I have no hesitation in saying my friend is clearly doing this quite deliberately.'

Mr Fairbairn used the same argument as he had with the evidence regarding Dick, that what Waddell had said to Macintyre was not proof of the truth of what he said, only that he had said it.

'I understand,' said Lord Grant, 'that you have a defence of incrimination under which you say that Waddell committed the crime. You are therefore attempting to prove that Waddell committed it and you are leading evidence, as I understand, or about to lead evidence, from this witness which would tend to show out of Waddell's own mouth that he was at any rate planning the crime . . . and that seems to me wholly improper.'

'If I may make the distinction,' said Mr Fairbairn (and he

had made it several times already), 'I am not trying to prove that what Waddell said was true. I am trying to prove it was true that Waddell said something.'

'In order to establish what?'

'In order to establish that Waddell said something.'

'You are bringing evidence of what Waddell said in order to show that he said it. But in order to establish what?'

'In order to show that he said it.'

This was too much for Lord Grant. 'Mr Fairbairn,' he said, 'would you *please* not be more stupid than you really are' – then thinking he'd gone too far, 'I mean, don't *sound* as if you are more stupid than you are.' And he asked again what fact Mr Fairbairn wished to establish from whatever it was that Waddell said.

Mr Fairbairn gave much the same reply, but after a further ding-dong finally agreed that what Waddell said would tend to establish his special defence of incrimination. Then Lord Grant said he should have called Waddell *before* not *after* Macintyre, as you couldn't discredit in anticipation, and anyway what was Mr Fairbairn's authority? So Mr Fairbairn quoted from Lewis, and Lord Grant said he hadn't heard Lewis referred to for years, and Mr Fairbairn said Mr Stewart would find the passage in Walker. And then, after another immensely long hassle, Lord Grant said that 'under very considerable reservations' he would allow Mr Fairbairn to proceed.

So Macintyre told of how, having heard from Waddell that it was to be a tie-up job on two elderly people, he backed down; how on the night of the robbery he had sat up with Andrew Dick in his house until two or three in the morning to give him an alibi; and how on that same Sunday afternoon Andrew Dick had given him £30 for the bill he owed him, £10 for being so patient waiting for it, and £10 for the alibi; and how, much later, when he'd asked Waddell for a loan of £10, Waddell had said that if he'd been with him on that job, he wouldn't have had need of a £10 loan.

Macintyre stepped down, and presently Mr Fairbairn said, 'Call Ian Waddell.'

He slouched into the court and up the little steps into the witness-box; and, as Lord Grant rose to give him the oath, there was a heightening of interest in court. For a long time people had been wondering whether perhaps it was this man rather than the one in the dock who had committed the crime. Now they would hear Waddell's story from his own lips.

'Before Mr Fairbairn starts asking you any questions,' said Lord Grant, 'I should warn you that you are not bound to answer any question the answer to which might tend to incriminate you. I should also explain that as you are called by the defence, you have no immunity against prosecution in regard to any matters about which you may give evidence in the box if these are matters which might be the subject of a criminal charge.'

Mr Fairbairn rose. 'What is your full name?'

'Ian Waddell,' whispered Waddell.

'Speak up,' said Mr Fairbairn, 'so that the jury can hear what you have to say.'

'Ian Waddell' – this time a little louder.

'What is your address?'

'Care of Barlinnie Prison, Glasgow.'

'Would you care to read to the jury the words which I asked you to read before?' He handed Waddell a piece of paper.

'Shut up, shut up, we'll send for an ambulance.'

'Have you ever said these words before, apart from in this court?'

For Waddell this was the crunch. If he admitted to that, then in less than no time Meehan would be out of the dock and he would be in it.

'I refuse to answer that,' he said.

Why, thought the jury? Why should an innocent man refuse to answer it?

'Well, tell me this. Have you ever heard anyone else say those words before I asked you to read them in court?'

'No.' And this was true enough; for it was he, and not McGuinness who had said them.

'You refuse to say whether you have ever used them

before, do you?'

'Yes.'

'Well,' said Lord Grant, 'we must leave it there, Mr Fairbairn, no persuasion is allowed.'

Mr Fairbairn asked Waddell about his movements before and after the crime, and his replies were so nervous and hesitant that at one moment Mr Fairbairn had to complain, 'I don't know whether we can hear this evidence.'

Waddell said that he had been living with Andrew Dick before he went to London and after he came back.

'How long had you lived with Andrew Dick?'

'On and off for about three months.'

'... When did you go and live with him?'

'The end of April.'

'Who did you live with before the end of April?'

'I refuse to answer that.' Why, thought the jury again – unless the man he was then living with was his accomplice in murder?

'I see. Who were you living with in February?'

'I refuse to answer that,' whispered Waddell, so faintly that Lord Grant, only a few feet away, could not hear.

'I am sorry, would you speak up, I didn't hear that.'

'I refuse to answer those questions.'

Next Mr Fairbairn turned to Waddell's relations with Carmichael, his alibi for the night of the murder. Carmichael, it will be recalled, had said that Waddell had unexpectedly turned up 'about midnight' (i.e. two hours after the pubs had shut) with a carry-out of wine and whisky. He had 'had a drink ... been arguing with whoever he was staying with ... and he didn't want to go home and he was drunk'. He had said that Waddell had stayed with him once before when drunk and after a row with the person he was staying with, but apart from that he had met him only two or three times since December 1968. He had passed him occasionally in the Gallowgate but not spoken to him. He was a friend, he said, but he didn't want to associate with him.

Now Waddell told a completely contradictory story.

'Have you ever stayed with Carmichael before?'

'Now and again, yes.'
'How often have you stayed with him?'
'Three times, four times.'
'Three or four times – and for what reason have you stayed with him for three or four times?'
'Because I was drunk.'
'Now, tell me this. Why, when you are drunk, do you go to stay with Carmichael instead of staying with Dick?'
'Why?'
'Yes.'
'No particular reason.'
Waddell said that before going to Carmichael's on the evening of July 5th, he had been in the Club Bar in the Gallowgate.
'The Club Bar is just near to Andrew Dick's house, is it not?'
'Yes.'
'Why didn't you go home?'
The true answer would have been, 'Because I wasn't in Glasgow that night, I was in Ayr.' He said, weakly, 'I don't know.'
'Carmichael's house is a mile or a mile and a half away from the Club Bar, is it not?'
'Yes.'
'What reason did you give to Carmichael for going to his house?'
'No reason, just went for a drink.'
'But you arrived according to you at half past eleven that night at this man's house. Did you ever suggest that you had a row with the person you lived with and that is why you were coming?'
'No.'
'Did you ever suggest in February you had had a row with the person you had lived with, and that is why you were coming?'
'No.'
'Is it true to say that you have only ever been in his house in February once and on this night?'
'No.'

'Is it true to say you had never drunk with him in a pub?'
'No.'
'How often do you think you drank with him?'
'Twice a week.'
'And about twice a week over what period?'
'Five, six months.'
'Up until July?'
'Yes.'

That meant that Waddell had drunk with Carmichael at least forty times since the beginning of the year. Yet Carmichael had denied having seen him at all.

'... You must have been quite a good friend of Carmichael's, were you?'
'Yes.'
'If you saw him in the street, what would you do?'
'Speak to him.'
'Did you ever just walk past him?'
'No.'
'Did he ever just walk past you?'
'No.'

Clearly either Waddell or Carmichael was telling fibs, perhaps both. It looked as though Carmichael was pretending that he hardly ever saw Waddell because, as his alibi, he didn't want to be tainted with his guilt. And it looked as though Waddell was pretending to know Carmichael better than he did to make the jury believe his extraordinary story of walking while drunk at midnight, with a parcel of whisky and wine, a mile and a half to visit him.

Now Mr Fairbairn came to the crucial matter of Waddell being wanted for interview by the police, of being taken by Mr Skivington, manager of the Club Bar, to see the solicitor Mr Carlin, and giving Mr Carlin £200 in notes to act for him. It must have been about this time that Waddell realised that replying 'I refuse to answer that' itself sounded incriminating, and the safest thing would be to lie.

'Had you seen Mr Carlin before you went to the police office?'
'Yes.'
'Who did you go accompanied by?'

'Skivington.'

'Did Skivington give anything to Mr Carlin on that occasion?'

'I don't know.'

It seemed an odd reply.

'Think carefully.'

'I have thought carefully. I don't know. I left the office.'

'Is it not the case that you gave Mr Carlin the solicitor £200?'

'No.'

'That is a lie ...' Mr Fairbairn started to reply when the judge intervened to say that dealings between a client and his solicitor were privileged. Mr Fairbairn said that he would be calling Mr Carlin for the defence, but Lord Grant said that only the client could waive the rule, not the solicitor.

'Are you willing,' said Mr Fairbairn to Waddell, 'that Mr Carlin should tell us whether or not you gave him any money on that occasion?'

Waddell knew that if he said he wasn't willing, then it would be obvious that he had given Carlin money. Furthermore there might be questions as to how and where he had got the £200. Much better to lie in his teeth, no matter what Carlin said.

'Your evidence is that no money passed from you to Mr Carlin on the occasion when you went to him and asked him to accompany you to the police office when you were to be asked about your whereabouts on the 5th–6th July?'

'Yes.'

'I suggest to you on that occasion – your Lordship must rule on this question – you gave him a substantial sum of money in £5 notes?'

Lord Grant explained to Waddell that as dealings with solicitors were private, he could refuse to answer the question if he wished.

But Waddell had now committed himself to lying and there was nothing for it but to go on.

'I will answer it,' he said stoutly, 'I never gave him any money.'

Next Mr Fairbairn turned to Macintyre's evidence of Andrew Dick approaching him from Waddell with a proposal; and Waddell answered mostly in the monosyllables so commonly favoured by the guilty.

'Have you ever asked Andrew Dick to approach William Macintyre for any purpose?'

'No.'

'Didn't you ask Andrew Dick to see whether William Macintyre would assist you in carrying out a robbery in Ayrshire?'

'No.'

'Didn't you meet Macintyre in Dick's house in early June?'

'No.'

'Have you ever seen Macintyre in Dick's house?'

'No.'

'Never?'

'No.'

'Didn't you say that you would describe to him a job which you wanted him to take part in Ayrshire?'

'No.'

'A tie-up job?'

'No.'

'Didn't Macintyre refuse to do it after he heard the details?'

'He didn't refuse to do it, no.'

It was the same when Mr Fairbairn turned to McCafferty, the untried prisoner in Barlinnie whose letter to Mr Beltrami had also provided evidence for the Special Defence of Incrimination.

'Do you know an untried prisoner in Barlinnie called McCafferty?'

'Yes.'

'Have you ever spoken to him?'

'In prison?'

'Yes.'

'No.'

'Never.'

'No.'

'Did you not on Friday the 10th of October in the exercise yard at the back of C Hall, Barlinnie Prison, about 2.30 o'clock have a conversation with McCafferty?'

'No.'

'And was not that a conversation about what sentence you and he might get? Are you untried at the moment?'

'Yes.'

'What are you awaiting trial for?'

'Housebreaking.'

'And didn't you say to him that you had done the Ayr murder?'

'No.'

'Didn't he ask you how you'd like to be in prison for something you hadn't done, like Meehan?'

'No.'

'And didn't you say you'd done it?'

'No.'

'And didn't you say that you didn't like to see Meehan in there any more than he did?'

'No.'

'But what could you do?'

'No.'

'And didn't you say it was not your fault if a man was wrongly convicted, it was the Police's fault.'

'No.'

'Didn't he ask you how you could leave old people tied up all the time, and never think of getting assistance to them?'

'No.'

'And didn't you say that [your accomplice] had phoned, but he only told the operator?'

'No.'

'You are lying, aren't you?'

'No.'

Mr Stewart's cross-examination was very simple – to take Waddell through all his past offences – theft, larceny, housebreaking, opening lockfast places – nine convictions in all – and then to say,

'You have no violence whatsoever in your record?'

'No.'

'No robbery?'

'No.'

Mr Stewart sat down. He had been very effective. It was unfortunate that the jury were not in a position to know that Meehan, a self-admitted criminal, had no record of violence or robbery either.

Then came Robert McCafferty to tell of the conversation he had had with Waddell in Barlinnie. He was very nervous and shook like a leaf throughout his evidence, and when Mr Stewart suggested it was a funny thing that this conversation had taken place on the very afternoon of the day that Meehan had pleaded at Ayr his special defence of incrimination against Waddell, he shook even more. But he stuck to his story: Waddell had confessed to him that he had committed the murder.

The last major witness was William Carlin, the solicitor to whom Waddell had denied giving £200 in cash to act for him. When he had taken the oath, Lord Grant told him that his position, unlike Waddell's, was not privileged, and he was bound to answer the questions that Mr Fairbairn put to him. Unlike his client too, his answers were clear, firm, and when necessary elaborate.

'In the course of your professional practice did a man Ian Waddell come to you in July of this year?'

'That is so, yes.'

'In what connection did he call?'

'Well, he was brought to my office by another client of mine [Skivington] who introduced him, and told me that he had received information that the Glasgow Criminal Investigation Department wished to question him. That is all he said.'

'Did he tell you about why they wished to question him?'

'I asked him if he knew why the CID in Glasgow wanted to see him, but he said he didn't know.'

'He said he didn't know?'

'He said he didn't know the reason for it, and I then pressed him further and asked him if he had any idea at all what it might be, and he did say that it had been told to him that it could well be in connection with a robbery which had taken place recently in the town of Ayr.'

Mr Carlin said he had rung Mr Macalister at Glasgow CID at Waddell's request, and told him 'that I had in my office a man whom he might wish to see regarding a serious crime, and that this man was prepared to come to the CID to give any statement or any assistance to the Police that they wished to have'. Later he had accompanied Waddell to the police station where Waddell had undergone a 'very lengthy interrogation'.

Mr Fairbairn came to the heart of the matter. On the occasion of Waddell and Skivington visiting him, did Waddell give him any money?

'He did.'

'Did Waddell as opposed to Skivington give you any money?'

'Yes, it was Waddell who gave me money.'

'... It wasn't Skivington who produced the money?'

'No.'

'Or Skivington who said the money was to be produced?'

'Well, I remember – Waddell certainly produced the money from his pocket, but I remember Mr Skivington saying to him, "If Mr Carlin is going to act for you then you had better give him a fee", and he then produced this money.'

'... And what did he give you?'

'He gave me £200 as a fee.'

'And in what form was the £200?'

'In £20 notes.'

'And were these new £20 notes?'

'Yes.'

'And did this surprise you?'

'Yes, to a certain extent it did surprise me. I didn't ask for a fee, no question had been raised at that time, but he did say to me that he wanted me to act in his defence if he was charged with the particular serious crime ...'

'... he wanted you to act for him if he was charged with the crime?'

'Yes.'

'Well, did he tell you whether or not he had anything to do with it?'

'He said he knew nothing at all about it.'

'But he seemed to think there was sufficient risk of his being charged on the Thursday of the week it was committed, to give you a fee of £200 to act for him if he was charged?'

He thought there might be a possibility that he might be charged with this offence.'

At the end of his examination Mr Fairbairn said:

'Do you think that a client would be likely to forget having given his solicitor a sum of £200 on such an occasion?'

'Well,' said Mr Carlin, 'I wouldn't think so.'[12]

In cross-examination Mr Stewart tried to explain away the Police interest in Waddell – inferring that even if he weren't guilty of the major crime, he might perhaps be guilty of a minor one – that while his alibi at Carmichael's might be true, yet he could still have had knowledge that such a crime was planned. Mr Carlin agreed. It seemed, on Mr Stewart's part, a surprisingly large concession.

Having also got Mr Carlin to agree that Waddell's account to the Police 'was apparently checked and found satisfactory', Mr Stewart sat down, and Waddell was taken out. He had left the jury with some disturbing questions. Why, if Waddell was innocent, had he been so eager for Mr Carlin's services? Why, without being asked, had he given him £200 in new notes? Where would a man like Waddell *get* £200 in new notes? And why had Waddell lied about giving Carlin the £200 unless he felt the action self-incriminating?

At this moment Meehan's chances looked good.

Lastly there came a succession of minor witnesses: first

[12] Much later Mr Carlin asked Waddell why he had lied about giving him the money when he knew that his evidence would be contradicted and might lead (as it subsequently did) to a charge of perjury. Waddell replied that he preferred a perjury charge to a murder charge.

Mrs Mary Meldrum of Lewis's Department Store who testified that when Meehan worked there, he was selling roofing material with a gravelly surface, for garages and outhouses (and the inference was that these stones had got into the heel of one of his shoes). Then came Thomas Bell, one of the men who had picked up the two girls. He had originally been called by the Crown, but after his cousin William Mackie had given evidence about the visibility favourable to the defence, the Crown had dropped him, and he had become a defence witness instead. He testified, as his cousin had done, that it was dark when they let Irene Burns out, dark when Meehan and Griffiths caught up with them on the outskirts of Kilmarnock, and getting light when they got home. And then, with a dying fall, came various Ayr locals (among them Mr Falconer and Mrs Mathieson) to tell of suspicious characters they had seen or thought they had seen in the vicinity of Blackburn Place before the crime was committed.

And that was the end of the defence evidence. It was unfortunate for Meehan that despite strenuous efforts, neither Dick nor Skivington could be found, and that Mrs Carmichael's soul and conscience certificate prevented her from corroborating or contradicting her husband's evidence of being Waddell's alibi.

* * *

That evening, after the court rose, Mr Fairbairn travelled to the Glasgow University Union to take part in Lord McLeod's Rectorial Debate. Another of the speakers was the author of this book. In the train that took them back to Edinburgh together, Mr Fairbairn said, 'Tomorrow I have to make my closing speech in defence of a man who is being tried for murder, and who I know is innocent.'

* * *

On the morning of Friday October 24th, Mr Ewan Stewart rose to make his closing speech. He stressed all the points that indicated Meehan's guilt, Pat and Jim, the bloodstains in Meehan's trousers, the tarry stones found in the heel of his shoe, the whisky and lemonade, the bits of paper in the safe. Then he moved to after the weekend. Why was it that Griffiths and Meehan seemed anxious to tell people about picking up the girls? Why too had Griffiths mentioned to Irene about staying outside a hotel until 2 a.m. or for two hours? It wasn't as though he had told her much else.

Of the defence's contention that it was not likely that two murderers would pick up someone so soon after the crime, he had this to say. 'The accused is cunning as well as crooked. He knew he was identifiable all over Stranraer. A child of five would know his route to Glasgow from Stranraer. He obviously didn't know the girl would be there, but why not stop and turn the incident to advantage, so it could be said they behaved unsuspiciously?' *Would* the jury believe anything so far-fetched?

The defences of Alibi and Incrimination, he suggested, were not defences, but diversions of the jury's attention. Referring to McCafferty he said, 'Who does Mr Fairbairn produce as his star witness, but a man wanted on a charge of Intimidation of Witnesses?'[13] And of both McCafferty and Macintyre he said, 'If enough witnesses pass through the witness-box, of however degraded a character, then you'll begin to think they've proved something. In fact they've proved nothing.' And wasn't it significant that McCafferty's story of Waddell's admission of guilt had taken place on the very same day as Meehan had named Waddell in his special defence of Incrimination?

The important points for the jury to remember, concluded Mr Stewart, were fourfold. Pat and Jim; the voice identification by Mr Ross; the bits of paper in the safe and Griffiths' car-coat; and the destruction of Mr Moir's car. Mr Stewart could not know that the first was pure coincidence; the second was untrue; the third was untrue; and the fourth, though true and damning, was to avoid charges of having stolen a car, not of having committed a murder at Ayr.

Then it was Mr Fairbairn's turn, and he concentrated

[13] McCafferty was subsequently tried on this charge and acquitted.

first on the Identification parade. 'From that moment onwards,' he said, 'all the vast forces of the CID tried to place the crime at the feet of Pat Meehan.' Yet what did the Identification parade amount to? Mr Ross had been unable to identify by build or size; he had just lost his wife by murder and himself been savagely assaulted; the six words he had heard Meehan say would be very emotive to him at the time. 'If Waddell had been number one in the parade,' said Mr Fairbairn, 'would Mr Ross have made the same identification as he had with Meehan in the same emotive circumstances?' It was as good an explanation as any at the time and may have impressed the jury; yet Mr Fairbairn did not know, any more than Mr Stewart, that Mr Ross had not 'identified' Meehan's voice just because the words were emotive to him, but because, from the conversation between Irene and Isobel, he had a fair idea of what the police suspect looked like.[14]

Mr Fairbairn made another good point when he referred to the shoot-out that had resulted in Griffiths' death. If Griffiths was a man who carried arms and had not hesitated to use them, would he not have taken a gun with him to the robbery in Ayr? Why go in for so much physical violence when the threat of a gun would have done the trick instead?

But it was the two points about the visibility and the voices that Mr Fairbairn stressed most. Three of the four witnesses who had been at Kilmarnock between 3.30 a.m. and 4 a.m. had emphasised that it was then dark, and yet Mr Ross had testified that only five or ten minutes after they had gone, it was 'quite full daylight'. How was that conceivably possible? As to the voices, 'the Crown rely on the voices, and it is from the voices that the whole accusation against Meehan begins'. They had been told that both the voices Mr Ross had heard were not only Scottish but Glaswegian. Yet they also had been told that Griffiths had an unmistakably English accent. Therefore it was im-

[14] It would be interesting to know how Mr Ross would have reacted if Meehan had been last on the parade, and said the words after six others.

possible that on the night of the murder Meehan and Griffiths had been in Blackburn Place.

* * *

During the lunch break there was much discussion of the case, in nearby pubs and in the courtroom corridors. Leaving aside Meehan's guilt or innocence, the general view, expressed by several people on either side was that the Crown's evidence was not strong enough to convict. But they had not reckoned with Lord Grant's charge to the jury.

* * *

Lord Grant's opening remarks concerned Griffiths' final hours, and death. Personally he didn't think the jury were very much concerned with that, though it was a matter entirely for them. However if they had read about it – and few people had not – would they forget it except where evidence about it was relevant to the charges they had to try? (This was perhaps rather easier said than done.)

If Griffiths had been alive, said Lord Grant, it would have been only under the most exceptional circumstances that his criminal record would have emerged in court. Yet had he survived to stand trial alongside Meehan, and gone into the witness-box, he would have been cross-examined on any evidence he gave. 'We have had evidence as to certain things he said, and so far as you rely on that evidence, will you remember that evidence as to what a dead man said, not being subject to cross-examination, must be looked at with considerable care and on the basis that there has been no cross-examination of it. I do not think there is much practical problem arising out of that because, as I understand, there is little dispute that the witnesses who gave evidence as to what Griffiths said were in fact telling the truth.' As Meehan was later to write in the margin of the trial transcript, was this meant to include Irene Cameron's evidence that Griffiths had told her that on the night of July 5th–6th he was sitting outside a hotel for two hours, or until 2 a.m.?

Next Lord Grant told the jury that basically all the evidence in the case, apart from Mr Ross's voice identification, was circumstantial. Circumstantial evidence could be very strong and sometimes was preferable to direct evidence, but they had to look at it as a whole. 'Do not take each individual item and consider it in isolation. It is easy enough to take each item singly and knock it down like a ninepin; that is a naturally common defence tactic, and a perfectly legitimate one. You must however look at the *cumulative* effect of the evidence....' Later when the jury retired to consider their verdict, they would remember these words.

Lord Grant dealt with presumption of innocence, burden of proof, reasonable doubt ('it means something more than mere balance of probability') and the need for corroboration of evidence. Emphasising that Meehan was charged while acting with James Griffiths, he said that when two men went out on a criminal enterprise together the law was that both were equally responsible. 'If two men go out together in a motor-car hired by the one man for the purpose of stealing another motor-car, and the driver of that motor-car drives his friend to a place where a motor-car is available, and in furtherance of that purpose the other man steals that car, then you would be entitled to hold them both guilty ...' He thought it clearly established that Griffiths was guilty of Charge 1, stealing Mr Moir's car. The jury would have to decide if on that charge Meehan was guilty also.

The same argument applied to Charge 2. It was not disputed that Meehan and Griffiths were together that night from the time of leaving Stranraer until reaching Glasgow early next morning. 'So if there is evidence which you accept and which tends to show that Griffiths was in the Rosses' house at the time of the crime – and of course there is no suggestion that he was there at any other time than the early hours of the 5th–6th July – that would be evidence which would be equally valuable for your consideration in assessing the guilt or innocence of the accused. I am thinking in particular of the pieces of brown paper and white paper which the Crown suggest link up Griffiths with the

Rosses' house ...' It was a powerful point, and the Police, when they produced the paper as evidence, intended it to be: judge and jury had no means of knowing its history.

Next, Lord Grant dealt with Meehan's two Special Defences. As regards the one of Incrimination he said, 'I propose to direct you that this Defence has not been established – indeed there is not even remotely sufficient evidence to establish it – and that you would not be entitled to hold it established.' What Lord Grant meant was that on a balance of probabilities the Defence had not even remotely made out a case that Waddell had been one of the perpetrators of the crime, and on the evidence this was true enough. Yet for those jurymen worried by Waddell's assertions of guilt and otherwise fishy behaviour, Lord Grant said that evidence in relation to the Special Defence of Incrimination still remained for consideration as other evidence in the case. In other words the jury were entitled to take this evidence into account when deciding on the guilt or innocence of Meehan.

Lord Grant then turned to the Special Defence of Alibi, and as what he said about it is open to criticism, it is here given in full:

> 'As regards the abili, it is very difficult to consider that in isolation. It is very much tied up with the whole evidence in the case about the Second Charge. In essence it comes to this, that the Accused did not leave Cairnryan until 1.45 or 2, that he picked up the girls seven miles north of Ayr around 3.30 a.m., and was home about 4.30. From Cairnryan to Blackburn Road on Production 24 I make about 45 miles. The police going at a sort of family Sunday afternoon speed took about an hour and fifteen minutes to do that, and I think one of the officers said if he had been in a hurry he would have done that, plus the journey from Stranraer to Cairnryan in about an hour[15] – I think that was what he said. If, as Mr Meehan

[15] For the police or anyone else to have motored the 52 miles from Stranraer to Blackburn Road in 60 minutes would have been a total impossibility, and is a remark that could only have been made by someone who had not attempted it.

says, the Triumph car was capable of speeds of 110 miles an hour it would seem that in the early hours of the morning, when traffic is presumably little, anybody driving a Triumph 2000 from Cairnryan to Blackburn Road, Ayr, could have done it in very substantially under an hour and fifteen minutes. So even leaving at 1.45 – and there is not very much evidence that it was even as late as that that he left apart from one or two things he said himself[16] – although, of course, if you accept what he said that is enough – even leaving at 1.45 I would work out that travelling reasonably fast he could have had half an hour or more at the Rosses' house and been at the Underwood Road lay-by at 3.30 or thereby. I should say this, that up to a certain point and up to a certain time it is quite right to say that Meehan derives some corrobation from the proprietor of the Lochryanhall Hotel, and you will keep that in mind. But as far as I can make out – although this is just a matter for you again – from 1.45 until 3.30 the alibi depends entirely on Meehan's evidence. As I have said, however, if you accept his evidence or if it raises a reasonable doubt in your minds that is the end of the case against him.'

It was all very well for Lord Grant to tell the jury to acquit Meehan if they had a reasonable doubt about his ability to break into the Rosses' house and commit the crime in the time available, but what was the judge asking the jury to consider?

> 'I would work out that travelling reasonably fast he could have had *half an hour or more* at the Rosses' house and been at the Underwood lay-by at 3.30 or thereby.'

There are a number of points to be made here. First, if Meehan and Griffiths were to have 'half an hour' in the Rosses' house, that would leave a total of one hour and a quarter for them to get from Cairnryan to the lay-by, a distance of 52 miles. From Blackburn Place to the lay-by is a

[16] Meehan's evidence was that he and Griffiths had left Cairnryan 'at 2 a.m., or just after'.

distance of seven miles, four of which are in a built-up area. Allow, say, eleven or twelve minutes for them to travel this distance, that left just over one hour for them to cover the 45 miles between Cairnryran and Blackburn Place. Although the road from Cairnryan to Ayr is in many places extremely twisty, with S bends, double white lines, and varying gradients, although it was night and raining, it would have been *just* possible for Meehan and Griffiths to cover the journey in the time, but only if they had driven flat out from start to finish – and then rushed breathless into 2 Blackburn Place for half an hour's assault and robbery before arriving fresh as daisies at the lay-by to pick up Irene Burns ten minutes later.

Now quite apart from evidence by Mr Ross and others that tended to show that the two intruders had prepared the ground beforehand and were in no hurry, there was one vital piece of evidence which, if true, showed that Meehan and Griffiths could not have travelled from Cairnryan to Ayr in the time the judge suggested. This was Meehan's evidence that when they got to Ballantrae,

> '... Griffiths slowed down and said, "I am going to look at that Jaguar", and I didn't see the Jaguar, and he turned the car round and drove back, drove down a side-street on the right-hand side and parked the car, and left me in the car actually ... I got out the car but he went on his own and I was parked next to a funeral directors or undertakers – it was more like a works shed with the words "Funeral Directors" written on it.'
>
> 'How long do you think you stopped in Ballantrae?'
>
> 'Oh, ten minutes.'

Now this description by Meehan was in all respects accurate. There is a side turn to the right in the middle of Ballantrae, there is a small wooden building that looks like a works shed some 150 yards down it, and written above the doors of the shed in not very large lettering are the words, 'Funeral Directors'. Lord Grant did not put any of this evidence before the jury, either to accept or reject. It was surely a grave omission. For had the jury accepted it (and they well might have done) they would have been forced to conclude either that Meehan and Griffiths had travelled from Cairnryan to Ayr in under 55 minutes which is impossible, or that the break-in and robbery had taken them only twenty minutes, which was absurd.

Indeed Lord Grant's time of half an hour was equally absurd. We know, from information supplied by Waddell after the trial, that he and McGuinness were in the Rosses' house or its vicinity for much of the night. We know from what Superintendent Struthers told the press on July 8th (but unfortunately was not asked about at the trial) that the intruders were in the house 'several hours'. Yet even on the evidence given at the trial, the intruders must have been there much longer than half an hour. Consider what they had to do: park the car at a safe distance from the house, then walk back to it; make sure, by looking through the windows that the Rosses were asleep; go to the back of the house and cut the clothes line for use later in the tie-up; go to the garage, fetch a pair of step-ladders and carry them to the side of the garage of 2 Blackburn Road where it forms the boundary wall; climb on to the garage roof; from there climb up the telephone pole in the corner of 4 Blackburn Place (no easy task, for the pole is two or three feet away from the garage, and the first rung in it is well above the head of anyone standing on the garage roof); cut the wires, return to the ground, re-enter the Ross garage and steal a weeding tool and iron bar for breaking in; creep round to the front of the house, force open the front bedroom window very quietly so as not to disturb neighbours, and climb in; tiptoe down the corridor to the Rosses' bedroom, burst open the door and jump on them; assault them and tie then up; hit Mr Ross and go on hitting him until he had given up the keys of the safe; open the safe and take out everything in it; search the bedroom drawers and all Mr Ross's clothes; search and ransack drawers and cupboards in every other room in the house (even, though this was not given in evidence, removing the side panel of the bath to see if anything was concealed there); help themselves to whisky and lemonade in the sitting-room, take it to the kitchen and drink it; tie Mr Ross's feet to his hands; throw bloodstained gloves into the next-door garden; take off masks and put on shoes, leave the house and go back to the car. All this in half an hour, followed by picking up a girl at a lay-by eleven or twelve minutes later! The idea was pure fantasy, but it was a fantasy the jury were not invited to consider.

After pointing out to the jury that, although Meehan had protested his innocence vigorously all along, his statements about his whereabouts *before* his arrest differed from his evidence in the box, Lord Grant turned to 'one matter which has bulked largely in the case', which was the time the intruders left the Rosses' house. First he said this:

> 'Mr Ross's evidence was that it was dark when the robbers entered and, to the best of his recollection, at some stage they put on a light. He does not recollect how long they were in the house, and I think probably, in the condition he was, he would have had some difficulty in assessing accurately the length of time between any one particular event and another, but that is a matter entirely for you. I do not think he really heard the intruders leave. I think he said that things got quiet and he assumed they had left, and then about five or ten minutes later he looked round and it was full daylight. Whether Mr Ross is accurate in his five or ten minutes may be a matter of some importance, and you will keep in mind what Mr Fairbairn said so forcibly about it. That is because of the evidence which there is about the state of visibility round 3.30 and 4 o'clock when it is clear that the Accused was some miles north of Ayr and was going on from the Underwood lay-by to Kilmarnock.'

Then he went on to the evidence about the visibility, and again because what he said is open to criticism, it is given in full.

> 'Now, we have had various references to the state of

visibility, and I am by no means certain that they all fit in together. I would only add two references, one is of Allan, who was the Meteorological man at Prestwick. I mention him because he was engaged in looking at the weather, so he was the only man really that morning whose attention was directed to whether it was light or dark or wet or dry. What he said was – he is asked about the night of the 5th–6th when he was on duty at the control tower from 10 till 5.30, and he is asked, "Was it ever completely dark?" and he said "It depends what you mean by completely dark. The darkest time is about one o'clock and it gradually becomes lighter after that." Q – Did it gradually become lighter after 1 a.m.? A – "Roundabout that time, yes." Then he is asked about the period between 3.30 and 4 a.m., and Brown Carrick Hill and says "By four o'clock we could see Brown Carrick", and that was eight odd miles away. Then he is asked, "When did full daylight come?" and he queries, he is not very sure what full daylight is – and I don't think any of us are – and eventually he says "By four o'clock, four or half past, it is as light as it will get before the sun actually comes up."

'One further passage: Irene Burns who is speaking of the time when the Accused's car overtook the white car, which would have been round about 4 o'clock – no, before 4 it would have been, and she said, I think, it was quite light by then. Anyway you will consider to what extent you accept as what I might call gospel, the five to ten minutes evidence of Mr Ross and sort out as best you can the evidence about what is daylight and when was daylight and so on, because it does have a bearing, and, as Mr Fairbairn said, an important bearing upon the ultimate decision in this case.'

Now there are three points to be made here. The first is that when the weatherman, Mr Allan, was talking about the visibility during the night, and it gradually becoming lighter after 1 a.m., he was not talking about darkness and light, but about *varying degrees of dark*. Lord Grant seems to have thought it significant that he should have been able to see Brown Carrick Hill, eight miles away, between 3.30 and 4 a.m. But as any sailor can testify, it is possible on even a dark night, when one's eyes, like Mr Allan's, have got used to the visibility, to see land and particularly hilly land several miles away.

The second point concerns Lord Grant's reference to Irene Burns' remark about the visibility when they overtook the Anglia at Kilmarnock '... which would have been round about 4 o'clock – no, before four it would have been, and she said, I think, it was quite light by then.' It is clear from reading the transcript that Lord Grant was purporting to quote Irene Burns as having said, 'It was quite light by then.' But in fact she had said something rather different, which was, 'I think it was quite light by then because I noticed the colour [of the Anglia].' Earlier she had confirmed that the Anglia had its red rear-lights on when the Triumph overtook it, and that the Triumph itself had been flashing its lights. Furthermore one of the boys, Mr Mackie, had said that it was not daylight that enabled him to spot the Triumph coming up behind *but the street lights of Kilmarnock.*

What makes Lord Grant's misleading interpretation of Irene Burns' remark so much worse is that three of the other witnesses present testified that when the Triumph overtook the Anglia in Kilmarnock, it was (apart from the street lights) still dark. Meehan himself said it was 'quite dark', Bell said it was 'dark' and Mackie said 'it was still very dark'. Mackie also said that both cars had headlights on and added, *'It wouldn't be pitch dark, but it wasn't much better than being pitch dark.'*

Why then did the judge not put before the jury this contradictory evidence? Had he done so, they might well have concluded that it would have been impossible for Meehan and Griffiths to have left the Rosses' house five or ten minutes before full daylight, and yet be twelve miles away on the edge of Kilmarnock when it was still dark.

Lord Grant turned to Mr Ross's evidence regarding the voices of the two intruders, and the use of the names Pat and Jim.

'Whether the intruders were cunningly using assumed names even in the heat of the moment – for it would appear that Jim was rather heated when he asked for Pat's assistance to get Mr Ross off him – or whether this was spontaneous, is a matter for your consideration.' In other words, had the intruders been other than Meehan or Griffiths, would the one who had called out 'Get this cunt off me, Pat' while struggling with Mr Ross, have remembered in the heat of the moment to use his colleague's assumed name? But, as Meehan points out in his comments on the trial, using the same argument, would Griffiths, if he was the man struggling with Mr Ross, have been clever enough in the heat of the moment to have put on a Glasgow accent?

The fact that Mr Ross was emphatic that both men had Glasgow accents was one of the Defence's strongest cards. But Lord Grant dismissed it in a few words:

> 'As regards the evidence by Mr Ross that both assailants had Glasgow accents there is, of course, the difficulty that Jim Griffiths undoubtedly had an English voice. Well, there again, you heard the argument pro and con from the Solicitor-General and Mr Fairbairn on this matter, the possible explanations and so on, and you will consider that matter as part of the whole evidence in the case and give it what weight you think fit.'

There remained the three strongest points of the Crown's evidence, Mr Ross picking out Meehan at the Identification parade, the bits of paper in the safe and Griffiths' car-coat pocket, and the dumping of the car. First the Identification parade.

> 'You heard the evidence of Ross's reaction, how he was visibly shaken as soon as the accused repeated those words, which must ten days after the incident have been deeply imprinted in his memory. That emotion and the staggering came, not when Ross himself used the words

to the policeman or the policeman used them to Meehan, but when Meehan himself spoke them, and here again one has this coincidence that the only man in the parade who was called Pat was the man whose voice Ross identified.'

Well not even Lord Grant, far less the jury, knew of the irregular way in which the Identification parade had been conducted, and that because Mr Ross was in a position to know what the Police suspect looked like, the coincidence of his picking out the only Pat in the parade was no coincidence at all.

Second the bits of paper, found in Griffiths' car-coat pocket.

> 'Mr Fairbairn said that on the evidence Griffiths was not wearing that coat at Stranraer and I think that may well be so. But it is a motoring coat and the fact that he was not wearing it at Stranraer does not mean necessarily that he was not wearing it when he was driving his car that night. It is true that the papers in question are nothing out of the ordinary. But there is the Police evidence first of all of brown and white paper being found in the drawers of the safe which had been burgled, and scientific evidence that the pieces in Griffiths' pocket were identical in all respects with the pieces of paper which were in the safe which had contained most of the stolen money.'

Despite the fact that Mr Ross didn't think he had any paper in the safe, and despite also the fact that Detective Superintendent Cowie and Detective Inspector Cook had found nothing in it on July 7th/8th, let us assume for a moment that what the Crown was suggesting and what Lord Grant was inviting the jury to consider was true. We know that the intruder called Jim was not wearing a car-coat but what Mr Ross described as 'a sort of all black nylon outfit'. If therefore the intruder was Griffiths, it would mean that in robbing the safe, he had taken time to tear off a little piece (the size of a shirt button) from some white paper lying in one drawer of the safe and put it in his pocket and then taken further time to tear off a piece from some brown paper lying in another drawer of the safe and put that in his pocket, and then at a later stage, and for some reasons best known to himself, carefully transferred both bits of paper to one of the pockets of his car-coat. The jury, not having the opportunity to work out the mad details of this evidence must have been immensely impressed by it – indeed it was one of the strongest pieces of evidence in the Crown's case. Yet so far as reality was concerned, it was part of Cloud Cuckooland.[17]

Third the dumping of Mr Moir's Triumph. When Meehan got back to Glasgow on the Thursday after the murder, said Lord Grant, 'it would appear that almost immediately after hearing that a Pat might be involved, he advised Griffiths to destroy or dump the Triumph car. You will have to consider what significance if any that has, and why it was necessary to destroy the car rather than merely to abandon it with new number plates or indeed its old number plates in some side street in Glasgow.'

This was a very powerful piece of evidence, and the jury must have been asking themselves the same question. The answers were twofold – though as there was no evidence in the trial to support them, one cannot criticise Lord Grant for not putting them to the jury. Firstly, the Triumph was covered in Griffiths' and Meehan's fingerprints. Had Griffiths left the car in some Glasgow side street, the Police would soon have found it and evidence that it had been stolen and that Meehan and Griffiths had been using it would, with their records, have been enough to send both to prison for some time. Secondly Griffiths did not choose the Highlands as a place to dump the car on some wild impulse; he had put it where he had put other cars in the past. Yet to the jury it must have seemed a most peculiar thing to do.

Lastly the judge asked the jury to consider why, when Meehan rang the Police to tell them about Irene Burns and

[17] For comments on the evidence about the pieces of paper, see note on page 269.

the two boys, he said that 'two friends' had picked her up and not himself and a friend. The answer, which Meehan had given in evidence, but which the judge did not put to the jury, was that he did not wish the Police to know that he and another man with a long record were returning from an unlawful enterprise in Stranraer in a stolen car. Lord Grant said that Meehan had also told the Police that he had picked up Irene at 4.30 a.m., when in fact he had picked her up much earlier: was there any significance to be attached to that? Well, what possible significance could be attached to that? What purpose would Meehan have had in lying to the Police about the right time when, in the same breath, he was inviting them to contact a woman, and through her three others, who would say what the right time was?

Why, asked Lord Grant, had Meehan and Griffiths picked up the girls in the first place? Was it, he asked, taking up Mr Stewart's point, an ingenious method of providing an alibi, and was the whole visit to Stranraer designed to that end? Now the reason that Meehan and Griffiths had picked up Irene Burns was because she was a young girl left stranded on a main road in the middle of the night. Presumably the judge did not invite the jury to consider this, because he did not think that two such ruffians were capable of a simple act of common humanity. And why did he not suggest to the jury the most convincing point of all in Meehan's and Griffiths' favour? Would two men, having ten or twelve minutes earlier committed the sort of crime that had been committed, with loot in the car and possibly blood on their clothes,[18] have been the least likely to pick up not one but two people who would subsequently identify them? This surely was a far more telling argument than the

[18] On July 11th there was an announcement in the Police Gazette asking all local police to inquire of dry cleaners and laundries whether any bloodstained clothing had recently been handed in. This shows that the Ayrshire police thought it likely that whoever had done the crime had bloodstains on their clothing. Waddell later admitted he had blood on his jacket, which he burned on Carmichael's midden.

Agatha Christie idea of Irene and Isobel being alibis sent from heaven?

After explaining to the jury the difference between murder and culpable homicide, the judge asked the jury to retire to consider their verdicts. The time was 3.50 p.m. They came back into court just under two hours later. Their verdict on the first count (of acting with Griffiths to steal Mr Moir's car) was guilty unanimously. The verdict on the third charge (the passport offence) was also guilty unanimously. The verdict on the second charge of assault and robbery and murder was guilty by a majority verdict. Despite the police evidence against Meehan, six of the fifteen-man jury did not think the Crown had made out a sufficiently convincing case (or else felt uneasy about the possible involvement of Waddell). The other nine returned a true bill. (Had only two of the nine voted the other way Meehan would have been acquitted.) It was exactly the same majority as that given by the jury which more than half a century earlier had in the same court sent the innocent Oscar Slater to prison for eighteen years. Mr Stewart rose. 'I move your lordship to sentence on Charge Two, and I put in a schedule for what it is worth of previous convictions.'

'It does show a deplorable record,' said Lord Grant, 'but that is not a matter which I take into account. There is nothing you really can say, Mr Fairbairn?'

'Nothing.'

The judge turned to the prisoner. 'Patrick Connolly Meehan, as you know, there is only one sentence which I can pass, and that is imprisonment for life.'

Meehan stood firm and upright, his hands lightly resting on the dock rail. 'I want to say this, sir,' he said, and he said it loudly and clearly. 'I am innocent of this crime and so is James Griffiths. You have made a terrible mistake.'

The court rose, the judge departed, Meehan was taken down to the cells. Mr Fairbairn and Mr Beltrami felt very depressed. But some on the other side were uneasy too. Mr Stewart's assistant counsel, Mr John McCluskey, had thought the voice Identification parade evidence very unsatisfactory, and on the whole had found Meehan's explanations of the evidence against him coherent and convincing; nor had he been happy about the charged atmosphere of the trial, and the angry interventions of Lord Grant.

And as the Crown Agent, Stanley Bowen, gathered up his papers, he too felt unease. He knew Meehan's previous cases as a racing tipster knows form. Never before had Meehan (or any other accused in his experience) passionately asserted his innocence in this way right from the time of his arrest until the very last moment of his trial.

Was it conceivable, he asked himself, that Meehan was right? Had they in fact all made a terrible mistake?

PART IV

Afterwards

Meehan's appeal was due to be heard in the High Court in Edinburgh on November 25th. When Mr Beltrami visited him in Barlinnie the day before, Meehan told him that Andrew Dick (whom the police had unsuccessfully tried to trace during Meehan's trial) was now also in the prison awaiting trial. Mr Beltrami urged Meehan to find out all he could from Dick, and Mr Fairbairn would ask the Court of Appeal to hear Dick as an additional witness, even though it was now too late to precognose Dick for a statement.

Meehan cornered Dick early next day, and after their conversation wrote at once to Mr Beltrami.

Dear Mr Beltrami,

I have spoken to Dick and he says he will come clean about everything. He confirms everything William Macintyre said. He is very worried that he might be charged with receiving money from the Ayr crime. It was part of this that he gave to Macintyre.... On Sunday morning 6th July Waddell came to Dick's house along with Donald Carmichael between 11 a.m. and 12 a.m. Dick asked Waddell what had kept him and Waddell said he was over at Carmichael's house fixing up an alibi, and he had to keep Carmichael sweet....

Dick is not only incriminating Waddell, he is also saying that Carmichael put up a false alibi for Waddell.... Dick says the police didn't look very hard for him to serve a citation, as the factor knew where he had moved to, and his children were still at the same school. He had merely moved to another house with his family, and had not disappeared. I can well imagine that the police wouldn't look too hard for Dick....

I don't recall Carmichael testifying that he and Waddell went to Dick's house on the morning of 6th July. Didn't Carmichael say that Waddell left the house alone ...?

Dick also says that when Waddell gave him the £100 on the morning of Sunday 6th July, he remarked, 'We got a nice turn', and *Carmichael was in the house at the time*!

Later that day Meehan was taken by police car from Barlinnie back to the High Court in Edinburgh where he stood trial, to attend the hearing of his appeal. He was accompanied by three police officers and a prison officer. One of the police officers, out of interest, decided to listen to the appeal himself rather than hang about in the precincts of the court.

The judges hearing the appeal were the Lord Justice General, Lord Clyde (the senior judge in Scotland) sitting with Lords Guthrie and Cameron. Mr Fairbairn based his appeal on four grounds. The first was that the recording of Griffiths' voice in the BBC programme recorded at Gartree had come to light since the trial, and proved conclusively that Griffiths had a very English voice. 'In my submission,' he said, 'Mr Ross should be given an opportunity to hear that voice in the witness-box, and if he says it is definitely not the voice of either Meehan or Griffiths, that would be critical new evidence. If Ross says the man with that voice was not in his house that night, then Meehan too was not there.' The second was that Andrew Dick was now in Barlinnie, and the court ought to take a statement from him. The third was that Lord Grant had been wrong in removing from the jury's consideration the Special Defence of Incrimination of Waddell; and the fourth was that Lord Grant had not put the defence case fairly to the jury.

As regards the BBC recording, Lord Clyde said that the question of Griffiths' voice was an issue at the trial and pointedly drawn to the jury's attention by both sides. Whatever Mr Ross might say on hearing Griffiths' voice, it would be impossible for the court to say the jury would have arrived at a different conclusion. This was true enough; and yet one cannot help wondering what Mr Ross's reactions would have been if he had heard the recording at the trial; and if he had said then, as he surely would have done, that he didn't think that that was one of the voices he heard, then surely the jury might have reached a different conclusion.[1]

As regards Andrew Dick, Lord Clyde said that Mr Fairbaird had admitted that he did not know what Dick's evidence would be [there having been no time to take a statement]. 'Where is this to end?' he asked. 'Are you asking us to have a kind of retrial to rake about in the hope that something emerges from a witness whose evidence you don't know yet?' In those circumstances that aspect of the appeal clearly could not succeed.

This was wretched luck for Meehan; for had Dick told the court everything he had told Meehan that very morning, had he confirmed Macintyre's evidence that Dick had acted as a go-between for Waddell when proposing the Ayr robbery and that Dick had also repaid him a long-standing debt shortly afterwards, the court might well have thought that had this evidence been before the trial jury, they might have reached a different conclusion.

In regard to Lord Grant removing the Special Defence of Incrimination from the jury's consideration, Lord Guthrie said that there was in fact no corroboration to support it, and therefore Lord Grant's ruling was unexceptionable. He pointed out that Lord Grant had specifically directed the jury to consider the evidence in regard to the special defence in relation to the case as a whole (i.e. it might tend to support a belief in Meehan's innocence if not Waddell's guilt). This was perfectly true, and it is difficult to see what point Mr Fairbairn was trying to make here.

On the last point, that of Lord Grant not putting the defence case fairly to the jury, Lord Clyde said, 'The court is quite satisfied that there is no basis for these criticisms.' Mr Fairbairn had concentrated on two main points, the voice identification and the visibility at Kilmarnock. Witness after witness had testified to the Englishness of Griffiths' voice, Mr Ross had stated forcibly that both men had Glaswegian

[1] Before his death Mr Ross made a recording of Griffiths' voice, when it was broadcast in a BBC programme, and declared that he did not think it was like either of the intruders' voices.

accents, and yet, said Mr Fairbairn, Lord Grant had dismissed this fundamental contradiction in a few words. But it was the court's ruling regarding the evidence about the visibility that was so hard to understand. Lord Grant had cited the evidence of Mr Allan, the meteorological officer, and Irene Burns as suggesting – on entirely false premises – that by the time the Triumph had caught up the Anglia in Kilmarnock, it was light. He had omitted to put to the jury the evidence of Mackie, Bell and Meehan that it was dark – a most material factor. How could the court then say there was no basis for Mr Fairbairn's criticisms that Lord Grant had not put the defence case fairly?

There were of course other instances of Lord Grant's not putting the defence case fairly, the most glaring being his quoting the very misleading police evidence that the journey from Stranraer to Ayr could have been made in an hour, and so inferring that it would have been possible for Meehan and Griffiths to have motored the 52 miles from Cairnryan to the lay-by *and* broken into the Rosses' house and assaulted and robbed them all in the space of an hour and three quarters. In fact as has already been shown, it would have been impossible; but it was not a point the court was asked to consider.

Betty Meehan was also in court, and after the appeal had been refused, she was allowed to walk with her husband to the police car and kiss him goodbye. With tears in her eyes she said to reporters, 'I am going to contact my M.P. as soon as possible. To me it's obvious that Paddy was not in that house that night. I know him too well.'

Meehan got into the police car, and said to his four-man escort, 'If there was still capital punishment, they would take me out one morning soon, and kill me.' That afternoon, as the car returned to Barlinnie, and the next day, as the same officers took Meehan north to Peterhead prison to begin his sentence, they talked with him about his case. By the time they were on their journey back to Glasgow, none of them had the slightest doubts about Meehan's innocence. The police officer who had been in court said, 'I work in one of Glasgow's toughest areas, and I've escorted many prisoners convicted of murder and other violent crimes. But I've never met one before who talked in the way that Meehan did, or who made me feel so strongly that I was with an innocent man.'

Mr Beltrami now knew that the man Meehan had named with Waddell in his Special Defence of Impeachment was not in fact Waddell's partner in the crime. But who was it? One person who might help was John Skivington, charge-hand at the Club Bar, who had accompanied Waddell on his visit to Mr Carlin. So after the failure of Meehan's appeal, he went to see Skivington, told him he was convinced Waddell was involved in the Ayr murder, and asked him if he knew the identity of the second man. Skivington hummed and hawed, then said it would have to be off the record as there were no witnesses present. 'I pressed him for the identity of the second man and he told me the second man was a client of mine and that he had a nickname. I don't have many clients with nicknames, and out of the blue asked him if the nickname was "Tank", as McGuinness was known as "Tank". Skivington smiled knowingly and said, "You're on the right track".'

This was helpful information to confirm Mr Beltrami in his belief in Waddell's guilt and Meehan's innocence; but, as he was McGuinness's solicitor it could be of no practical use.

The Governor of Peterhead prison at this time was Mr Alexander Angus, a man who had spent all his professional life in the prison service, who in his time had met and interviewed thousands of prisoners, and who knew Meehan from past sentences. During Meehan's early days at Peterhead Mr Angus saw him regularly, and like all others who had been brought into close contact with him, was soon convinced of his innocence. 'It was a crime that was completely out of character for him,' he said, 'and it was the way he spoke about it that convinced me. Guilty men when they reach prison don't go on insisting on their innocence. Meehan's continued protestations in my experience were unique.'

During the first few months Meehan believed that it would be only a matter of time before the mistake was discovered and justice belatedly done. He knew that both his wife and Mr Beltrami were working hard on his behalf, and also that his M.P., Frank McElhone, had expressed a wish to help. He himself wrote to Mrs Ross's nephew, Dr Maurice Miller, the M.P. for Kelvingrove, asking for his assistance. As someone commented at the time, had he murdered Mrs Ross, he would have been hardly likely to have sought the help of her nephew in order to prove that he hadn't.

The story of Meehan's next five years is the story of one man's efforts, at first almost unaided, and latterly with an increasing number of supporters, to get his innocence accepted by the authorities. During this period he wrote literally hundreds of letters to all manner of people, as well as making a close study of the law books. To relate in detail everything that took place would fill another book. Here we will follow only the main threads.

In February 1970 Mr Beltrami, who from the very beginning had been tireless in Meehan's cause, prepared a dossier on the case for the Secretary of State for Scotland. Nothing happened. Two months later a more dramatic development occurred when Ian Waddell was tried in the High Court for committing perjury at Meehan's trial in denying he had given Mr Carlin £200. He pleaded guilty, and in sentencing him to three years' imprisonment Lord Cameron said of his evidence at the Meehan trial: 'Supposing he had told the jury the truth, they might have taken a very different view of an unemployed labourer handing over a substantial sum of money' – in other words the jury might well have found Meehan not guilty. In the light of this Mr Beltrami immediately prepared a fresh dossier on the case for the Secretary of State, Mr William Ross, who three weeks later agreed to look into the matter again.

But May and June went by without anything happening, and Meehan continued to rot in Peterhead.[2] At the end of June, in protest against the complacency of the authorities,

[2] In July Griffiths' Scunthorpe friend, the fence John Matthews, was convicted of receiving at Nottingham Assizes.

he decided to embark on a policy of non-co-operation. One morning at 8 a.m., when the prisoners were ordered to march to work, Meehan refused to join them. He was sent for by Mr Angus, and explained what the reasons for his non-co-operation were. Normally, when a prisoner refuses to work, he is deprived of certain privileges, such as loss of smoking, for a fixed time. But Mr Angus thought it would be more appropriate in Meehan's case if he were sent to the Observation Block, where he could continue his privileges, be able to smoke, have newspapers and library books, and receive visitors, but otherwise be in solitary confinement. After a month of this Mr Angus sent for Meehan again, and asked him if he was ready to return to work. But Meehan had now decided that refusal to co-operate with the system was the only protest left to him, and he declined. He was therefore returned to solitary confinement, and apart from one period of a few months has remained there ever since. Whatever one may think of Meehan as a member of society, for such a gregarious man voluntarily to forgo the company of his fellow prisoners year in and year out rather than to submit to rules which, he felt, had no relevance to him, showed courage and endurance of a high order. By 1975 Meehan had been in solitary confinement longer than any other prisoner in the United Kingdom in modern times.

At the end of July Mr Beltrami prepared a fresh dossier on the case for Mr Gordon Campbell[3] who, as a result of a change of government, was now the new Secretary of State. In October Mr Beltrami, Mr Fairbairn and Mr McElhone travelled together to Peterhead to discuss further developments, and a few days later Mr McElhone announced that he was taking the matter up with the Secretary of State and the Lord Advocate. In the New Year Mr Beltrami petitioned Mr Campbell for exercise of the Queen's Pardon, and also asked if Meehan could be transferred from Peterhead to Barlinnie where it would be more convenient for discussions and less expensive for his family to visit him.

Meanwhile Meehan's family had been doing some detective work on their own. It had seemed to Meehan that the

[3] Now Lord Campbell of Croy.

police evidence at his trial, that Ross had viewed the parade first when in fact he had seen it last, was so strange that it warranted further investigation. So his son Pat went to interview various witnesses, and from them emerged for the first time the story of Mr Ross being taken to the Interview Room before viewing the parade and asking questions of those who had viewed the parade, in particular the girls who had identified Meehan. Once again Mr Beltrami took up this new evidence with the authorities and once again nothing happened.

So Meehan, who during his long hours of solitary confinement, had been studying law books, now proposed to apply for a Bill of Criminal Letters against the detectives in charge of the parade, alleging perjury at his trial. Bills of Criminal Letters, which allow a private individual to bring a prosecution where the Crown Office has refused to, are a relic of Scottish law which last succeeded in 1909. Mr Beltrami declined to act for Meehan in this matter, for his view was that while there would be no difficulty in showing that Inglis and Struthers had made a mistake, in law it would be impossible to prove perjury (i.e., that the detectives, in testifying that Ross had seen the parade first rather than last, had lied with malicious intent). So Meehan removed his case from Mr Beltrami and put it in the hands of Mr Ross Harper of the Glasgow firm of Ross, Harper and Murphy.

Mr Harper started reading the papers with what he described as 'a certain amount of suspicion and cynicism' but within a week or two he wrote that he was 'reasonably convinced that there was a miscarriage of justice'. Like Mr Beltrami he petitioned the Secretary of State for exercise of the Royal Prerogative of Mercy, wrote to the Lord Advocate requesting an interview, and again asked the Scottish Home and Health Department for Meehan to be transferred to Barlinnie so as to be available for consultations about the new evidence. In mid-May, when Mr Harper was about to combine a visit to Meehan in Peterhead with attendance at the Conservative Party Conference in Aberdeen (he had stood as a Conservative candidate at the previous election), he suddenly got word from Meehan that he was to be transferred next day to Inverness. He wrote at once to the Home and Health Department to protest, and in return received a terse and unsympathetic reply:

'I refer to your letter dated 10 May that Mr Meehan be transferred to Barlinnie or Edinburgh Prison for consultations with yourselves or be retransferred to Peterhead where he could be seen by one of your partners who will be in Aberdeen shortly.

'Mr Meehan has been transferred to the Segregation Unit at Inverness Prison because of his continued non-co-operation with the prison authorities since July last year, and for a more recent serious breach of prison regulations. It will not therefore be possible to transfer Mr Meehan as you request.

'Mr Meehan's return to Peterhead will depend on his response to authority, and on his conduct and industry while in Inverness Prison.

'I regret I am unable to give you a more helpful reply at this time.

'Yours faithfully,
'T. Melville.'

This brought a somewhat tart rejoinder from Mr Harper:

Unfortunately it is not our client who suffers as a result of your transfer, but his solicitor who has to travel all the further. We wonder whether it would be possible for you to arrange for him even temporarily to be brought somewhere nearer civilisation at any time in the near future – even if he was segregated or put on bread and water, or whatever happens to the non-co-operative prisoner.

He wrote to Meehan, too, asking what the serious breach of prison regulations was, and Meehan said it was only smuggling out of prison letters and a draft pamphlet about 'the terrible injustice of my position'. Meehan also wrote:

'As I see it, giving an undertaking to be of future good conduct would imply willingness to work. I have nothing against work – but I feel that by not working I register my protest.' ('I have no wish to complain about my treatment here. Why complain about too much salt in the porridge, if I should not be eating it to start with?') But later that day he wrote again to Mr Harper, 'In order to remove any objection to a transfer I have decided to end my strike as from today. This is in keeping with your wish, and I must be guided by you.'

* * *

It was about this time that I first came into the case. Mrs Meehan had written to me soon after Paddy's appeal had been refused, and I was naturally interested because of my conversation in the train with Nicholas Fairbairn the night before Meehan was found guilty. However I was very busy at the time with a book, and I told Mrs Meehan that I regretted there was nothing I could do. The following year, 1970, and in 1971, she wrote to me again, and then I began receiving letters from Meehan himself.[4] In April 1971 Mrs Meehan wrote: '... I would appreciate it if you could do anything to bring all that happened into the open. As I say again, Paddy or Jim had never heard of Mr Ross until after this crime, and I know that if not this week or this year, he will clear himself some day. Meantime it's a living hell for all of us, and I need all the help we can get to shorten the time he will be in prison.' Such an appeal was not to be resisted, and Meehan's letters also had about them the ring of truth. With a busy television and writing life, I did not feel able to commit myself to a book, but hoped, having investigated the case, to write an article about it for the *Scotsman*.

But first there was one matter to be got out of the way, and on June 11th I wrote to Meehan:

> I hope it may be possible for me to write an article on

[4] Meehan's first letter to me – the first of scores – began as follows: 'Dear Mr Kennedy, I am serving Life Imprisonment for a horrible murder in which I was never involved....'

your case. You, I know, have always consistently declared that you were not guilty of the charge, and it may very well be so. But before I go any further, I must tell you frankly that I must consider myself free ... to come to whatever conclusions that my investigations lead me – whether in your favour or not.

Please let me know whether you are willing to take this risk.

Meehan's reply was unequivocal.

I am certainly willing to give you a free hand in the investigation of my case, and to express whatever conclusions you come to ... as to guilt or innocence. If there are any questions you wish to put to me, then do not hesitate to do so.

This convinced me that it was unlikely that I was dealing with a guilty man.

So from Mr Ross Harper I obtained a copy of the transcript of the trial (more than 700 pages) and in the course of the next few months made notes from it, as well as travelling to Glasgow to talk to Mr Beltrami and Mr Harper. It soon struck me, as it had already struck others, that the only really convincing piece of Crown evidence (albeit circumstantial) was Mr Ross having heard the intruders call each other Pat and Jim (or Jimmy), and Meehan and Griffiths being in the neighbourhood. Without this evidence it is inconceivable that Meehan would have been brought to trial (indeed as we now know it was from this evidence that other evidence – the Identification parade and the bits of paper – followed): it was the foundation of the whole case against Meehan.

Meehan himself, no less than his prosecutors, believed the Pat and Jim thing to be beyond coincidence. But whereas the Police thought the explanation was to be found in Meehan and Griffiths' guilt, Meehan himself believed the Police had manufactured it. Superintendent Struthers had issued a statement on July 9th that the Police were looking only for 'Pat'. When had the name 'Jim' first been introduced, Meehan wanted to know. Had Mr Ross mentioned it to the officers who had first interviewed him, and if so was the fact contained in the telex the Ayrshire Police had sent out immediately after discovery of the crime? If not, argued Meehan, then the Police, having heard that Meehan and Griffiths were in the neighbourhood, had deliberately introduced it. I myself, believing with everyone else that Pat and Jim was beyond coincidence yet also believing in Meehan's innocence, felt this could be the only explanation.

Now, at this time the defence did not have a copy of the telex of July 7th, and early in May 1971 Mr Ross Harper wrote to the Crown Office asking for one. I also was naturally anxious to see this, as the whole structure of my article depended on it. The Crown Office took their time in replying, despite numerous prods from Mr Ross Harper. June, July, August, September, October went by without an answer, and then finally, in December, the Crown Office sent copies both of the telex of July 7th and the Police Gazette of July 15th. Both contained the information that Mr Ross had heard the intruders call each other Pat and Jim (Jimmy by this time seems to have been abandoned).

As a result of this information I must confess (to my eternal shame) that I now had strong doubts – despite all the contrary evidence – about Meehan's innocence, and these were reflected in a letter I wrote to him on December 30th 1971:

30th December 1971

Mr Patrick Meehan 279/71,
H.M. Prison,
Inverness.

Dear Mr Meehan,

I have now at long last been able to see a copy of both the Police telex for Tuesday July 7th and also of the Police Gazette for Wednesday July 9th. Although the copy of the Police telex is not altogether satisfactory these two pieces of evidence clearly show without a shadow of doubt that the Police were after two men called Jim and Pat at a time before they had any knowledge that you and

Griffiths were anywhere in Ayrshire that night. This combined with Mr Ross's evidence in the witness box that he heard the two men address each other as Pat and Jim is, I am sure you will agree, devastating evidence.

I have not got your various letters with me at the moment, as I have lent them to Mr Raeburn Mackie who, I think you know, is also taking an interest in your case, so I cannot recall in exact detail your various explanations of how 'Pat and Jim' came to be used if as you say, Griffiths and you were not there. I do not seem to remember your saying at any juncture either that you knew that the crime at Ayr was going to be committed or if anybody else knew that you and Griffiths were intending to go to Stranraer and whether there could be any connection between the two. Please let me know the absolute truth about this. Did you know anything about the possibility of Mr and Mrs Ross being robbed, and was your trip to Stranraer in any way connected with this? I do not know if I can be of any help in your case, but I do know that I can only be if I know exactly what happened.

I am sending a copy of this letter to Mr Mackie and to your new solicitors, Messrs Levy and McRae. I am also enclosing a copy of the Police Gazette for Wednesday 9th July.

Yours sincerely,
Ludovic Kennedy

This letter shows clearly that I had not been able to accept – any more than the Police or the Crown Office, or Meehan himself – that Pat and Jim were no more than a strange coincidence. And here let me add that it is the inability to accept this coincidence that forms the basis of belief of all those who still think Meehan guilty today. I do not blame them, for until one has studied the case in depth, it is a belief which is very hard to overcome.

Meanwhile Meehan himself had been active, pouring out a stream of letters to myself, Mr Frank McElhone and others; and instructions to Mr Harper to precognose a variety of witnesses – Mr Ross's nurse to get confirmation of the irregularity of the Identification parade, Mr Ross to confirm that it wasn't until full daylight that the intruders had left, the doctors at Ayr Hospital to find out if Mrs Ross had said anything relevant before she died. In August Meehan was transferred to Barlinnie, which made things easier for Mr Harper as regards consultations, and a dossier on the Identification parade was sent to the Crown Agent in the hope that he would consider action against Inglis and Struthers for perjury. When he declined to do this, Meehan reverted to his old idea of a Bill of Criminal Letters. 'There have been very few cases in the past,' he wrote to Mr Harper, 'which means there is very little law involved. "A substantial and peculiar personal interest" is the main factor ... I will be reading up Baron Hume's *Criminal Law of Scotland*: I think the old authorities are what we need here.'

In the beginning of September Meehan was transferred back to Peterhead. He had now been in prison nearly two years. By the end of the year, there had been no further progress in his case, and Mr Harper, notwithstanding his goodwill, was beginning to wilt under Meehan's almost daily flow of instructions. Meehan had already sensed this himself, and despite a feeling of personal gratitude to Mr Harper, decided to change to another firm of Glasgow solicitors. Accordingly he instructed the firm of Levy and McRae, to act for him, and one of the senior partners, Mr Leonard Murray, took over. 'My information about the case is terribly scanty,' Mr Murray wrote to me on December 20th 1971, 'and I wondered if you were to be in Glasgow ... you could possibly fill me in on a considerable number of aspects.' Early in 1972 having briefed himself thoroughly on the case, and seen and corresponded with Meehan, Mr Murray was as convinced as Mr Beltrami and Mr Harper that his client was an innocent man.

During the first six months of 1972 Meehan remained in Peterhead Prison. He had gone back to solitary confinement in the Observation Block in renewed protest against his imprisonment, but this time the authorities decided to let things be. During this period very little of moment happened. My article, as the result of seeing the telex containing Pat and

Jim revelations, was in abeyance, no other outside agency was expressing an interest in him and, so far as the Crown Office and Secretary of State were concerned, the case was closed.

But there was one man who hadn't forgotten Meehan, and that was Tank McGuinness. Meehan was popular in the underworld, and the underworld knew, and let McGuinness know they knew, how unjust was Meehan's continued imprisonment. But there was nothing he could do to right the situation without himself inviting certain arrest and imprisonment. The thing preyed on his mind, said Agnes, his hair began to go grey, he suffered from alopecia. She herself, knowing that she was harbouring a murderer, began increasingly to suffer from nerves, and had to go to the doctor for sedatives. The doctor asked what was worrying her, but naturally she couldn't bring herself to say.

However, McGuinness continued with his life of crime – there was no other business he knew – even venturing back to the Ayr area where he appeared in the High Court on a housebreaking charge, was sentenced to three years, but released on appeal. In September 1972 he and a man called James Farrell were taken into custody in connection with a murder. Two months later the authorities decided not to proceed against them, and informed Mr Beltrami. He went to Barlinnie Prison, told them of the news and then drove them from Barlinnie to Glasgow. On the way McGuinness, grateful to be out of prison, said spontaneously to Mr Beltrami that Meehan was entirely innocent of the Ayr murder and he was much concerned about him. 'He also,' in Mr Beltrami's words, 'indicated in an indirect manner that he was involved in the Ayr crime.'

Because of the solicitor/client relationship this private confession by McGuinness to Mr Beltrami had to remain confidential. But now, from another source, came an unexpected turn up for the book. McGuinness's partner in the Ayr murder, Ian Waddell, was ready publicly to confess.

Ian Waddell had been released from prison, after serving

his sentence for perjury, in the early summer of 1972. But on June 4th he was arrested again, this time on a charge of being in possession of a loaded revolver. Waddell nominated as his legal aid solicitor Mr William Dunn, Mr Beltrami's partner, who attended him in Barlinnie Prison. But when the time for his Pleading Diet came up in the Sheriff Court on July 28th, Mr Dunn had gone on holiday. So Mr Beltrami took his place. He asked Waddell if he had any objections to him representing him, in view of Waddell having been impeached by his client Meehan. Waddell said he had no objections, and Mr Beltrami said he would do his best for him.

When the case was called, Waddell pleaded guilty on Mr Beltrami's advice, and then Mr Beltrami tendered a plea in mitigation. Waddell was sentenced to 12 months imprisonment, to run from the time of his arrest, which meant that he would not have to serve more than nine months, and with remission for good conduct only six. This was less than he expected, and later that morning he sent word from the cells that he wanted to see Mr Beltrami. They met in the Solicitors' Consulting Room. Waddell thanked Mr Beltrami for what he had done, and said he would like to do something for Meehan. He had recalled that before Meehan's trial Mr Beltrami had applied for Meehan to take the truth drug, but that the High Court had ruled that this could not be accepted as evidence. If that was so, and one could not be prosecuted for anything said under the truth drug, he would like to take the truth drug himself when he was released from Barlinnie. He would talk about the Ayr murder, and he expected that what he said would help Meehan. He wanted the experiment to take place in the BBC Studios and for the press to be present.

Mr Beltrami saw Waddell on several further occasions and Waddell repeated his willingness to take the truth drug. However he said he would require a considerable sum of money for doing so, as he would probably have to leave Scotland and start a new life in England. How much Waddell was motivated by a genuine desire to help Meehan and how much by a desire for money and notoriety, it is impossible to say – probably something of both.[5]

Mr Beltrami had informed Mr Murray of these developments and the two of them drove to Peterhead to tell Meehan about it. Meehan then asked Mr Beltrami to join with Mr Murray in acting for him, and Mr Beltrami accepted. On return to Glasgow Mr Beltrami informed Waddell that because of this he could no longer act for him, and he arranged for Waddell to have the services of another Glasgow solicitor, Mr Robert Gibson. He also alerted the BBC as to the date of Waddell's release.

Just before 7 a.m. on the morning of February 2nd 1973, the BBC reporter David Scott and producer Ken Vass met Waddell on his release from Barlinnie prison. They got into Scott's car. Scott had a tiny tape-recorder concealed in his tie, and here is a précis of the more important things that were said.

SCOTT: We just wanted a wee chat to establish with you who we were, so that if we see you this afternoon, you'll know who we are ... and really if you, you know, felt at this stage ... just more or less what it was you had to say, you know, – if anything?

WADDELL: Ah, well I'll need to see my lawyer and a' that.

SCOTT: That's Mr Gibson?

WADDELL: Aye ... He'll discuss everything ... I've got to see what the questions are before I say anything.... The only question I don't want asked is who my accomplice was. That's all.... Every other question I'll answer regarding the murder, everything else ...

SCOTT: I mean, you would be quite prepared to give the details of the murder. Will you?

WADDELL: Everything, aye everything.

VASS: It would exonerate, do you think, Meehan altogether? Would it?

[5] The news that Waddell was ready to confess spurred me on to take up again the article I had put aside, and it was published in the *Scotsman* of December 14th. So lacking was public interest in the Meehan case at the time that I received not one single letter about it.

WADDELL: I don't know, that's up to them you know.
SCOTT: No, but I mean basically ... you would be quite prepared to give the details of what happened that night?
WADDELL: Every detail, aye.
SCOTT: Except who was there with you?
WADDELL: Aye.

Waddell agreed to a further meeting to discuss the truth drug experiment later that day. This was to be in Mr Gibson's office. Joe Beltrami, Scott, Vass and myself all waited there for Waddell, but he never turned up. However a day or two later Scott, Vass and the tape-recorder tracked him down again.

SCOTT: So what are your plans now, Ian?
WADDELL: I want to get all this finished as soon as possible.... I'll need to get my money back, I'll need to leave before I get assassinated. The police'll assassinate me first chance they get.
VASS: See, we'll have problems persuading our colleagues what the outcome might be before we start talking to them on any other basis. Our people keep asking me, does this mean in fact that you will establish that Paddy Meehan is innocent or not?
WADDELL: Aye, I will establish that. It must be under the truth drug. That is the only way I can't be charged, as far as I know.
VASS: But you will certainly establish his innocence?
WADDELL: I'll establish that.
VASS: Why were the names Pat and Jim used? Were they not used deliberately? It wasn't to incriminate them?
WADDELL: No, I didn't know them. That's been established.
SCOTT: I think it's been fairly well established that there were only two in the house at the time.
WADDELL: There was two of us, aye.
SCOTT: Can you describe the inside of the house at all?
WADDELL: Oh aye, I can describe it.
SCOTT: What happened to the cash that was brought out

of there?
WADDELL: That was spent.
SCOTT: And what was the share-out, roughly ...? Can you remember?
WADDELL: Aye, three thousand five hundred or so.
SCOTT: So there was a lot more taken than was actually revealed at the time?
WADDELL: Eighteen hundred, the figure was.
SCOTT: And ... later on when you gave evidence. Was it Mr Carmichael ... where you said you'd been that night? That was wrong too?
WADDELL: Aye, that was wrong too.
VASS: Was it daylight when you left, in fact? ... The old man ... thought he saw daylight before you left the house?
WADDELL: Aye, that'll be right, probably.
SCOTT: You've not seen Meehan since the murder, have you?
WADDELL: I was in C hall then. I've never seen him since the trial.
VASS: You didn't know him before the trial?
WADDELL: I didn't know him before that ...
SCOTT: You must have heard of him though.
WADDELL: I'd never heard of Griffiths, but I'd heard of Meehan, just in conversation. He's a bit of a known character.
SCOTT: And how did you get into the house? There was a question of a ladder being used at some point?
WADDELL: No, there was nae ladder ... the ladder was used for cutting the phone's wires.
SCOTT: What would be the greatest thing that you could say that would sway people to believe that Meehan was innocent?
WADDELL: I done the murder.
VASS: You actually tied them up, did you?
WADDELL: Uh, huh.
SCOTT: You and this other fellow?
WADDELL: Aye ... I still maintain she wasn't murdered ... she wasn't murdered, know what I mean?

SCOTT: Yes.

WADDELL: ... she wasn't intentionally murdered ...

SCOTT: And how much did it cost you for an alibi then, as a matter of interest?

WADDELL: I never paid for my alibi.

SCOTT: And why, Ian, are you now confessing about it, then? I mean, what's brought this on?

WADDELL: It's hard to say. I mean, I feel sorry for the bloke.... If the public believes Meehan's innocent, then the police have framed him.

VASS: Either that, or a mistake's been made.

WADDELL: Cannae be a mistake.

VASS: You're not afraid that you'll be charged with the murder after you've taken this drug, then?

WADDELL: ... the evidence they'd need to use against me would under this drug be illegal, as far as I know.

Lastly Scott said, 'You've said you'd have to leave town because you'd be assassinated, I mean who would be after you in that case?'

WADDELL: The police.

SCOTT: Just the police? I mean, not your accomplice?

WADDELL: Aye, probably him and all.

That afternoon Scott and Vass went to see Mr Gibson, who told them that if the experiment was successful and Waddell said things under the truth drug that would be helpful to Meehan, he wanted £30,000; if he said nothing helpful, he would not expect anything. Later still I came to Mr Gibson's office, and heard David Scott repeat, in front of Waddell and Mr Gibson, what Waddell had told to Scott and Vass. Waddell did not interrupt to correct or deny any part of what Scott said.

After this Scott and Vass took Waddell away for a couple of days, while inquiries were made as to whether any newspaper or broadcasting organisation was interested in paying Waddell the huge fee he was asking. Meanwhile Waddell told Scott and Vass more details to confirm his story that he had been inside the Ross house. He said the lounge had a highly polished floor, he had seen a lighter in the lounge and an alarm clock in the kitchen. These things were all followed up and found to be true.

On return to Glasgow, Waddell learnt that no paper or broadcasting organisation was interested in paying Waddell what he wanted, or anything like it; and so the truth drug experiment was dropped. But Vass and Scott now had sufficient material for a television programme. It was to contain the information that Waddell had given Scott and Vass, interviews with Beltrami and Murray affirming their belief in Meehan's innocence, an extract from the BBC religious programme in which Griffiths said he would not hesitate to kill rather than be arrested, statements from Gillies Falconer that Mr Ross had been taken out of the witness room to view the Identification parade first, and from Peter McCann and Rooney that he had in fact viewed it last. It would be a comprehensive and convincing précis of the main points of the case.

The programme was due to go out in April, but when Waddell realised that what he had told Scott and Vass was going to be made public and might be used in any future proceedings against him, he got Mr Gibson to apply to the Sheriff Court to prevent the programme being screened. He was successful initially, but when the case was referred to the Court of Session, Lord Wheatley (Lord Grant's successor as Lord Justice-Clerk)[6] reversed the decision (Waddell, he said, could always raise an action for defamation), and the programme finally went out in mid-July.

All the new evidence regarding Waddell had been collated in a fresh dossier on the case, which was sent by Mr Murray to the Secretary of State, Mr Gordon Campbell, in a further appeal for the Royal Prerogative of Mercy. In October 1973 Mr Campbell announced that after consultations with the Lord Advocate he had decided there was no further action he could take. These continued refusals by the authorities to recognise that justice had miscarried were now occurring with monotonous regularity and are one of the case's most

[6] Lord Grant was killed in a road accident in 1973.

depressing features.

But one result of the Waddell confession was to renew the interest of the press and politicians. Early in 1974 the *Sunday Times* sent Peter Watson to Scotland, and he wrote a long interesting article setting out the case for Meehan's innocence. In March Mr Frank McElhone, Meehan's M.P., spoke on the matter in the House of Commons and asked the Secretary of State for Scotland 'to appoint an impartial inquiry to recommend the Queen's Pardon'. In reply Mr Bruce Millan promised that the matter would be looked at again, although it had already been looked at several times before. Other television programmes broadcast items on the case, and both press and broadcasting newsrooms were now regularly reporting latest developments.

In February 1974 the Conservative government was defeated: Mr Campbell lost his job as Secretary of State (and his seat as M.P.) and Mr William Ross came back. In August 1974, after Meehan had been in prison for almost five years, Mr Ross announced that 'after careful and exhaustive consideration', in consultation with the Lord Advocate, he had 'come to the conclusion that there are no grounds that would justify [him in] recommending the exercise of the Royal Prerogative of Mercy or taking any action in the case.'

I thought this a shocking and perverse decision. It should have been clear to the authorities by now that the time for stone-walling was over, that there were, to put it at its lowest, the gravest doubts about Meehan's guilt, and the only way to resolve them and allay public unease was not by secret consultations which smacked of a cover-up, but through an officially appointed independent inquiry, whose findings would be made public. I knew then that until somebody wrote a comprehensive book setting out the case for Meehan's innocence, he would rot in Peterhead for ever. I was as familiar with the case as anyone, and therefore, in spite of previous resolutions, decided to write it myself.

It was after I had started my researches in the late autumn of 1974 that the most penetrating inquiry into the question of Waddell's guilt was undertaken by two newspaper reporters, Gordon Airs (Chief Reporter) and Charles Beaton of the *Scottish Daily Record*. For a time we joined forces. With them I interviewed Abraham Ross for the first time at 2 Blackburn Place and was shown the bedroom in which the crime took place (and where, strangely, Mr Ross still slept). Later, in their company, I interviewed Waddell, both to get background details of his life as well as confirmation of certain things said to them by Waddell in an amazing interview they had had a few weeks earlier.

This interview, at which Mr Leonard Murray was present, took more than two hours. Subsequently Mr Airs wrote articles which showed devastating evidence of Waddell's participation in the Ayr murder. Here is an extract from one of them:[7]

> ... during two weeks of intensive investigation we have confirmed through different witnesses, the following significant factors in Waddell's confession which would only have been known to one of the raiders in the house that night.
>
> 1. A gold bracelet watch was ripped from the bound wrist of Mrs Ross. *Mr Ross confirms this fact has never emerged during the trial or its aftermath in any way.*
> 2. The colour of the quilts that night was *pink*. Mr Ross confirms. Again this was never known publicly.
> 3. The bedroom door had an old workable lock. Mr Ross confirms. Again this was never mentioned in public.
> 4. An accurate and detailed lay-out of the bedroom and its contents. Mr Ross confirms.
> 5. Hundreds of pounds of the £1,800 haul were in new £10 notes numbered in sequence. Mr Ross confirms. This was never mentioned in the trial.
> 6. Travellers cheques contained in a black plastic folder were taken. Mr Ross confirms the black folder was never disclosed publicly.
> 7. The safe key was accurately described as a long-mortice type. Mr Ross confirms. Again this was never made known before.
> 8. An alarm clock in the hatchway of the kitchen was

[7] Reprinted by kind permission of the Editor of the *Daily Record*.

perfectly described with its black face and green luminous hands and figures. Mr Ross confirms.

9. The divan beds didn't match the rest of the furniture. Mr Ross confirms. Not revealed before.

10. There was a bedside light with a round shade and an overhead light. Mr Ross confirms. Again, never described in public.

11. A light tan suit was in the bedroom wardrobe. Mr Ross confirms. This never emerged before.

12. A photo in the room of a man with two young children was described. Mr Ross confirms there were similar photos. Again, not publicly known.

13. There was a dark-coloured highly polished wooden floor in the hallway. Mr Ross confirms.

14. Waddell says a woman next door at her garage spotted him outside the Ross house about 11 p.m. The woman, Mrs Scott, confirms that that night she was at her garage shortly before 11 p.m.

15. Waddell's accomplice hired a silver car with what Waddell thought was a black roof, for the job. The car hire firm confirm they had silver cars at that time.

16. A key lock was on the back door. Mr Ross confirms.

17. They left in broad daylight. Mr Ross confirms.

Despite having got a first-class journalistic scoop, the *Record*'s editor, Mr Bernard Vickers, was himself not sufficiently convinced of the truth of Waddell's confession to publish, and instead sent all the papers to the Crown Office for consideration by the Lord Advocate. In time the Lord Advocate announced that the Crown Office would not be making any prosecutions but that the papers would go to (guess where?) the Secretary of State for further consideration. They went early in 1975 and gathered dust there for the next year.

It was about this time that Agnes McGuinness and her daughter Elizabeth underwent a very frightening experience. One evening after midnight, when McGuinness was out, there was a knock on the door. She called out, 'Who's that?' and a voice replied, 'It's me'. Thinking it was her husband, she opened the door, whereupon two hooded men burst in, one with a shotgun. Agnes screamed. One of the men put a hand over her mouth and tried to drag her out of the door. Her daughter Elizabeth opened her bedroom door to see what was happening and began screaming too. The two men threw Agnes at her daughter, then searched all the rooms. In one they fired a shot at a wardrobe and riddled it with holes. Then they left.

Whether the men intended to kill McGuinness, or, knowing he was out wanted to frighten him into owning up to the Ayr murder in order to free Meehan, or whether the raid had some other object, is not known. What is certain is that from about this time onwards, and as the campaign for Meehan's release gained momentum, McGuinness was becoming a nervous wreck. He sarted going to a psychiatrist in Oakley Terrace to expunge his guilt and because, as he told Agnes, 'psychiatrists cannot divulge information to anyone'.

He became more confiding in Mr Beltrami too, and during 1975 saw him no less than eight times, though there were no charges against him. He told Mr Beltrami he felt sorry for Meehan and that he would be willing to make a statement confessing to the Ayr crime providing he could be given immunity from prosecution. During these meetings McGuinness elaborated on his part in the crime, telling about hiring a car for the job, being stopped by the police, hiding the keys and the rings in the street drains, going to London immediately after the murder, depositing a large sum of money in his bank. From this information Mr Michael McDonald, Mr Beltrami's office manager, drew a plan, and a few days later Mr Beltrami, Mr McDonald and myself searched some of the drains, hoping to find the car keys and rings but – inevitably after four years – without result.

On September 24th 1974 Meehan at long last brought to the High Court his application for a Bill of Criminal Letters against the three detectives involved in the Identification parade. The hearing took place in the same court where Meehan had been sentenced nearly five years earlier, and was heard by Lords Wheatley, Fraser and Kissen. Although his new solicitor, David Burnside of the Aberdeen firm of Clark and Wallace, was there to assist him, he presented his case in person. Those of us who were in court were as impressed by the vigour and lucidity of his plea, as by his research among the law books. Indeed at one point the judges had to adjourn because Meehan's law books were different from theirs. But in the end they turned him down. If they allowed the application, they said, this 'would open the floodgates to private prosecution which our system of criminal prosecution has been devised and developed to prevent....' In the spring of 1975 Meehan made a further application for another Bill of Criminal Letters, and this too was refused.[8]

At the beginning of June 1975 the Secretary of State asked to see a manuscript copy of this book, and it was sent to him with the approval of the Patrick Meehan Committee in the hope that it would persuade him to set up the independent inquiry into the case for which they had long been pressing. Four months later, on October 10th, Mr Ross once more announced that 'in consultation with the Lord Advocate ... he has come to the conclusion that there are no grounds that would justify the exercise of the Royal Prerogative of Mercy, or taking any other action in the case'.

This decision was even more disgraceful than the one given eighteen months earlier. It must surely have been obvious to the Secretary of State, and even more so to the Lord Advocate, that if the Meehan jury had known what we know today about the Identification parade and the bits of paper, they would not have dared to convict (indeed Lord Grant might well have directed them to acquit); and that this, coupled with Waddell's persistent and detailed admissions of guilt, made an inquiry essential. Why did the Secretary of State refuse an inquiry? As his decision was arrived at in secret, it is impossible to say. But it looks as though

[8] See note on page 274.

either – and this I found hard to believe – that he had not the slightest doubts about Meehan's guilt, or that he was afraid what such an inquiry might reveal. What other explanation could there be?

Yet if Mr Ross thought that after his decision the Meehan affair would go away, he soon found he was mistaken. It is true that when the news was broken to Meehan – who had been setting high hopes on the decision and whose health after more than five years in solitary confinement was deteriorating steadily – he burst into tears; and that fellow prisoners and some staff at Peterhead prison who had long believed in his innocence, were shaken too. But for others the decision only strengthened their resolve to fight on. Next day the Scottish National Party, meeting at Stirling, passed a unanimous resolution calling for an independent inquiry, and so did that Sunday's *Sunday Times*. During the following week Waddell, secure in the knowledge of the Lord Advocate's assurance that he would not be prosecuted for his previous confessions (and possibly also as a result of pressure from the underworld), walked into the offices of the Scottish *Daily News* and gave them yet another full and detailed confession.[9] Subsequently the *Daily News* and ITN interviewed Abraham Ross who said that he now believed that Meehan was not one of the intruders.

In October 1975 extracts from my book were published in the *News of the World*. By this time, although Mr Beltrami had been scrupulous in respecting his confidential relationship with his client McGuinness, the Committee had begun to form from other sources the view that McGuinness was in fact Waddell's accomplice – a view that Mr Beltrami did not contradict. To save Mr Beltrami any embarrassment it was decided to call McGuinness McTurk,

[9] Published as Appendix III. One of the most bizarre aspects of this case is that from the beginning Waddell rarely departed from admitting his guilt with a wealth of detail to support it, while Meehan never wavered in asserting his innocence. Yet with amazing persistence the authorities continued to cling to the opposite view. Could perversity go further?

and I used this name to describe him in my book. On November 21st I received the following letter from the Crown Agent (the solicitor for the Crown in Scotland), Mr W. G. Chalmers.

21st November 1975

Dear Sir,

Patrick Connelly Meehan

I have been advised that in your book on the above case you state that Waddell was a passenger in a car driven by a person called for the purpose of the book 'McTurk' and that his real name is no secret to anyone who knows the case. Are you prepared to give his name to me in order that further investigation may be made?

W. G. CHALMERS,
Crown Agent.

As the Lord Advocate had refused either to prosecute Waddell for the Ayr murder, despite a wealth of detail in his confessions which could only have come from someone who had been there, or alternatively to prosecute him for attempting to pervert the course of justice the Committee found it difficult to take the Crown Agent's letter seriously. After several discussions, and as a result of information from Mr Beltrami, I replied to the Crown Agent on January 5th 1976 as follows:

5th January 1976

Dear Mr Chalmers,

I refer to your letter of 21st November in which you ask if I am prepared to give the name of Waddell's accomplice in the Ayr murder.

I much regret that I am unable to do this. If the man were to be interviewed by the police he would naturally deny all knowledge of the crime and indeed there is no legal proof that he committed it. Had there been evidence capable of proof his name would have been given to you long ago.

From information received however, we have reason

to believe that in the interest of justice for Meehan, this man would be willing to give you personally and in the presence of a solicitor acting for him, a full and detailed account of his part in the Ayr murder, provided that he and anyone else he might name in the statement were given immunity from prosecution. The Meehan Committee are convinced that such a statement would go a long way towards persuading the Crown Office that this man and Waddell, and not Meehan and Griffiths, were responsible for the crime. Admittedly this is an unusual proposal, but as the Lord Advocate has twice indicated that he does not intend to institute criminal proceedings against Waddell, despite his many detailed confessions to the crime, there would presumably be no difficulty in extending the same concession to his accomplice. The prime concern of the Meehan Committee, as I am sure you understand, is to get an innocent man released from prison.

This information would have been put to you by the Meehan Committee before but as you know, the Secretary of State for Scotland, the Lord Advocate and the Solicitor General have all refused our requests to see them.

Please let us know if we can assist you in this matter further.

Yours sincerely,
LUDOVIC KENNEDY.

To which the Crown Agent replied on January 7th:

7th January 1976

Dear Mr Kennedy,

I thank you for your letter which I received yesterday and note that you are not prepared to name the person alleged by you to have been involved in the Murder of Mrs Ross.

The Lord Advocate has not granted Waddell any immunity from prosecution. He has said only that having had regard to all the evidence available, he has decided that prosecution of Waddell would not be justified. But other evidence could emerge and if there were evidence, sufficient in law to establish that he had committed a crime, it would be necessary to consider the matter afresh. The same would apply to anyone else who stated that he was involved in the murder. Accordingly the Crown cannot enter into the arrangement put forward in the third paragraph of your letter.

I suggest, however, that you and your committee reconsider the matter and if you have any information bearing on the crime, which has not been previously disclosed to the Crown authorities you reveal such information to me. I assure you that a thorough investigation will follow. Neither you nor I can predict what such an investigation might disclose.

It is not easy to understand how you can on the one hand call for the release of Meehan yet on the other refuse to give the Crown information which might point to his innocence, or at least allow matters to be further investigated.

Yours sincerely,
W. G. CHALMERS,
Crown Agent.

Any doubts in my mind that I had not made out a strong enough case for Meehan's innocence, or at least one that merited an immediate public inquiry, were dispelled when reviews of my book appeared in the national press. With the exception of a notice in the *Scotsman* which read like a hand-out (and in parts clearly *was* a hand-out) from the Crown Office, the reviews were unanimous in calling for action. First, and most encouraging of all, came the offer of an unsolicited testimonial from Lord Devlin, the distinguished former judge (he had been sent a proof copy of the book in connection with his committee inquiring into Identification Rules).

'It is a very disturbing book. It needs to be answered one way or the other if confidence in the processes of justice is to be maintained.'

The reviews that followed were no less heartening:

Louis Blom-Cooper, Q.C. in *The Listener*.

'One states categorically that this is a case of a double miscarriage of justice, because Mr Kennedy has made out an overwhelming case for it ... It is so beyond the sense of fair-minded men that they cannot concede a public inquiry?'

T. A. Sandrock in the *Daily Telegraph*.

'No reader of the book can come to any conclusion that at best Meehan is innocent or at worst the whole affair demands an impartial review.'

Lord Snow in the *Financial Times*.

'It is impossible to pretend there is not a case to answer.'

Julian Symons in the *Sunday Times*.

'... an overwhelming case for saying that Meehan is innocent. There is every reason why the Royal Prerogative of Mercy should be used.'

Mervyn Jones in the *New Statesman*.

'Patrick Meehan was convicted of a crime ... which he did not commit. The truth about the affair is now absolutely certain. If Meehan's conviction ought to astonish credulous boys, his continued imprisonment should jolt even cynics.'

Tom Bentley in the *Yorkshire Post*.

'... an independent and full-scale inquiry is now the only proper course ... it would be an injustice to refuse one.'

Bernard Levin in *The Observer*.

'... it is clear that certain irregular aspects of the investigation ... make some kind of inquiry now imperative.'

Leo Abse, M.P., in the *Spectator*.
'... necessitates a new independent inquiry ... there is too much in this case for matters to rest.'

And finally the former police officer and eminent writer on judicial affairs, C. H. Rolph, in *The Times Literary Supplement*.

'If I was Secretary of State for Scotland ... without further ado I would recommend to the Queen that she grant what we still so oddly call the "free pardon" by which the innocent are forgiven for what they have not done. For me that is the measure of the book's authority and power.'

And later the Council of JUSTICE, consisting of some of the most senior counsel at the English Bar, issued a statement demanding an official inquiry.

Always an optimist, I sent the Secretary of State for Scotland, Mr William Ross, and the Lord Advocate, Mr Ronald King-Murray, Q.C., those extracts from the reviews, hoping that even their prejudices might be dented, that even they might have second thoughts in the face of such unanimous opinion. I should have known better. From the Secretary of State's office came a brief acknowledgement of my letter, from the Lord Advocate's office nothing. The rest was silence. So far as they were concerned, it seemed, Meehan, guilty or innocent, could rot in Peterhead for ever.

On January 23rd 1976 the Lord Advocate compounded his errors of judgment when in the High Court Meehan sought permission to bring a private prosecution against the man Carmichael (Waddell's alibi during the night of the murder) for committing perjury at Meehan's trial. He also for the first time publicly named McGuinness as Waddell's accomplice. Now this was a perfectly well-founded application, for Carmichael had lied in his teeth at Meehan's trial. But, said the Advocate Depute, appearing for the Crown, 'the Lord Advocate has fully investigated the allegations in the bill ... and has decided not to prosecute Carmichael for perjury, and not to grant his concurrence with a private prosecution.' He went on blandly, 'Carmichael and his wife have been interviewed by the Crown Agent, and the Lord Advocate has decided there is nothing to satisfy him that Carmichael committed perjury.' In the light of this the three judges had no option but to refuse Meehan's application. It was a travesty of justice, but by this time none of us expected much else.

Two days before this Mr Alex Fletcher, Conservative M.P. for Edinburgh North (to whom, as to all other Scottish M.P.s I had sent a copy of the book) asked Mr Ross in the House of Commons if he would order an inquiry following publication of my book. Predictably Mr Ross refused. He had discussed the book with the Lord Advocate, he said, and was satisfied that an independent inquiry would be unlikely to bring out any facts not available to him. 'The Lord Advocate,' he went on, 'has examined very thoroughly the statements by Ian Waddell on which much of Mr Kennedy's book is based. He has decided on the evidence available to him that prosecution of Waddell would not be justified.' Later in the Commons, a Conservative M.P., Mr Malcolm Rifkind, informed the Lord Advocate that 'the alleged new evidence that is presented in Mr Kennedy's book is almost entirely obtained from those who have substantial criminal convictions'. Mr Ross, and Mr Rifkind (who is a lawyer and should have known better) were talking nonsense. The case for Meehan in this book, as the reader will have observed, is not based mainly on Waddell's statements, nor on information from others with criminal convictions. It is based on untrue evidence given by police officers and others at the trial, and on Lord Grant's inaccurate and misleading summing-up. Without these Meehan would not have been convicted. Waddell's confessions do not prove Meehan's innocence; but they certainly confirm it.

And there, as they say, the case rested. The Meehan Committee and I, not to say Meehan himself, were profoundly depressed by the prolonged, wilful stubbornness of the Secretary of State and Lord Advocate. We had done everything in our power that we could do, and we had failed. There was no other avenue open to us: Meehan would have to continue to decay for further years in solitary confinement in Peterhead.

February and part of March went by without any further developments. And then in this extraordinary tangle of events, a most dramatic and unexpected thing happened, the key that at long last was to unlock for the disbelieving the ultimate truth of the case. On March 12th Tank McGuinness was found unconscious with severe head injuries in Springfield Road, Glasgow. He was taken to hospital where, thirteen days later and without regaining consciousness, he died. That evening Agnes McGuinness and her elder son telephoned Mr Beltrami to tell him they had something important to say in relation to Patrick Meehan.

Next day Mrs McGuinness and her son came to see Mr Beltrami, and confirmed in greater detail the information McGuinness had already given him of his and Waddell's participation in the Ayr murder. Having obtained a waiver of confidentiality from them, and having written to the Law Society of Scotland for their approval, Mr Beltrami informed the Crown Agent of this latest development in the case. The Crown Agent later interviewed the McGuinnesses himself and appointed two senior Strathclyde police officers to make further investigations. From Mr Beltrami they obtained a full statement of everything that McGuinness had confided to him over the years.

The ultimate outcome was now a foregone conclusion, although the authorities, having clung to their false beliefs for so long, took their time in admitting an injustice had been done. At the end of April, facing the inevitable, they did something typical of their shoddy conduct in the past – offered Meehan parole, or release on licence, in the knowledge that he was about to be freed unconditionally anyway. The temptation for Meehan to accept must have been great, but wisely and courageously he rejected it, seeing no reason why he should agree to terms in relation to a crime that he had had no part in committing.

By now Mr William Ross had been retired as Secretary of State, and on May 20th his successor, Mr Bruce Millan, announced to the House of Commons that he had decided to exercise the Royal Prerogative of Mercy. It would have been agreeable if Mr Ross, who was also in the House, could have been gracious enough to admit his past errors of judgment and congratulate his successor on his decision. But all this blinkered man could grudgingly say was, '*Was this the only action open to you?*' Mr George Younger, Conservative M.P. for Ayr, who until now had shown no public interest in the case, said he hoped there would not be a 'witch-hunt' against the Ayr police. As the Ayr police were as responsible as anybody for Meehan's wrongful imprisonment, this was somewhat comic.

The same day the gates of Peterhead prison opened, and Meehan walked out a free man, his long ordeal (two months short of seven years, mostly in solitary confinement) at last over.[10] He was spirited away by the *Daily Record,* and his picture was later to be seen in that paper's pages being served bacon and eggs in bed by his son Garry while on a fishing trip to a Highland hotel. Later he and Betty went on holiday to Majorca, then moved back together to the flat in Old Rutherglen Road where Meehan began writing his memoirs. Later he was awarded an interim payment of £2,500 compensation, with a promise of more to come.

Now attention shifted away from Meehan and on to Waddell and the investigations being carried out by the two senior Strathcylde police officers, Assistant Chief Constable Bell and Chief Superintendant McDougall, both officers of the highest integrity and calibre. For the next six months these two devoted their time and energies almost exclusively to the task assigned to them, nor in their determination to reach the truth did they consider that any source, including the files of the Ayrshire police, should be denied them. As a result of their inquiries, there was now a strong case against Andrew Dick for planning, and against Waddell for

[10] Throughout his time in Peterhead Meehan never lost his sense of humour. When I visited him there after publication of the book, he told me that his son Garry had told him that he preferred the picture of him with the blanket over his head (plate 9) to the one at plate 1.

planning and taking part in the Ayr murder along with William McGuinness; and accordingly both Dick and Waddell were charged, Waddell in Barlinnie, where he was already serving a sentence for stabbing a man with a knife and saw.

Under the presiding judge, Lord Robertson, the court first met in the High Court in Edinburgh in October to hear legal arguments. Lord Robertson was one of the few judges before whom Meehan, in his numerous court appearances, had never appeared. Mr Beltrami, Meehan and myself turned up at the court to hear the legal arguments, but although neither the Crown nor the defence raised any objections, Lord Robertson would not allow us into the court. On the way to a café in the Royal Mile Meehan said, 'That's the first court in my life that I've ever been turned away from.'

The trial proper opened in No 9 Court in Edinburgh on November 15th, 1976. Waddell's defence was a special defence of impeachment against Meehan, just as Meehan's defence at his trial had been impeachment against Waddell. This meant that despite Meehan's pardon, the trial would to some extent be a retrial of Meehan as much as a trial of Waddell; and one of its more lunatic aspects was hearing the Lord Advocate, who for two years had strenuously opposed all our efforts to have Meehan's case re-opened, now deploying as prosecutor the arguments of this book to show Meehan's innocence and Waddell's guilt; and conversely to hear Mr James Law Q.C., who appeared for Waddell, echoing Ewan Stewart's arguments at Meehan's trial to show Waddell's innocence and Meehan's guilt. Mr Michael Morrison Q.C. appeared for Dick, but as very little in the way of hard evidence emerged against him, he was eventually discharged.

The new evidence against Waddell, however, was damning; and by far the most damning was that of Mrs Agnes McGuinness. She wasn't long in the witness-box but what she said, if true, was conclusive proof of her husband's and Waddell's participation in the Ayr murder. 'My husband went out on the Saturday and I didn't see him again until the Sunday morning. He told me that he had done a job at Ayr. He said that the police had picked him up and dropped him at the bus station. Later he said that Ian Waddell was with him. Later he also told me that he had told Mr Beltrami about it.'

The next most damaging new evidence was that of Donald Carmichael. Carmichael, it will be recalled, had testified at Meehan's trial that Waddell had stayed with him on the night of the murder, and so couldn't have been in the Rosses' house in Ayr. Now at long last he admitted to have lied. 'He came to my house at about 10 am on the Sunday morning of July 6th and said he had done a turn.' At that time, Waddell hadn't said what the turn was. Waddell had asked him, if questioned by the police, to say he had stayed the night, and Carmichael said he would. The police did question him and he told them that. A few days later he had met Waddell carrying a newspaper with news of the Ayr murder, and Waddell had said, 'I was involved in that.'

Then he was asked about being a witness at Meehan's trial. Did he think *then* that Waddell was involved in the Ayr murder? Yes, but he couldn't go back on his written statement; and when interviewed by the Procurator-Fiscal in 1974 he had stuck to his false story. It wasn't until Bell and McDougall interviewed him in 1976 that he admitted to having lied: this was because he learnt that if he continued to lie, he might be prosecuted for perjury.

He was followed by his wife Martha. She confirmed that Waddell hadn't stayed the night, but had arrived next morning. Asked if she would have told a lie at Meehan's trial, she said probably, as she had been told to say that Waddell had stayed the night: she hadn't turned up to give evidence at Meehan's trial because of fear and the fact that she was pregnant. She too had lied to the Fiscal, and had told the truth for the first time to Bell and McDougall.

The Carmichaels had come clean just seven years too late. Had they told the truth at Meehan's trial and so shown that Waddell's alibi on the night of the murder was a lie, it is unlikely that Meehan would have been convicted.

The next important evidence to have been discovered by Bell and MacDougall emerged from three women witnesses; Sarah McKay, sister of Waddell's friend James McCusker; Waddell's girlfriend Jean Casey and Rosanne Wills, a friend of Jean's. Sarah McKay was looking after Jean Casey at the time of the murder (Jean had been injured in a fire) and Waddell called to see Jean the day after he had given Sarah £30 for looking after her. He had also left a parcel for Sarah to look after while he and Jean were away in London with the Carmichaels. When he had gone, she looked in the parcel and found £1,700.

Then Jean Casey was called and said that shortly after the murder Waddell said he had had a big win at the bookies and was going to buy her a house. She had been given £600. Her friend Rosanne Wills came into the witness-box and said she had been given £595 to help Jean Casey purchase the house.

And finally came John McMullen, a Glasgow barman, who said that soon after the murder Waddell had come in with Donald Carmichael. Waddell had told him that he had won £1,250 on the horses, and asked him to keep £1,000 for him. *The money was all in new £10 notes.* Every day Waddell came in and withdrew forty or fifty pounds at a time. In about a week's time all the money had gone.

The total sum of money which according to these witnesses was in Waddell's possession at this time amounts to nearly £3,000. When we add the £200 given to Mr Carlin and smaller sums given to Dick, McIntyre and others, Waddell's statement to David Scott and other journalists that Mr Ross had much more money in the safe than he ever let on, is amply confirmed. I recalled what Lord Cameron had said when sentencing Waddell to three years imprisonment for denying at Meehan's trial that he had given Mr Carlin £200 for defending him if charged with the Ayr murder: 'Supposing he had told the jury the truth, they might have taken a very different view of an unemployed labourer handing over a substantial sum of money.' What would the jury's view have been if the unemployed labourer had told them that not only had he given £200 to Mr Carlin but nearly £3,000 to others!

The third most important piece of information had come from the files of the Ayrshire police. It will be recalled that when Mr Beltrami, who believed in Meehan's innocence from the beginning, received a letter from him in Barlinnie saying that 'wee McGuinness' had been picked up by the Ayr police in the early hours of the morning (see page 130) he at once contacted the Chief Constable's office in Ayr to find out if anyone *had* been picked up, and received an unsatisfactory answer.

Now the two officers who picked McGuinness up, Inspector Hepburn and Sergeant McNeil, appeared in the witness-box in person. They confirmed that at about 4.30 am on July 6th they had picked up a man 'with a slight build and a Glaswegian accent' some 600 yards from the Rosses' bungalow, and taken him to the bus station. From photographs recently shown, they had identified the man as William McGuinness. On the Monday after the murder they sent a report of the incident to the CID, *but had not been asked to make a statement about it until October*. A statement by Detective Constable Gall found in the files of the Ayrshire police confirmed that Mr Beltrami had telephoned him on October 7th to ask if a man had been picked up in the vicinity of the crime in the early hours of July 6th, and if so the names of the officers concerned. Mr Gall in the witness-box confirmed this, and added that he had immediately telephoned the information to Detective Superintendant Struthers.

And what had Superintendant Struthers done, the officer in overall charge of the case, and to whom all relevant information would have been sent? He appeared in the witness-box as a nervous, muddled witness who rarely answered any question directly.

He was asked if he had received Hepburn's and McNeil's report at the time of their submitting it, and replied, incredibly, that he hadn't. He agreed that Gall had passed him the message from Mr Beltrami, and was asked if he had collected the names of the two officers and their statement. After much questioning he admitted he had, and said he had given the original to the Ayr Procurator-Fiscal and a copy to Mr Beltrami's office manager, Mr McDonald. No one from the Fiscal's office was called to confirm or contest this, nor was Mr McDonald. Had he been asked, Mr McDonald would have vigorously denied having received anything of the kind. Nor could he have been mistaken; for it was what he and Mr Beltrami had been waiting for.

Here, once again, was evidence which if it had reached the ears of the defence in 1969, would not only have preempted Meehan's indictment but, if followed through, have ensured that McGuinness, and with him Waddell, would have stood trial in his place.

The fourth fresh piece of evidence to associate Waddell with the crime concerned certain marks found on Mrs Ross's face when taken to Ayr Hospital. In Waddell's confession to the *Daily Record* he admitted to having thrown ammonia in the face of Mrs Ross when attacking her, and inquiries had since been made to see if this could be true. Dr Neil Bremmer, of Ayr County Hospital, who had attended on Mrs Ross, now gave evidence that while at the time he thought the marks on her face had been caused by assault, the suggestion put to him recently that ammonia might have been the cause was a much more likely explanation: the marks were more consistent with ammonia than assault, and ammonia would also account for the chest symptoms.

Dr Bremmer was followed by an eminent pathologist, Professor Gilbert Forbes, who went even further; in 1975, having been asked to study the reports of Mrs Ross's death, he had come to the conclusion that the cause of death was definitely ammonia poisoning. Dr McLay a pathologist at the time of the murder, said that ammonia hadn't occurred to him at the time, but now he agreed it could have been a contributory factor.

And lastly, as regards new evidence against Waddell, Bell and McDougall had been through the records of Carnie's Car Hire firm in view of Waddell having said that he and his accomplice travelled to Ayr in a hire car; and an employee of the firm testified that on the day before the murder she had made out hire documents for a Ford Cortina in the name of William McGuinness.

This new evidence against Waddell was of course in addition to the evidence already there. This included that of William McIntyre who, it will be recalled, had told at Meehan's trial of how Andrew Dick had approached him with an invitation from Waddell to join him in a robbery at Ayr; of how he had gone to Ballachulish to buy a car for the job; of how he had backed down when he heard from Waddell that it was going to be a tie-up job, but had stayed in Dick's house during the night of the murder in order to give him an alibi.

Now he expanded on this in more detail, and for the first time mentioned McGuinness. Who was present, he was asked, at a meeting when the use of the car was being discussed? Dick was there, he said, Dick's wife, Ian Waddell and William McGuinness. He was shown a photograph of McGuinness and identified it. Did they say where the job was going to take place? Yes, in Ayrshire. Did they say anything about the nature of the job? Yes, a small safe had to be lifted. Later, when questioned about giving Dick an alibi on the night of the murder, he said that Dick had said, 'Ian is away a message.' Asked what a message meant he replied it was slang for a crime.

Until now McIntyre had given evidence in almost a whisper. But when questioned as to whether he thought Meehan was innocent of the crime, his voice suddenly grew in strength. 'I've been telling the police that for seven years,' he said. Had he written as much to Mr Beltrami before Meehan's trial? 'Yes,' he said, 'and I also told McGuinness that I was writing to Meehan's lawyer, and this was only a few days before the trial.' He was asked by defence counsel, 'Wasn't this a last minute attempt to assist your exceptional friend Mr Meehan?' This got him on the raw. 'Just a minute sir,' he replied. 'None of this "exceptional friend Mr Meehan", Waddell is a friend and Dick is a friend. I am not throwing one friend to the wolves to save another. I told the truth at Meehan's trial, and don't you beat about the bush with me. If you can get the jail for telling the truth, I'm quite willing to go to jail.' It was an impressive because spontaneous outburst.

Lastly he was asked directly by the Lord Advocate who he would say committed the murder, and he raised his finger at the dock and pointed at Waddell.

In addition, all Waddell's confessions were introduced; those to David Scott and Ken Vass of the BBC, Gordon Airs and Charles Beaton of the *Daily Record*, George Forbes and Jack Wallace of the *Scottish Daily News*, and the television confession for the BBC Birmingham programme *Night and Day*. Although these confessions were remarkable for the correct description of details in the Rosses' house, the defence inevitably emphasized the few things that didn't tally. Chief of these was the room through which McGuinness and Waddell entered the bungalow, and which Waddell had described as 'a lounge with a polished floor' when in fact it was a carpeted bedroom. But, as one police witness said, his description of the rooms was 'a very accurate description' of the sitting-room opposite the bedroom, and when one remembers that at the time of the confession Waddell was recalling an event of five years earlier that had taken place in the middle of the night, it is hardly surprising that he should have mistaken the position of one room for another. Inevitably too the defence made much play of the fact that Waddell had been paid for his confessions.

Many people have raised the question as to why Waddell confessed so often and so freely when such confessions were clearly an invitation to prosecution. There are a number of possible reasons: a desire for money, a desire for notoriety, a desire to expunge guilt, both as regards Mrs Ross (whom he had not expected to die) also Meehan and pressure from the underworld (with whom Meehan was popular) to get Meehan released. How far any or all of these factors influenced him it is impossible to say. But it is worthwhile recollecting the sequence of events.

It will be recalled that Waddell first expressed a wish to confess to Mr Beltrami, who he knew had been Meehan's solicitor, when Mr Beltrami had successfully acted for him in 1972. But he said he would only do so under the truth drug, as he knew from the failure of Meehan's application for the truth drug, that such a confession could not be accepted as evidence, *and he therefore could not subsequently be prosecuted.* He would like the experiment to take place in the studios of the BBC and he wanted a considerable sum of money for it.

Accordingly when Waddell was released from Barlinnie in February 1973, he was met by David Scott and Ken Vass of the BBC, who were empowered to enter into discussions about the experiment taking place. It was to them, driving away from Barlinnie, that Waddell admitted his part in the Ayr murder, *not knowing that Scott had a microphone concealed beneath his tie.* The negotiations for the experiment fell through, but when Waddell learnt that Scott intended to use his taped conversation in a BBC programme, and that this might result in arrest and prosecution, *he applied through the courts to have the programme stopped.* In this he was unsuccessful.

The programme went out, and Waddell must have been delighted to find that no action from the Crown Office resulted. Possibly the wish for money, possibly pressure from the underworld, encouraged him to repeat his confessions to other papers, and the more he confessed without reaction from the Crown Office, the more he was encouraged to confess the more. By the time he reached George Forbes and the *Scottish Daily News* in October 1975 he had come to realize, with every justification, that the Crown Office did not believe him, and that the probable reason was their reluctance to admit that in prosecuting Meehan, they had made a dreadful mistake. 'I'll never be charged,' he told Forbes, 'because it would mean the police would have to be charged for framing Meehan.' Indeed, had Tank McGuinness not died, Waddell would probably be confessing to this day. And for all we know he may continue to do so yet.

The reader may have concluded that the evidence against Waddell so far was massive enough to convict. It would have been even more massive had two further pieces of evidence been introduced. Both were available, but one was not led by the Lord Advocate, and the other was disallowed by the judge.

The evidence not led by the Crown concerned Meehan's identification parade. It will be recalled that the police who conducted the parade testified at Meehan's trial that Mr Ross had viewed the people first, and that when this evidence was given, Meehan had leaned over to Mr Beltrami to say that in fact Mr Ross had viewed it last. As a result of inquiries made after the trial, several of those present at the parade (including Meehan's then solicitor and Glasgow's present Lord Provost, Peter McCann) had given statements confirming that Mr Ross had viewed the parade last (see pages 292–3): after further inquiries from those who had viewed the parade, there was strong evidence to show that before viewing the parade, Mr Ross had heard from witnesses who had already viewed it what the police suspect (Meehan) looked like. Irene Burns had said, 'The old man asked me if I picked out anyone. I told him I had ... Isobel [Smith] came in and together we discussed the parade and I described Mr Meehan to Isobel. The old man was sitting near us as we were talking. Isobel and I agreed we had picked out the same person.' Another witness, Mr Falconer, had said, 'I remember one of the girls discussing the fact that she had picked out someone in the parade ... Mr Ross asked them if they had identified anyone, and one of them nodded, "Yes."' Mr Falconer also stated that Mr Ross had asked if he had identified anyone.

Incredibly none of this evidence was led, though both Mr Falconer and one of the girls, Isobel Smith (now Mrs Manson), were questioned on other matters. Mr Peter McCann was not called nor any of the other witnesses listed on pages 292–3. The Crown cannot have considered it irrelevant, so one can only assume that the Lord Advocate omitted it to save embarrassment to the Ayrshire police. Whatever the reason it was a most unfortunate omission.

As no evidence was called to cast doubts on the police account of the parade, the police could then be asked, as Superintendant Struthers and Sergeant Inglis were asked, whether they had heard of allegations that the parade had been rigged; and naturally they answered that such allegations were absurd. Mr Struthers did let in a chink of light when he was asked if the two girls *followed* Mr Ross, and he replied, *'I would have to say I can't be positive.'* But his was not taken up, and so the judge was in a position to say that 'over a period of years very senior and experienced policemen had been maligned, defamed and accused by Meehan of very grave dereliction of duty, including perjury and planting of evidence, without *as it turns out*, any shred of justification whatsoever'. It had turned out thus because evidence which might have told a different story had been omitted.

The evidence disallowed by the judge was even more vital. This was the information given by Mr Beltrami to the Crown after McGuinness's death that in private conversation with him between 1972 and 1976 McGuinness had told him on numerous occasions of his participation in the Ayr murder, information that Mr Beltrami had kept scrupulously and often agonisingly to himself. It was largely this information that had led the Secretary of State for Scotland to recommend Meehan's free pardon. The judge disallowed the evidence on two grounds, first because conversations between a client and his solicitor were confidential and could only be waived by the client. McGuinness could hardly waive it as he was dead, but Mr Beltrami had done the next best thing which was to obtain waivers both from Mrs McGuinness (who wanted the truth to come out) and the Law Society for Scotland. It turned out however that the Crown Office had not lodged the waivers in court. Whether their presence would have made any difference is not known but one can only say that if a rule such as this leads, as on this occasion it did lead, to a denial of the course of justice, the sooner it is changed the better.

The second reason for disallowing the evidence was that, although McGuinness had been named in the indictment as acting with Waddell, evidence against McGuinness was not competent against Waddell, as Waddell was not in a position to rebut it. But this was just the same grounds of complaint that Meehan had unsuccessfully raised at his own trial. Crucial evidence had been allowed relating to the dead Griffiths, the bits of paper found in his coat pocket, his conversations with Irene Cameron, which Meehan was in no position to rebut. Why was it allowed? Or conversely, why was the evidence that could have been given by Mr Beltrami relating to the dead McGuinness, not allowed? After all, we had heard evidence of McGuinness's movements from the Ayr traffic officers and the girl at Carnie's Car Hire, and from his wife Agnes of what he had said to her. It seemed that one ruling was in operation at Meehan's trial and the opposite at Waddell's.

There were other vital pieces of evidence omitted or disallowed. Mr William Carlin, in the witness-box, was not permitted to recount how Waddell had lied at Meehan's trial in denying that he had given Mr Carlin £200 to defend him for the Ayr murder. Mr Bell and Mr McDougall, who as the trial progressed, saw the case they had laboriously built up against Waddell dissolve in ashes and their six months work wasted, were not permitted to describe documents they had found in the files of the Ayrshire police. And I myself could have given evidence, had I been called, to show that Mr Ross, when he read the manuscript of this book, had accepted my account of how he knew before he viewed the identification parade, who the police suspect was.

In addition there were two questionable pieces of evidence, both relevant to a belief in Meehan's innocence, and neither of which was challenged by the Crown.

They were concerned with the vital question of the time available for Meehan and Griffiths to have got from Cairnyan to Blackburn Place, committed the murder and then picked up Irene Burns at the Underwood lay-by. Firstly, the police added to the evidence they had given at Meehan's trial that they could have driven the 52 miles from Stranraer to Blackburn Road in an hour by now saying they could have driven the 45 miles from Cairnyan to Blackburn Road in 50 minutes. No one challenged this absurdity.

Secondly, there was the evidence of Isobel Smith (Manson). It will be recalled that both Isobel and Irene and the two boys – four witnesses in all – had testified at Meehan's trial that Irene had said that Meehan and Griffiths had come by 'a couple of minutes' later. But now under questioning by Waddell's counsel, she was persuaded to agree that the time might have been 4.15 or even later. This was the moment for the Crown to challenge the evidence, to argue that the statement taken from Isobel Smith soon after the crime was infinitely safer than her memory seven years later. They signally failed to do so, with the result that in his charge to the jury Lord Robertson could refer to this erroneous time of 4.15 and so stretch the time available for Meehan and Griffiths to have committed the murder.

There was one further important piece of evidence that the Crown did not challenge. It will be recalled that in his statement of facts before Meehan's trial, Superintendant Cowie had declared that he had searched Mr Ross's safe and found it 'empty'. Now he told a quite different story. *There was money and brown paper in the safe*, he said, and although he hadn't seen the white piece of diary paper then, he *'thought it was further down the drawer'*. Had the Crown asked him to square these contradictory statements, it would have been interesting to know what he would have said.

The forensic officer, Detective Chief Inspector Cook, also gave some revealing evidence about the pieces of paper. He said that it was 'just possible it could be coincidental' that the brown paper was the same. But the small piece of paper found in Griffiths' car-coat pocket was *'definitely part of a page of the diary found in the safe'*. This evidence, if true, was proof positive that the pieces of paper were planted, and furthermore tended to show that Cook himself (who was hardly likely to have indulged in self-incrimination) had nothing to do with the planting.

And what in the last analysis told most heavily in favour of Waddell and against Meehan, what made Waddell's acquittal a virtual certainty, were the views of the presiding judge, Lord Robertson. I do not think I am misinterpreting Lord Robertson when I say that before the trial ever started, he was of the belief (held by most of the Scottish bench), that Meehan had been properly convicted, and that efforts over the years to show otherwise had been a sort of conspiracy to pervert the course of justice.

First indications as to the direction in which Lord Robertson's mind was moving came at the beginning of the trial when he called in two other judges to rule as to whether or not Meehan's free pardon quashed his conviction and after hearing legal arguments they came to no conclusion.

Now this was an extraordinary decision, contrary both to common sense and English precedent. In 1963 in the House of Lords the Lord Chancellor ruled that a free pardon wiped out a conviction and all its consequences and an accused so pardoned was to be regarded as having been acquitted. Again in 1966 when considering the posthumous free pardon granted to Timothy Evans, the Lords ruled that its effect was to say his conviction had been expunged and that he had been wrongly put to death. Why then should the effects of a free pardon granted by a common sovereign be any different in Scotland from in England?

Yet the failure of the three judges to come to a conclusion was to have far-reaching consequences of which they must have been well aware. Had they ruled that a free pardon *does* quash a conviction, Waddell's special defence of impeachment – that Meehan and not he had committed the crime – would have been greatly weakened. Now it was enormously strengthened.

Mention has already been made of evidence disallowed by the judge. There were also occasions throughout the trial when, by question or comment, the judge seemed to indicate where his own feeling lay. For instance, during the examination of Detective Superintendant Struthers reference was made to Meehan's vehement denials to the police in 1969 that he had committed the crime. The judge asked Mr Struthers if criminals did make vehement denials of crime with which they were charged, and Mr Struthers replied that it depended on the experience of the criminal: the more experienced the criminal (a nice side swipe at Meehan this) the more vehement the denial. But neither the judge nor the Lord Advocate nor anyone else followed this up by asking, 'And would you also expect vehement denials from a man who was innocent?'

Again, there was this exchange between the judge and Meehan on the subject of Meehan's compensation.

'How have you been living since your release?'

'I've been living on compensation of £2,500 paid on account.'

'Do you expect to get a lot more?'

'I expect so.'

'Did you know when you were in prison you would get a lot of money when you came out?'

'I would expect, having got a free pardon, I would get compensation. I was offered £6,000 from the *Daily Record*, and refused it. I got £2,000 from them.' (This was because he had given an interview to David Scott of the BBC at the prison gates.)

'Why was that?'

'For my story.'

'Are you getting any other money . . . from television?'

'Yes, two cheques for about £1,000.'

To which the judge replied, *'A pretty lucrative affair, this, of yours.'*

It would be hard to imagine such a question being put by anyone who entertained even the smallest belief that Meehan might be innocent, and if so, was entitled to every penny he could get.

And as a last small example, when Gordon Airs was giving evidence about Waddell's confession to the *Daily Record*, he suggested that this had been a very different case from others he had experienced. What was different about it, asked Lord Robertson? 'We thought perhaps Waddell was telling the truth,' said Airs. To which Lord Robertson replied, *'Perhaps'*, in tones that seemed to indicate his doubts.

But it was when all the evidence was over, and it came to the judge's charge to the jury (in England the summing-up) that Lord Robertson's sense of fairness was most absent; and what should have been an impartial review of the evidence (and God knows if any case needed an impartial review, it was this one) became almost a direction to the jury to acquit.

Indeed, it was much more. Such was the certainty of Lord Robertson's belief in Meehan's guilt (which all the new evidence against Waddell had done nothing to shake) that he felt confident enough to make an unprecedented three-pronged attack, first on the integrity of those of us who had campaigned on Meehan's behalf over the years, secondly, against the Lord Advocate for having brought the case, and thirdly, against the Secretary of State for having ever recommended the free pardon.

He recalled that seven years earlier Meehan had been found guilty by a jury 'on evidence which was amply justified'. He went on, 'Some public support was whipped up over the years *for reasons which were not entirely clear, and for motives which might be imagined.*' This would seem to suggest that the Meehan Committee knew all along that he was guilty, but had continued to campaign on his behalf for ulterior motives. What possible motives could his trial counsel, all four of his solicitors and myself have had other than in wanting to see a wrong put right? Yet in the phrase 'for motives which might be imagined', Lord Robertson seemed to suggest that so clear was Meehan's guilt that all right-minded people would recognize our unworthy motives immediately.

For a long time, he said, the Lord Advocate and the Crown Authorities had paid no attention to 'this clamour', but in 1976 a decision was 'apparently' taken to advise on a free pardon. 'The reasons for this decision,' he said, 'have not become apparent at this trial' (some of them had, but he had chosen to ignore them), and he went on to attack the Secretary of State for usurping the functions of the judiciary. 'If the Executive,' he said, 'are going to interfere in such a way in administration of justice, *there is no end to it ... because of course it could be done in every and any case.*' Finally, he said that a pardon was, in ordinary sense of language, for something you had done, and not for something you hadn't done.

There are several points here. Firstly, the recommendation of a free pardon without reference back to the courts has always been vested in the Executive, a right which the judiciary has never questioned. Hundreds of free pardons have been granted in England in recent years, mostly for minor traffic offences, and not even in the most serious of them did the English judiciary take issue. In Scotland, in 1975, a free pardon was granted to a man who had served over a year in prison for a bank robbery, and the Scottish judiciary did not protest.

Secondly, as regards his complaint that a free pardon 'could be done in every and any case', Lord Robertson did not seem to have appreciated that it is only done when the Secretary of State, acting on the recommendation of his legal advisers, finds overwhelming reasons for doing so; or that in Meehan's case, because of the strict rules of evidence, many of the overwhelming reasons could not be given.

Thirdly, as regards a pardon being given for something you have done rather than something you haven't done, Lord Robertson did not ask why, if this was so, Meehan had suddenly been released from prison and given £2,500 compensation with the promise of more to come. One gained the impression from all of Lord Robertson's remarks that he took the view that the Secretary of State *had* responded to 'clamour', and had no overwhelming reasons at all.

Lord Robertson turned to the evidence, and prefaced his remarks by saying, 'There is no legal justification whatever in saying that Meehan was wrongly convicted, and having heard all the evidence in this case [quite untrue], you might well have come to the clear conclusion that he was in fact rightly convicted . . .' It would be difficult to think of a more clear-cut direction to acquit.

Step by step he went through some of the evidence against Waddell, step by step he offered alternative explanations to show Waddell's innocence. There was no evidence linking Waddell with Ayr, he said, no fingerprints or stolen articles found in his possession. He did not add that this was true of Meehan too.

He spent some time stressing the discrepancies in

Waddell's confessions about the details of the Rosses' house but did not emphasize the far greater number of things that tallied ('I think the Lord Advocate said over 40 which appear to tally with the lay-out of the house, the articles in the house and things of that sort . . .'). Indeed he tried to explain these away by suggesting that 'all the evidence given at the first trial . . . was there, written down for anyone who cared to read it. Productions were available . . . photographs . . . *and no doubt there would have been extensive publication in all the newspapers of the details of the murder and of the Rosses' house*.' The jury must have found this specious explanation very plausible, but in fact *hardly any of the details supplied by Waddell to the Daily Record had appeared either in the notes of evidence at the first trial nor in the newspapers*. Indeed it was because of the fact that the details supplied by Waddell and subsequently confirmed by Mr Ross were entirely new evidence that led the BBC, the *Daily Record* and the *News* to institute their own inquiries.

On the same point he suggested that Waddell's confessions were based on 'information fed to him over a period of time by inducements of drink and money', but he did not add that Waddell's first confession to David Scott and Ken Vass of the BBC was made neither for drink nor money. (The reader will also recall that his confession to McCafferty in 1969, and the evidence of McIntyre at both trials, were also given neither for drink nor money.)

Lord Robertson then turned to the large sum of money in Waddell's possession after the crime, and explained it by saying that it was 'considerably more than was said to have been taken from the house', reminding the jury of Waddell's evidence that he had won it on the horses. He did not also remind the jury that in his confession to David Scott and George Forbes, Waddell had already said that there was a lot more taken from the house than was actually revealed, nor did he ask them to consider the likelihood of 'an unemployed labourer' having the stake money to win such enormous sums.

And then he left Waddell and built up in considerable

detail the case against Meehan (and after a time Meehan stormed from the court in protest, saying his pardon wasn't worth the paper in was written on); and he gave a strong impression of emphasizing those things that told against Meehan more than those that favoured him. For instance he spoke at great length – five pages of the official transcript – of evidence given by long-term prisoners from Peterhead (dangerous men, they were led manacled into court) who said that Meehan had admitted to them his part in the Ayr murder.

But when it came to one of the most vital pieces of evidence in Meehan's favour – Mr Ross's insistence that the two men had Glasgow accents – he dismissed it in a single paragraph. 'It is quite true that Ross said that Pat and Jim both had Scottish voices, and we have been told that Griffiths was a Lancashire man and spoke with a Lancashire accent. Well, ladies and gentlemen, it is for you to say what you think the explanation of that may be, whether it is true, whether it is not, whether you think Mr Ross may have been mistaken . . .'

Double standards were used too in the judge's assessment of Isobel Smith's (Mrs Manson's) evidence about the time that Meehan and Griffiths picked her up at Underwood lay-by. 'There is a bit of doubt as to what the time of that was. The girl herself says in her evidence, I think she got it at about 4.15, I recollect . . . she certainly got it a good bit later than I think it had been in the previous trial . . . assuming that they did pick up the girl at four o'clock, even 4.15, there is really no alibi for Meehan between at least midnight and four o'clock, *and it only takes 50 minutes to drive from Stranraer to the bungalow in Ayr*' (a total impossibility and a claim unsupported by any evidence).

Now right at the beginning of his charge to the jury Lord Robertson had suggested that evidence given at the time of the first trial was more reliable than that given at the second. 'Ladies and gentlemen, to go into a witness-box and depone on oath as to what happened seven and a half years ago on some things which may have been very small incidents at the time, I should think you may have some difficulty in remembering or really remembering the thing at all ... the recollection of many of the witnesses may have been saying things that they think happened ...'

But later, in referring to specific witnesses, Lord Robertson did not stress his earlier warning. Mr McMullen, the barman to whom Waddell had given £1,000, had said that Waddell and Carmichael had been in his pub between 6 pm and 8 pm on the night of the murder. 'Well, if Waddell was there, if you accepted that evidence, it would of course have a distinct bearing upon the whole story told by Mr Carmichael and indeed Mrs Carmichael.' Not a word about the possibility of McMullen's memory being dimmed. And again with Mrs Manson. Not a whisper of a suggestion to the jury that her evidence at the first trial, *confirmed by three other witnesses and given within three months of the murder*, was likely to be more reliable than that coaxed out of her at a second trial seven and a half years later.

Finally Lord Robertson referred to Meehan's long list of convictions, but did not add that none was for violence. The jury of course could not know that Waddell at that very moment was serving a sentence for violence in Barlinnie – nor as regards the second charge against him of committing perjury at Meehan's trial, that he had already served one three-year sentence for doing that very thing.

All in all it was not surprising that the jury took only an hour to find Waddell not guilty.

A few days later in the House of Commons, the Secretary of State for Scotland took Lord Robertson to task for his remarks. The decision to recommend Meehan's pardon, he said, had been his alone, and was not as the result of 'clamour'. On information not all of which was before the court he had concluded that Meehan should not be held in prison for murdering Mrs Ross. That was still his view. He was considering an inquiry and the form it should take. Two M.P.s suggested that Lord Robertson should either resign or be removed from the bench.

In a statement in reply Lord Robertson said that his comments had arisen only from the evidence that was before him. If the evidence the Secretary of State had had, had been before him, his comments might have been different.

When I read this, I could not recall any evidence having been given to justify his remark that those of us who had campaigned for Meehan had been activated 'for reasons which were not entirely clear and motives which might be imagined'.

Since Lord Robertson has publicly questioned the motives of others in this case, it is not unreasonable to question his own. What made him ignore the massive evidence against Waddell, and seemingly direct the jury to acquit? What made him go out on such a limb in his remarks about the Lord Advocate and the Secretary of State?

I think the answer is simple. It is that the judiciary – all judiciaries everywhere – have a strong deep-seated and perfectly understandable reluctance to admit that they can err. The Meehan verdict was initially a straight-forward miscarriage of justice; but the longer that Meehan remained in prison and the more often the judiciary turned down his applications for Bills of Criminal Letters and the Lord Advocate and Secretary of State refused to re-open his case, the more convinced the judiciary became that they must be right and Meehan wrong. By 1976 to have admitted otherwise would be to admit that they had made not just one mistake but a whole series of mistakes, indeed were very near to thwarting the course of justice; and such an admission, for such men, would be intolerable. No wonder that Lord Robertson approached the case in the belief that Meehan was Mrs Ross's murderer, and that the ends of justice (not to mention faith in the judiciary) would best be served by seeing that view prevail.

There is, oddly enough, almost an exact parallel in this case to the Evans/Christie case, the Waddell verdict coming at about the same point in events as the Scott-Henderson report in the other. In 1950 Timothy Evans was hanged for strangling his daughter in 10 Rillington Place. In 1953 John Christie was found to have strangled several women there. After his trial the Home Secretary instructed Mr John Scott-Henderson Q.C. to inquire whether in Evans' case justice had miscarried. But the thought of justice miscarrying was as unacceptable to Mr Scott-Henderson as to Lord Robertson. He concluded blandly that nothing had gone wrong, and that only the two male occupants of 10 Rillington Place were both strangling women on the premises in much the same way without either knowing what the other was doing. Such a preposterous conclusion was unacceptable to public opinion, and eleven years later as a result of prolonged 'clamour', another inquiry was convened under a judge. This did find Evans innocent of the charge for which he had been hanged, but added, to save the conscience of the Bench, that he probably had strangled his wife, on which charge he had been indicted but not tried. By this equivocal conclusion the judge no doubt hoped to muddy the waters; but the Home Secretary of the day, Mr Roy Jenkins, being a man of courage and imagination, at once recommended a free pardon.

The conclusion is clear: judiciaries everywhere, and at all times, close ranks and prepare to fight long rear-guard actions when they think their virtue is in question.

At the time of writing (January 1977) the Secretary of State has not yet announced an inquiry, but we have every hope that he will in the near future. This should clear up once and for all a case that has dragged on far too long already. It should not only clear Meehan finally but also, which is even more important for the good name of Scottish justice, expose and define the irregularities, especially as regards the identification parade and the bits of paper, that led to his conviction. The inquiry may also conclude, if its terms of reference allow, that had all the evidence that was before the Secretary of State been before the court at Waddell's trial, the verdict might have been very different.

That Meehan's conviction and Waddell's acquittal was a double miscarriage of justice, I have no doubt at all. Waddell, as he serves out the remainder of his term for violence in Barlinnie, must be thanking his lucky stars. To have confessed in detail to his part in the Ayr murder, then to be tried for it, and despite a mass of evidence against him, to be acquitted, was for him an astonishing piece of good fortune. He may when he is released, choose to sell the detailed story (not that he can have many details left) of how he and McGuinness committed the Ayr murder, to the highest bidder, thus indulging in the cheque-book journalism that Lord Robertson so deplored.

On the wider front, some reform seems necessary. Part of Lord Robertson's confusion in being unable to decide what a free pardon meant, lies in the absurdity of the phrase itself. It is high time it was abolished, and some simpler expression such as 'exoneration and apology' substituted.

So far as the conduct of the two trials is concerned, I begin increasingly to wonder whether the accusatorial system of justice is the best we can do. Twelve years ago I concluded a book on another case with these words:

'Let no one pretend that our system of justice is a search for truth. It is nothing of the kind. It is a contest between two sides played according to certain rules, and if the truth happens to emerge as the result of the contest, then that is pure windfall. But it is unlikely to. It is not something with which the contestants are concerned. They are concerned only that the game should be played according to the rules.

'There are many rules and one of them is that some questions which might provide a shortcut to the truth are not allowed to be asked, and those that are asked are not allowed to be answered. The result is that verdicts are often reached haphazardly, for the wrong reasons, in spite of the evidence, and may or may not coincide with the literal truth.'

Had we in Scotland, and in England, some form of inquisitorial system, such as they have in the first instance in France, this book might have never needed to be written. A recent report by Lord Thomson on Scottish Criminal Procedure recommended that the Procurator-Fiscal should regain his ancient powers of personally questioning the suspect in front of the Sheriff and the man's solicitor, in much the same way as the *juge d'instruction* is empowered to in France. Had the Ayr Fiscal at the time of Meehan's apprehension been able to examine him and others in this way, and considered whether there was a case against him in the light of all the circumstances, it is probable that Meehan would never have come to trial. A Fiscal with such powers would be the greatest safeguard a suspect could have against the over-zealousness of the hard-pressed police, as well as provide a useful shortcut to the truth.

I finished the other book with this paragraph:

'It is time not only for the rules of the game to be revised; but also, if (accused people) are to have a just trial in future, to ask ourselves whether the game we have chosen is the one that we wish to go on playing.'

After the trials of Patrick Meehan and Ian Waddell that thought is surely no less relevant to-day.

Postscript June 1977

As the page proofs of this book go to the binders, a number of important events have recently occurred.

Firstly, Meehan has rejected as 'ridiculous' total compensation of £7,500 (an additional £5,000 to the £2,500 already received) awarded by an independent assessor for his six and a half years of wrongful imprisonment. He cites a similar case of a man who in Scotland recently was awarded a total of £5,000 *for only eleven months* wrongful imprisonment, and whose record was just as bad as his own.

Secondly, the Secretary of State has ordered an inquiry into the Ayr murder under a High Court judge, Lord Hunter, with the following terms of reference:

(1) The inquiry will take place in private.
(2) It will not have any powers of subpoena.
(3) Its report will be published.
(4) It will not be able to consider

(a) The guilt or innocence of Meehan or Waddell.
(b) The Secretary of State's reasons for recommending a free pardon for Meehan.
(c) The Lord Advocate's reasons whether or not to institute criminal proceedings.

Soon after this announcement, the Lord Advocate issued a statement that he would not prosecute any witness who in the course of the inquiry admitted to having committed a crime connected with the investigations of the murder and the prosecutions of Meehan and Waddell. This presumably was so that the identification parade-riggers and whoever planted the bits of paper in Griffiths' car-coat pocket could come clean for the first time. But it was somewhat ironic to find the Lord Advocate now accepting the idea of waivers of immunity from prosecution. The reader will recall (pages 256–8) our efforts to persuade the Lord Advocate to grant a waiver of immunity from prosecution to Waddell's colleague at the end of 1975, and our subsequent rebuff from the Crown Agent. Yet had the Lord Advocate arranged for McGuinness to be given immunity from prosecution then, not only would the truth have emerged for the first time, but all of us, including the courts, would subsequently have been saved a vast amount of time and trouble.

Soon after this announcement the Meehan Committee met to decide whether or not to give evidence to Lord Hunter's inquiry. At first sight the depressingly restrictive terms of reference seemed to us to be establishing a good base for whitewash – on no account must people in high places be blamed! Further, if Lord Hunter was not to be allowed to pronounce on Meehan's or Waddell's guilt or innocence, what was the inquiry's object?

On the other hand Lord Hunter was represented to us as a man of great intellectual integrity and independence of mind who would in no way be influenced by the views of anyone, including his colleagues on the Scottish bench. The inquiry being in private also meant that Lord Hunter would not be bound by the normal rules of evidence, and could ask any questions of any witnesses invited to appear: there would be no reporters present, so future witnesses would have no knowledge of what past witnesses had said. Finally, as it was our Committee who had over the years repeatedly called for an inquiry, it would seem somewhat contrary, not to say churlish, not to attend it. We agreed therefore to offer Lord Hunter any assistance we could, and to advise Patrick Meehan (who had already announced he would boycott it) to do the same.

Finally, in the spring Waddell was once again released from Barlinnie, and once again lost no time in confirming his guilt, this time, and without payment, to the *Glasgow Evening Times.*

'He said, "I want to tell the truth. I want the whole thing finished. If I told the whole story, it would show that I did it."

'Waddell said to-day he was prepared to take a lie-detector test or be hypnotized along with Paddy Meehan. He added, "I'm willing to get round the table with everyone involved in the case to get the truth told. I want to start a new life."

'Waddell said that while admitting responsibility for the crime, he had no conscience about his actions. Because he left them bound but alive, he does not consider that amounts to murder.

' "But it was me all right," he said.'

Stop Press

From the *Scotsman* of June 7th, 1977.

'Ian Waddell (39) appeared in private at Glasgow Sheriff Court yesterday, charged with being in possession of a gun with intent to commit a robbery . . .

The charge states that the offences took place within five years of his being convicted on charges of attempted murder and breach of the peace – at the High Court in Glasgow in June last year – contrary to the Firearms Act.'

NOTES

Page 133

Meehan's Indictment charged him with 'acting along with James Griffiths', and he wrote forcefully about the injustice of this to Mr Beltrami.

'It seems to me that there is something wrong with my indictment. An indictment charging me "along with James Griffiths (now deceased)" is, in my view, hardly competent. Is it not a cardinal principle that the accused is only answerable for evidence against himself?

'An indictment "acting along with a man unknown" is quite valid, but an indictment naming the man would surely require his presence if evidence is to be led that only he can answer.

'Were Griffiths alive he may well have had an explanation consistent with innocence for the paper alleged to have been found in his jacket. Surely it would be for the jury to accept or reject this?

'But Griffiths is dead and therefore cannot give an explanation. How then, can I? Does the Law allow me three guesses or six? Although I have tied myself in with Griffiths, it does not follow that I am answerable for what Griffiths had in his possession. This would be an unfair burden on me, since it prevents me from contesting the Crown evidence. The evidence at my Trial cannot by its nature or source be such as to prevent me defending myself.

'Had Griffiths had £1,000 in his pocket this would be damning evidence unless a perfect explanation could be put forward by Griffiths. But Griffiths being dead cannot explain anything.

'Don't you think Mr Beltrami that there is an argument that the indictment is incompetent? Surely Mr Fairbairn can prevent the Crown leading this evidence? Griffiths has never been convicted of this crime, and cannot be tried in his absence. If Griffiths were still alive but "on the run" would the Crown still be able to charge me "while acting along with James Griffiths" and lead evidence against him – for me to answer? I feel my indictment should read "while acting with a man unknown". Will you please consider the above as I do feel we may have an argument, and I am sure you have already entertained some doubt about the point.

'As I understand it, persons charged together should be tried together except under special circumstances when the Court may order separate Trials. But you can't order a separate Trial for a dead man. Were he alive he may have testified that the paper had been planted by the Police; this would have been for the jury to consider. Whether it would have been acceptable is another point. I cannot explain what Griffiths had in his pockets and I can't see that the Crown can call upon me to give an explanation. After all the evidence must surely be that I can challenge it.

'The indictment may be competent, but evidence which I am prevented from challenging is not.'

Page 154
The evidence that has come to light since the trial that Mr Ross viewed the parade last and not first is now overwhelming.
1. *Peter McCann* (Meehan's solicitor) 'I cannot swear if there were no other witnesses after Mr Ross, but I am perfectly satisfied that Mr Ross was not the first witness to enter that room.'
2. *Cornelius McMahon* (Mr McCann's assistant) '... it is my recollection that after this [Ross's 'identification' of Meehan's voice] the parade broke up.'
3. *Thomas Haxton* '... his recollection is that Mr Ross left the room first.'
4. *Gillies Falconer* 'He is quite certain that Mr Ross was taken from this room first, and was under the impression that Mr Ross was going to see the parade.'
5. *Irene Burns* 'The old man was taken out of the room first.'
6. *Isobel Smith* '... she remembered Mr Ross being taken out of this room first, and she assumed that he was going to see the parade.'

7. *James Durand* (on the parade with Meehan) 'I am quite certain that Mr Ross did not see the parade first.' After describing Mr Ross's collapse: 'As far as I can remember, the Parade was then dismissed, and after collecting our expenses, we all left.'
8. *Laurence Rooney* (on the parade with Meehan) 'I can say definitely that Mr Ross was certainly not the first man to view the parade. In fact my recollection is that after Mr Ross collapsed, there was a bit of a commotion, and we were all dismissed. . . .'
9. *Gerald McMail* (on the parade with Meehan) 'Mr Ross was the last witness to be brought into the Identification Room.'
10. *Patrick Meehan* 'I can swear that Abraham Ross was the last witness to view the parade.'

Mr Ross has denied that he learnt anything from other witnesses; yet, in a precognition taken by Mr Ross Harper in 1971, he admitted that he did not go straight from the first room to the Identification parade. 'I went into one room, *and then went into another room*, and then to the Identification Parade.'

The statements from the first eight witnesses were taken by Mr Joseph Beltrami or a member of his staff, and the one from Gerald McMail was taken by Meehan's son, Patrick Meehan.

Pages 157 and 223
The evidence of Detective Superintendent Cowie and Detective Inspector Cook about the pieces of paper found in the safe and in Griffiths' car-coat pocket is highly unsatisfactory.

In his statement of facts made before the trial Detective Superintendent Cowie declared that he had looked at the safe when called at the Ross house on July 7th and found it empty. The next day, July 8th, Detective Inspector Cook visited the house and made a thorough examination everywhere. Had he found any pieces of paper in the safe, he would have taken them away for analysis and recorded the fact in his statement of facts. That he did not so do is corroboration of Cowie's statement that the safe was empty.

Six weeks then go by, during which the safe, presumably still empty, sits in Ayr Police Station. On August 18th Mr Cowie returns from leave, and learns that there has been no further progress in the case. However Mr Struthers tells him that on July 31st Mr Cook found two bits of paper, one white and the size of a shirt button, the other brown, and also tiny, in Griffiths' car-coat pocket. This news makes Mr Cowie 'recollect having seen something similar in the safe'. So he goes to the safe and opens it; and the safe that was empty on July 7th when Cowie looked at it (and according to Mr Ross's evidence had no paper in it) now has brown pieces of paper in both drawers and a white piece of paper in one drawer. How and when did those pieces of paper get there?

So Mr Cook is informed in Glasgow, and on August 21st he comes down to Ayr, and Mr Cowie takes him to the safe and they look at the pieces of paper together. They then go round to 2 Blackburn Place, where they find brown paper similar to the brown paper in the safe, lying on the floor of the safe cupboard. Mr Cook takes all the pieces back to his laboratory in Glasgow, and here he finds the brown pieces and white piece in the safe to be 'of common origin' to the brown piece and white piece in Griffiths' car-coat pocket.[1]

Page 158

Mr Murdo Beaton, then a detective sergeant and Mr Cook's assistant, and now Warden of the High School at Portree, Isle of Skye, has made this comment to me in regard to the phrase 'of common origin':

'When summing up our findings in any scientific investigation we had to think about how much importance we should attach to any piece of evidence found. We usually considered the following four categories based on our own

[1] I am grateful to Mr Nicholas Fairbairn for pointing out how strange it is that when the non forensic expert, Mr Cowie, *hears* about Mr Cook having found little bits of paper in Griffiths' car-coat on July 31st, this makes him 'recollect' having seen something similar in the safe; yet when the expert, Mr Cook, *finds* the bits of paper in Griffiths' coat, he has no recollection of having seen anything similar in the safe.

view of the statistical probability of these pieces of evidence having been picked up in some other innocent way, and that is obviously a very subjective view:

'1. "They could have a common origin"
2. "They probably have a common origin"
3. "It is highly probable that they have a common origin"
4. "There is no doubt that they have a common origin"

'The first category means that the materials found, although identical to the samples from the locus, are very common. The accused could have become contaminated with these materials other than by his having been at the locus, but scientific evidence even in this category sounds very impressive to a layman sitting on a jury, although it is really no more than a bit of "window-dressing".

'The second category means that the materials found are identical to the samples provided, and moreover that these samples are in some way unusual, although not unique.

'The third category means that the materials found on the accused are identical to the samples taken from the locus, and also that this material is in some way unusual to such a degree that it is difficult to imagine how the accused could get such a contamination except by his having been at the locus of the crime.

'The fourth category means that the material is unique or it can be physically fitted to the sample.'

The reader may well think that Mr Cook's declaration, 'I am of the opinion that they have a common origin', coming from so experienced an officer, falls within the third category of Mr Beaton's interpretations, i.e., that his view was that 'it is difficult to imagine how the accused could get such a contamination except by his having been at the locus of the crime.'

Mr Beaton, incidentally, believes Meehan innocent of the Ayr murder.

For a further comment on the pieces of paper evidence see pages 222–3 (Judge's charge to the jury).

Page 159
Nearly two years later, when preparing a memorandum on the case for the author, Meehan wrote of his own explanation of the evidence of the bits of paper in relation to the Crown Office statement.

'It is safe to say that the Crown Office issued their statement [that with the death of Griffiths and arrest of Meehan they were not looking for anyone else in connection with the Ayr murder] because they were assured by the Police that the case was closed.

'But what was the evidence at that time? Against me there was a voice identification, achieved (as we now know) by a phoney Identification parade; and against James Griffiths there was not one iota of evidence. Indeed there was evidence to say that James Griffiths could *not* have been one of the men who committed the crime; because Mr Ross said the raiders had Glasgow accents, and Griffiths was English.

'The Police and the Crown Office were in a bit of a fix. Because of the statement to the press, they were committed to bringing me to trial – and to bring me to trial along with the dead James Griffiths. But as things were, there was not sufficient evidence to take me to trial, and there was no evidence to implicate James Griffiths. Something had to be done, and it was!

'Five weeks after issuing their statement the Police claim that paper found in the pocket of James Griffiths was identical to paper from the drawer of the Ross safe. These fragments of paper served a double purpose. (1) They implicated Griffiths, enabling the Crown Office to name him on the indictment and (2) they served to corroborate the phoney voice identification and convict me.

'One can well imagine the state the Police – and the Crown Office – were in before they made this remarkable discovery about the bits of paper. What would their position have been had they not made it? They could hardly have taken me to trial charged with acting along with a man unknown, when they had already named Griffiths as the man in their statement. Equally they could not have dropped the charge against me without making themselves look ridiculous.

'It should be noted that at the time the Crown Office statement was issued, I was charged "while acting with a man unknown". It was not until the 10th October that I was charged "while acting with James Griffiths".

'The Crown Office statement was highly prejudicial to my trial; and having made it, the Crown Office became a party to their own cause. They could not draw back without leaving themselves open to attack. They carried on, and in the search for two men with Glasgow accents, the Police produced evidence from the pocket of an Englishman with a Lancashire accent. Sherlock Holmes was definitely not involved in this case!

'From the moment the Crown Office made their statement, the search for evidence must have been intensive; and it would become more intensive as the days passed into weeks. Any halfwit would know how that paper got into the Crown evidence.'

Page 187

Meehan's comments on the Crown argument that he was in Stranraer 'to set up an alibi'.

'Setting up an alibi (to my mind) means either that one produces false evidence that one was at A when in fact one was at B; or when one knows a crime is to be committed by someone else, one makes a point of being somewhere else. Griffiths and I were outside the hotel at the time stated, therefore we could not have been setting up an alibi. We could not have been in two places at once; Stranraer and Ayr.

'The fact of the matter was that the Crown, realising that they could not dispute that we had been outside the hotel – the evidence was overwhelming – threw in this phrase about setting up an alibi in order to confuse the jury. They were saying to the jury: "We do not dispute that Meehan and Griffiths were at the hotel. We know they were there: they were setting up an alibi to prove they were there and not in Ayr. They were at the hotel setting up an alibi. Because they were not really at the hotel at all. They were in Ayr."

And no doubt the jury would think "This is all double dutch to us, but that chap with the wig must know what he is talking about – even if we don't." '

Page 254

For Meehan to succeed in his application for a Bill of Criminal Letters, he had to prove to the Court that he had 'suffered injury of a substantial, particular, special, and peculiarly personal nature beyond all others ...' In this he failed, and his wry comments on it are worth recording:

'Visualise yourself standing on the scaffold, and the hangman is about to throw the lever. Suddenly your solicitor enters the Death Chamber and says, "We have just discovered that you were wrongly convicted as a result of police perjury. But it is a question if you have a substantial and peculiar personal interest." You would wonder why you were standing on the trap if you did not have a substantial and peculiar interest – just as I wonder why I am serving a life sentence if I don't have a substantial and peculiar interest.'

Appendix I

IDENTIFICATION PARADE

Held at 11.40 am *on* Monday 14th July, 1969

within Det/Const's Rm, Central Police Office, Glasgow.

**Suspect or Accused*
- *Name* PATRICK CONNOLLY MEEHAN
- *Age* 42 b. 12.4:27
- *Address* 474 Old Rutherglen Rd., Glasgow C.5
- *Dress* Blue pin-stripe lounge suit, black shoes, green checked shirt and tie.

Crime Murder and Robbery.
Officer in Charge of Parade D/Sgt. J. Inglis
Other Officers conducting Parade D/Const. D. Gall.
Law Agent of Suspect/Accused (state if present)* Present – Peter McCann Solicitor, 101 St. Vincent Street, Glasgow.
Objections raised by Suspect/Accused or Law Agent and the action taken thereon:*
Both objected to No's. 2 + 5, who were withdrawn. A third man who entered room was objected to because of age and he too was withdrawn.

Officer in Charge of Case (state if present) Present: D/Supt. Struthers, D/Ch.Insp. McAlister + D/Insp. McAllister.

Names, Ages and Addresses of Persons in Parade

1. Patrick Connolly Meehan (42) 474 Old Rutherglen Rd. C.
2. John Richard Meoghan (26) 86 Frankfield St., Glas. E. — Objection – too tall
3. Gerald McMail (20) 115 Summerhill Rd., Glas. W.5.

4. Laurence Rooney (28) 33 Langholm St., Glas. W.4.

Objection – too small +dark

5. Robert Burns (34) 47 Inglefield St., Glas. S.2.
6. Thomas Thomson (34) Whitelees Cottage, Greenock.
7. James Durand (27) 42 Inglefield St., Glas. S.2.
8. Charles Lane (24) 40 Highburn Rd., Glas. W.2.
9. James Fallon (41) 14 Monteith Rd., Glas. S.4.
10.
11.
12.

Signature John Inglis *Rank* D/Sgt. *Date* 14/7/69

ORDER OF PARADE

Witness (Name, age and Address)	1 2 3 4 5 6 7 8 9 10 11 12	*Words used by Witness*
Abraham Ross (66) 2 Blackburn Place AYR	1 4 3 8 7 6 9 √	'That's the voice. I know it, I know it. I don't have to go any further.' 'Oh, that's him, that's him.'
Gillies Morris Falconer (21) 20 Westfield Rd., AYR	4 8 3 1 7 6 9	'Can I see their profile?' 'No.'
Catherine Porter or Mathieson (68) 19 The Squire, CUMNOCK	4 8 1 3 7 6 9	'No I don't think there is any of them there, really.'
Thomas Haxton (51) 19 Springwell Rd., STRANRAER	4 8 3 1 7 6 9	'Do you want it in answer? The men I saw are not there.'
Irene Burns (16) 81 Hillhead Ave., KILMARNOCK	4 8 1 3 7 6 9 √	'Can I see them from the side? That's like him but I am not sure.' (Pointing to No 3)
Isobel Smith (16) 37 Boyd St., KILMARNOCK	4 8 1 3 7 6 9 √	'I think number three.'

But what makes a man who has served a long sentence in prison, return to crime: knowing what will happen to him, if he is caught?

In my own case I could answer in one word — stupidity. But I think that would be avoiding the question.

I should think a number of factors are involved here.

In my own case the word criminal means nothing, if by criminal you mean someone who is not normal; although I grant that my way of life is not normal. I have the same emotions as any other man. What would shock a normal man would shock me. I dont beat my wife and children. If I read in the press that some old woman has been beaten up and robbed; that some child has been molested; that some idiot Irishman has blown up innocent people. These things make me angry. But if I read that someone has robbed a bank or a train I say good luck to them. Most people do. But I bitterly regret the years wasted in prison; most of all the years spent away from my family.

Extracts from one of Patrick Meehan's many letters to the author. Note how the writing shifts from upright to sloping and back again – a regular feature of all Meehan's letters.

Appendix III

Confession by Ian Waddell published in the *Scottish Daily News* of October 14th, 1975, and reprinted by kind permission of the Editor. It follows fairly closely the account given on pages 71–4 and 78–82, except that Waddell states that on return to Glasgow he went to a cousin's house and not to Carmichael's.

'I first learned about Mr Ross's house from my accomplice.

He said there was bound to be a lot of money in Mr Ross's house on a Saturday night because he was a bingo hall owner.

We went down to the bungalow on a Saturday night. We knew Mr Ross arrived home around midnight.

When we arrived and looked at the house we found he was already there. There were only two people in the house as far as we could see, a man and woman watching television.[1]

We were in a hired Cortina or Corsair parked outside an hotel half a mile away.

Just before midnight Mr and Mrs Ross went to bed. We sat for an hour or an hour and a half in the back garden.

My accomplice cut the telephone wires. He stood up on the shed and cut them from there.

We were kneeling down beside a hedge facing the back of the kitchen.

We then waited for half an hour. We entered the house through the front window. We used an iron jemmy to prise it open.

The room we entered looked like one you would use for visitors.

There was a big shiny floor and a table in the middle of it with flowers on it.

[1] Confirmed by Mr Ross and not revealed publicly before. See page 76.

We went out the door, up the small corridor and into the room on the right where the couple were in separate beds. Mr Ross was nearest the window.

I went for the woman and my accomplice went for the man. Mr Ross struggled and got out of bed and they both landed on the floor.

My accomplice shouted "Get this ... off me." He either called me Pat or Jim.

These were names we deliberately adopted before we went in. Most housebreakers do it.

It meant if we had to talk to each other we could not identify each other.

The reason the names had to be used was because Mr Ross put up a struggle.

It was pure coincidence that Meehan and Griffiths first names coincide with this. I didn't even know them.

Mr Ross continued fighting so I hit him with the jemmy.

Mrs Ross just lay there in bed. She kept shouting if her husband was all right but never got out of bed.

We tied them up. We used a clothes rope which had been hanging up in the garden.

I stayed with the two people and he searched the house. He came back with a small case full of money.

I found £1,800 in the hip pocket of the man's trousers which were hanging over a chair.

It was in new £10 notes all numbered. As far as we knew it was his bingo money.

We asked where his wall safe was and he said he didn't have one.

It was dark but we put the light on. We had masks on cut out from balaclava hoods.

We flung a quilt over Mr Ross's head and a pillow slip over Mrs Ross.

It was very warm and difficult to breathe and we wanted to take our masks off. My accomplice continued searching the house.

There was a safe under the stairs which Mr Ross told us about. I never saw the inside of the safe.

My accomplice came back with the case which had £2,500 in it.

But there was a lot of stuff we did not touch.

There was a lot of old coins and premium bonds and a travellers cheque book which we threw away and left.

I can remember quite a bit about the house.

A wee alarm clock sat on the kitchen window and I think there was a fridge on the left-hand side. The back door was green in colour with a key in it.

We had a drink from a bottle of whisky in the kitchen which had been opened and used.

I gave them some lemonade out of a small bottle straight from the neck.[2]

We put the masks on then to give them the lemonade.

We waited two or three hours. We would probably have got pulled up by the police if we had set out at that time in the morning.

We waited until it was daylight so that they would think we were tourists or wouldn't bother so much.

We broke in about one o'clock and we left after five.

My accomplice went into the garage to steal Mr Ross's car. I think it was a red Vauxhall or a red Jaguar, but he couldn't get it started so we left it.

He then walked to where our car was, came back and picked me up.

I said to Mrs Ross that I would phone for an ambulance, she kept asking if her husband was all right.

We went back to Glasgow by the long route joining up to the A74.

We split up the cash on the Edinburgh road. I got out and got a taxi home to my cousin's in Parkhead.

The first I knew about the couple being found was when I heard it on the news on the Monday night.

I lay low for three days. The police interviewed me on either the Wednesday or the Thursday after the murder.

They said it was routine inquiries and I was allowed to go.

I didn't know Meehan or Griffiths and I had no idea where they were on the night of the break-in.

[2] Denied by Mr Ross.

When Meehan was arrested I didn't bother too much because I was certain – as he probably was – that he would get off with it.

I felt it a bit after he was sentenced. But it was just one of those things.

Later I spoke to Mr Beltrami. You get particular feelings and reasons at particular times. Maybe I felt sorry for Meehan.

I still get mixed feelings about it, and I would like to see him get released as long as I don't go in.

I never regarded it as a sadistic murder.

Mrs Ross was not assaulted. She was just tied up.

Mr Ross was not tortured but he received eye injuries and was hurt in the struggle with my accomplice.

I was surprised when I learned it was the woman who had died.

I thought it would have been the man. He was in a pretty bad way.'

Appendix IV

Many of Meehan's fellow prisoners at Peterhead knew of his innocence, and in 1974 composed this song about him.

PADDY'S SONG

To the tune of *Come Back Paddy Reilly*

In Peterhead prison locked up in the hole
There's a man well known for his pranks
No shining halo encircles his head
'Cause he's blasted too many banks
Five long weary years alone in the hole
Protesting that justice went wrong
And the convicts sing loud when they reach the refrain
Why don't they let Paddy go home

Chorus

Free Paddy Meehan, free him today
Don't leave him to rot down the hole
Free Paddy Meehan, free him today
Why don't they let Paddy go home

Whatever his sins there's one thing for sure
And there's many prepared to declare
The man has a heart and was never involved
In the murder committed at Ayr

Chorus

He has argued for justice in the courts of the land
And everyone knows he is right
But the Law Lords of Scotland have turned him down flat
Yet Paddy won't give up the fight

Chorus

Is there no one on high who will end his ordeal
No one who will right this great wrong
All join in together, sing out the refrain
Why don't they let Paddy go home

Chorus